Reconstructing Criticism

Reconstructing Criticism

Pope's *Essay on Criticism* and
the Logic of Definition

Philip Smallwood

Lewisburg
Bucknell University Press
London: Associated University Presses

© 2003 by Rosemont Publishing & Printing Corp.

All rights reserved. Authorization to photocopy items for internal or personal use, or the internal or personal use of specific clients, is granted by the copyright owner, provided that a base fee of $10.00, plus eight cents per page, per copy is paid directly to the Copyright Clearance Center, 222 Rosewood Dr., Danvers, Massachusetts 01923. [0-8387-5544-5/03 $10.00 + 8¢ pp, pc.]

Associated University Presses
2010 Eastpark Boulevard
Cranbury, NJ 08512

Associated University Presses
Unit 302, The Chandlery
50 Westminster Bridge Road, London SE1 7QY, England

Associated University Presses
P.O. Box 338, Port Credit
Mississauga, Ontario
Canada L5G 4L8

The paper used in this publication meets the requirements of the American National Standard for Permanence of Paper for Printed Library Materials Z39.48-1984.

Library of Congress Cataloging-in-Publication Data

Smallwood, Philip.
   Reconstructing criticism : Pope's Essay on criticism and the logic of definition / Philip Smallwood.
     p. cm.
Includes bibliographical references and index.
   ISBN 0-8387-5544-5 (alk. paper)
1. Pope, Alexander, 1688–1744. Essay on criticism. 2. Pope, Alexander 1688–1744—Knowledge—Literature. 3. Literature—History and criticism—Theory, etc. 4. Criticism—England—History—18th century. I. Title.

PR3626.S63 2003
821'.5—dc21

                                                      2003000297

PRINTED IN THE UNITED STATES OF AMERICA

But some will say critics are a kind of tinkers, that make more faults than they mend ordinarily. See their diseases and those of grammarians. It is true, many bodies are the worse for the meddling with; and the multitude of physicians hath destroyed many sound patients with their wrong practice. But the office of a true critic or censor is, not to throw by a letter anywhere, or damn an innocent syllable, but lay the words together, and amend them; judge sincerely of the author and his matter, which is the sign of solid and perfect learning in a man. Such was Horace, an author of much civility, and, if any one among the heathen can be, the best master both of virtue and wisdom; an excellent and true judge upon cause and reason, not because he thought so, but because he knew so out of use and experience.

—Ben Jonson, *Timber or Discoveries*

Contents

Acknowledgments	9
Abbreviations	11
Introduction	15

Part I: Logics of Definition

1. Defining Literature/Defining Criticism — 29
   - Paradoxes of Definition in Literature and Criticism — 29
   - Defining Literature: Four Theories — 31
   - Defining Criticism — 38
   - Philosophical Method and the Problem of Criticism: Collingwood on Definition — 45
2. On Definition and Debate — 49
   - Uniqueness and Plurality in the Definition of Criticism — 49
   - Definitional Conditions for Critical Debate — 53
   - Empirical and Transcendental Concepts of Criticism: The Logic of Circularity — 60
3. Criticism, Function, Category, Complement — 63
   - Ordinary and Proper Meanings of Criticism — 63
   - Three Limits of Definition — 67
   - The Durability of Terms — 73

Part II: Whole and Part in the Description of Literary Criticism

4. "Outside the Academic Fold": Radical Theory and the Modern "Men of Letters" — 77
   - Polemical Representations of Theory and Theorists — 77
   - Identity, Difference, and the Communities of Critical Practice — 81

	"Grub Street and the Ivory Tower": Critical Institutions and the Communities of Social Valuation	85
5.	Criticism, Valuation, and Useful Purpose	90
	Valuation and Criticism	90
	The "Debate" on Value	93
	Value, Politics, and the Law	96
	Value, Marginality, and Canon Formation	97
	Useful Purpose	99
6.	Criticism and the Meanings of "Theory"	102
	The Rhetoric of Mediation: Criticism and the Theory Guides	102
	Theory in Criticism and Criticism in Theory	105
	The Logic of Theory in Practice	111
7.	Criticism, Interpretation, and Judgment	114
	Criticism and the Limits of Interpretation	114
	The Idea of Judgment and the Scope of Criticism	120
	Varieties of Judgment	123
	The Limits and Uncertainty of Judgment	126

Part III: The Idea of History and the Idea of Criticism

8.	Truth, History, and Literary Criticism	131
	History as Definition	131
	The History of Criticism and the History of "X"	132
	Literary and Fictional Form in the History of Criticism	140
9.	Pope's *Essay* and the Poetic "Idea of Criticism"	143
	Four Platitudes and Pope's *Essay*	144
	Seeing and Supposing Criticism	147
	The Priority of Ideality	156
10.	Conclusion: Pastness, Presence, and Pope's *Essay*	159
	Definition and Temporality	159
	Conclusions	167
	Summary of Conclusions	173
Afterword: The Logic of Cultural Studies		176
Notes		183
Bibliography		206
Index		216

Acknowledgments

Particular debts to published work are recorded in the notes, but I have benefited throughout this study from the thought and writings of H. A. Mason, a past coeditor of *Scrutiny* and of the *Cambridge Quarterly*, on the subject of Pope and criticism. Mason's thinking on Pope's *Essay* and its classical, French, and English critical background under the rubric of "Reason, Truth, and Nature" first taught me to attend to the poetic resonances of the poem and to comprehend its value in the analysis of literary criticism today.

Parts of this book were delivered in a different form as guest lectures at the University of Virginia in 1997, at Bucknell University in 1998, and as one of the series of "Churchill Lectures" at the University of Bristol, England, in 2000. I should like to express my thanks to Ralph Cohen, Greg Clingham, and Andrew Bennett for their kind invitations to me to speak to their colleagues and students.

The second part of chapter 2 of this book originally appeared as "The Definition of Criticism" in *New Literary History* 27 (1996): 545–54. Chapter 5 is a slightly amended version of my "Criticism, Valuation, and Useful Purpose," first published in *New Literary History* 28 (1997): 711–22. Both are reprinted with the permission of Johns Hopkins University Press. Chapter 3 appeared in its original form in the *British Journal of Aesthetics* 36, no. 3 (July 1996): 252–64 as "Problems in the Definition of Criticism," and part of chapter 6, "Criticism and the Meanings of 'Theory,'" in the *British Journal of Aesthetics* 37, no. 4 (October 1997): 377–85. Both are reprinted here by permission of Oxford University Press. Chapter 4 of this book, "'Outside the Academic Fold': Radical Theory and the Modern 'Men of Letters,'" has been published in an earlier version in *English: The Journal of the English Association* 47, no. 187 (spring 1998): 41–52, and is reprinted by permission of the English Association. I am grateful to the editors of the journals in which these articles appeared.

ACKNOWLEDGMENTS

Permission to quote material has been granted as follows. The quotation in chapter 1 from R. G. Collingwood's *An Essay on Philosophical Method*, first published by Oxford University Press in 1933, is made with the permission of St. Augustine's Press. The quotation in chapter 7 from Leonard Cohen's "Suzanne Takes You Down" is © 1967 Stranger Music, Inc., renewed 1995 Leonard Cohen, and is used by permission/all rights reserved. The extract in chapter 7 from *The Common Pursuit* by F. R. Leavis, published by Chatto and Windus, is used by permission of The Random House Group Limited. The quotation from Terry Eagleton's *Literary Theory* in chapter 8 is made with the permission of Blackwell Publishing. The quotations from H. A. Mason's essay "An Introduction to Literary Criticism by Way of Sidney's *Apologie for Poetry*," first printed in the *Cambridge Quarterly* 12, nos. 2 and 3 (1983): 79–173, are made by permission of Oxford University Press. The epigraph to chapter 10 quoted from the second revised edition of Joel Weinsheimer's and Donald G. Marshall's translation of Hans-Georg Gadamer's *Truth and Method* is reprinted by permission of Sheed and Ward (publishers), an imprint of Continuum. The quotation from Richard Rorty's *Contingency, Irony, and Solidarity* in chapter 10 is reprinted with the permission of Cambridge University Press. The dust jacket illustration of *The Critic* is reproduced courtesy of the Print Collection, Lewis Walpole Library, Yale University.

For reading parts of this study and offering useful advice on revisions, I should like to thank Susan Butterfield.

Abbreviations

AJ   *The Age of Johnson: A Scholarly Annual*
BJA *The British Journal of Aesthetics*
CQ   *The Cambridge Quarterly*
JEGP *Journal of English and Germanic Philology*
LRB *The London Review of Books*
NLH *New Literary History*
NYRB *The New York Review of Books*
PQ   *Philological Quarterly*
TLS *The Times Literary Supplement*

Reconstructing Criticism

Introduction

> Inquiry, as a kind of seeking, must be guided beforehand by what is sought. So the meaning of Being must already be available to us in some way. As we have intimated, we always conduct our activities in an understanding of Being. Out of this understanding arise both the explicit question of the meaning of Being and the tendency that leads us towards its conception. We do not *know* what "Being" means. But even if we ask, "What *is* 'Being'?," we keep within an understanding of the "is," though we are unable to fix conceptionally what that "is" signifies. We do not even know the horizon in terms of which that meaning is to be grasped and fixed. *But this vague average understanding of Being is still a Fact.*
> —Martin Heidegger, *Being and Time*

> Modernity exists in the form of a desire to wipe out whatever came earlier, in the hope of reaching at last a point that could be called a true present, a point of origin that marks a new departure. This combined interplay of deliberate forgetting with an action that is also a new origin reaches the full power of the idea of modernity.
> —Paul de Man, "Literary History and Literary Modernity"

Aesthetics, the History of Criticism, and Critical Theory: Outline and Aims of This Book

THIS BOOK ENTERS AND EXTENDS DEBATE ABOUT THE CONCEPTUAL RELATIONS OF literary criticism at the present time; and it tackles the problem of the modernity of criticism in its theoretical relation to that part of the critical past which finds aesthetic and poetical elaboration in the *Essay on Criticism* of Alexander Pope. To this end, I argue that the concept of criticism—for those concerned to weigh and measure and test the meaning of the word—is best explained by reference to criteria based on an aesthetic or literary-artistic model that stands over and against a model convened from theories of universal textuality, from social, psychological, political, economic, or other culturally or naturally determined sources. The book by this means draws antiabolitionist and far-reaching conclusions about the relation of the critical present to the critical past. In its methods, likewise, it seeks an unusual rapprochement between the techniques of aesthetics, theory, and the practice of criticism.[1]

The drift of my argument is to resist a pervasive "historicist" approach to the criticism of the eighteenth-century past (exemplified here by one defining text of that period), as this is productive of a dubiously "pure" or hermetic conception of historical value. I contend that it is a mistake is to suppose that a "historicist" or even "New Historicist" view of criticism *could* exist outside an immediate critical problem; and that it is possible to ignore the sense in which old or ancient critical works are indispensably party to the here and now of criticism. Such isolationist perspectives almost certainly stem from a misconception of the historical status of "criticism" and from its externalization as an "object" of historical study in its own right.[2] My case thus links Pope's *Essay* to a call to "reconstruct criticism" in its fullest possible ideological range, inwardness, and temporal variety.

Nowhere else, to my knowledge, have these arguments about theory and history been subsumed within an attempt to construct a systematic account of problems in the definition of criticism, or to bring the *Essay on Criticism* into this theoretical fold; but it is, I believe, important that such connections be made. The motive to engage what may appear an esoteric concern (submerged in the unglamorous backwaters of aesthetics) is in part to reimagine an "idea of criticism" from the recalcitrant logical and expressive materials surviving intact in the poststructuralist and materialist landscape with its counteremphasis on the politically and culturally constituted literary and critical work. But the chapters that compose this study are also an attempt to overcome the self-defeating partiality that arises from overspecialized aesthetic or author-centered critical theories. There are studies of old literary critics and of eighteenth-century literary criticism; and there are studies of the theory of criticism. Yet neither, to my mind, sufficiently takes us back to the texts of criticism in their *literary* aspect, or conveys a sufficiently urgent critical approach to the representational devices of form and language from which definitions of criticism can be inferred: the problems of historical narrative, the meanings of theory itself, the unique resources of poetical tone, the implications for understanding criticism of vocabulary and syntax, and so forth.

This book makes no *explicit* contribution to "critical theory" in the "race-gender-class"[3] sense of the term. Little is said to forward the cause of Marxist criticism, feminist approaches, deconstruction, postmodernism, postcolonialism, gay and lesbian theory, and so on. The method and conclusions of the book are offered as a methodological aside or integrated "other" to that whole Western middle-class quest for social, moral, religious, and linguistic redemption, and they express one "posttheoretical" alternative to the homogeneous and fiercely defended definition of criticism implicit within it. Nor is the book an attempt to work over the whole of criticism from the point of view of its multifarious internal problems and local controversies: intentionality, metaphor, the question of fiction and fact, the nature of character and plot, the pleasures of tragedy, and so on. It is rather a reflection on how, granted the materialist developments of the theoretical model, "criticism"—a term that remains in use—may yet be conceived. Given the disputed territorial identities of literary criticism, the question of definition is currently a more marginal problem in critical studies than it ought to be. Philosophical investigations tend not to engage with difficulties at a sufficiently textual level to satisfy the sort of literary and critical audience that might benefit from them, and I do not attempt to provide a history of the problem in this book. Indeed, it is part of my point that historical representations of literary criticism are problematic as to events, objects, and narrative materials. The subhistory of attempts to define this term, from the seventeenth century to the twentieth,[4] makes a long and interesting tale, and of necessity in the light of my central claims, I adopt a work from an earlier period (the eighteenth century) as a reference point. But my approach is analytic, not historical or narrative. In focusing ultimately on the *Essay on Criticism*, what follows is not a "contribution to eighteenth-century studies" in the established sense of that phrase.

Any analytic account of the problem of criticism will confront current orthodoxies in a number of ways. In the present case, I do not concede (indeed, I explicitly argue against) the view that criticism must be *wholly* explained according to extraliterary social, political, or linguistic agendas of the here and now. My account does not suggest that criticism can be viewed from a secure philosophical distance and is of necessity immune from the perfectly legitimate and exceptionally interesting concerns of society, politics, or language, or exempt from scrutiny in terms of its bourgeois commitments. But in admitting an aesthetic conception of criticism the book attempts rather to reestablish the right of works composing the critical past to exist on terms that are also proximate to the definition of art.

From the beginning, therefore, I discuss the strengths and defects of different approaches to defining criticism, go on to relate theory to other constituent parts or subordinate modes of criticism, and at a later point describe in more or less precise terms the theoretical problems faced by efforts to construct historical narratives of critical "events." Chapter 1 sets the scene by defining the problem of criticism in relation both to literature and to the definition of philosophical concepts. Chapter 2 analyzes some accounts of what criticism "is" from the point of view of debate about it, and draws conclusions about the reflexive nature of defining, the distinction between "empirical" and "transcendental" concepts, and the occasional nature of criticism. Chapter 3 continues the discussion of defining criticism and comes to some conclusions about how far definition is possible or desirable. Chapter 4 deconstructs the cultural division between academic and journalistic criticism. Chapter 5 considers the relationship between "criticism" and two meanings of "theory," and blames the recent tradition of "theory guides" for obscuring certain established truths. Chapter 6 critiques the distinction between evaluative and nonevaluative criticism and suggests a preferred footing for this. Chapter 7 discusses attitudes to "interpretation" and "judgment" and objects to reductive conceptions of the latter. Chapter 8 discusses a number of standard histories of criticism and examines the reality of criticism as historical object. Chapters 9 and 10 bring Pope's *Essay on Criticism* of 1711 under the defining aspect and suggest that its aesthetic and poetical qualities throw a unique light on the conceptual status of criticism.[5] Finally, an afterword considers the "redefinition" of criticism by cultural studies and gives reasons why its widely influential logic is ultimately self-defeating.

Studies focusing tangentially on many of the critical issues raised by this book are manifold, but there are known to me only two works of book length, published in recent years, that share its explicit and sustained emphasis on definition. One is Paul Hernadi's *What Is Criticism?* (1981); the other F. E. Sparshott's *The Concept of Criticism* (1967).[6] Hernadi's book is a collection of essays by different hands, and though valuable in numerous ways, it is not a connected, systematic account of a single problem that comes to a general conclusion of stated consequence for critical history and humanistic study. The inquiry by Sparshott nominally covers some of the ground, but now seems dated; it lacks reference to, and quotation from, the actual literature of criticism, and is unable to focus the problem in relation to challenges posed by post-Saussurean literary theory. It is aimed more exclusively at philosophers than the wider, interdisciplinary readership that I have in mind. The same can be said of M. C. Beardsley's more ambitious and seminal "new critical" *Aesthetics: Problems in the Philosophy of Criticism* (1958).[7]

The balance that is by comparison sought in this book is more accurately anticipated by Stein Haugom Olsen's *The Structure of Literary Understanding* (1978) and *The End of Literary Theory* (1987). To these studies I would add, as partial inspirations for the present work, the growing list of (mainly 1990s) literary-theoretical books written for the English-speaking world. They include John M. Ellis's *Against Deconstruction* (1989) and *Literature Lost: Social Agendas and the Corruption of the Humanities*

(1997), Richard Freadman's and Seumas Miller's *Re-Thinking Theory* (1992), Peter Lamarque's and Stein Haugom Olsen's *Truth, Fiction, and Literature: A Philosophical Perspective* (1994), John Harwood's *Eliot to Derrida: The Poverty of Interpretation* (1995), and Wendell V. Harris's *Literary Meaning: Reclaiming the Study of Literature* (1996). I would also like to draw attention to Peter Lamarque's *Fictional Points of View,* published by Cornell in 1996, to Valentine Cunningham's *Reading After Theory* (2002); and to such seminal essays as Frederick Crews's "In the Big House of Theory" (1986). The essays collected in W. W. Robson's *The Definition of Literature* (1982) have provided further suggestive determinants for this work.[8] These studies lack stated prior political or social commitments, and though they vary quite widely in difficulty, tone, and formality, they place a high value on articulating theoretical concerns in fairly direct and accessible language. They are nicely poised between theorizing and analyzing. They are "humanist" in a sense that expresses political values incidentally, and makes way for "theory" in a broader (sociopolitically uncommitted) meaning of the term. Such works have a natural place in most bibliographies of "post-theory" reading.[9]

I do not in the present context aim to retrace the arguments of all of the studies I have mentioned above; nor do I recount their sometimes severe, often highly particularized, and detailed critique of post-Saussurean and postmaterialist theory seen from the inside. Valentine Cunningham has described the tendency of different theories to collapse into each other, and to constitute a "gumbo" or "olla podrida" that is Theory with a capital "T."[10] I, too, for reasons outlined in chapter 6, have found it useful to treat Theory en masse. However, I have also tried to work in a pluralist spirit from the conclusions of commentators over the last twenty years about the limits of Theory towards a broader, historically inflected account of the idea of criticism. In this my method engages the values of Enlightenment culture in their more limited, testable, and textual specificity, which anchors grand generalizations and is therefore open to criticism. The recovery of the critical past needed to define "criticism" is, I suggest, a necessarily more piecemeal and perfunctory task than allusion to the vast cultural oppositions in Ellis's book on the "corrupting" social agendas of criticism, and my authorities here are themselves part of Theory: underlying my argument will be found the temporal hermeneutics of such thinkers on the narratives of history as Hans-Robert Jauss, Hans-Georg Gadamer, and Paul Ricoeur.[11] The present study tries to imagine what a merging of the "horizon of expectations" of critical present and eighteenth-century past might actually look like, and the keeping open of this prospect is itself Pope's greatest gift to the analysis of literary criticism. His negotiations between the "other" and the "same" in the poetical terms of the eighteenth-century are not at all at odds with leading concepts in post-Saussurean literary-historical theory.[12]

As a context of reflection for comprehending the durability and aesthetic value of the *Essay on Criticism* of Pope, *Reconstructing Criticism* sets out to contribute to critical theory and practice at a point of tension and potential growth: its traditionally antagonistic interface with philosophical and literary aesthetics. What follows will probably be found to contain a somewhat higher incidence of illustrative quotations from the literature of criticism (drawn from different periods of critical history) than readers will likely encounter in most pure aesthetics or philosophically oriented texts. But if the work looks "after theory" from its own occasion in history, I have not attempted to dismantle the post-Saussurean concept of criticism further,[13] and, doubtless, an addition to the body of writings critical of Theory would not in any event persuade the presently unpersuaded.[14] My aim is to *move on* from this impasse, to shift the spotlight elsewhere, probing the rifts and gaps left on the outside of Theory. I therefore observe what is telling in the grammar, vocabulary and sociology of certain popularizing texts, and reopen a space for "literary criticism" as a language in use. And with its concluding focus on Pope's *Essay*, reread in the light of determinants that have *not* been extinguished, the study seeks to carry an important literary- and critical-historical point. While I am arguing that the reasons for comparative neglect of the *Essay* are part of the problem we urgently need to discuss, the poem is itself of acknowledged importance to valuation of eighteenth-century criticism and to our estimate of Pope and his critical successor Samuel Johnson.

Finally, as a contribution to criticism's philosophical context, I claim a special role for work on and about definition and history by the English philosopher R. G. Collingwood, and for the significance of the movement unpromisingly known as "British idealism." My intention here is to encourage appreciation of the explanatory relevance of Collingwood's "idealist" thought to an English literary study grappling with recent critical and cultural trends, reviewing the available options, and looking before and after the pervasive periodization and culturalization of eighteenth-century studies.[15] The link between poststructuralist notions and Collingwood's own is one of the lost threads in the recent history of criticism. I hope such coincidence may persuade the skeptical that a historicist turn to Collingwood and a rediscovery of his work in terms of present problems are qualitatively different things: as Frank Kermode has recently noted in his review of two "flagship" volumes, *Practicing New Historicism* (by Gallagher and Greenblatt) and *Shakespeare after Theory* (by David Scott Kastan), a necessary amnesia about the history of the philosophy of history seems part of the current scene. Kermode observes that Kastan "thinks the moment of New Historicism has passed":

> Yet he admittedly owes much to New Historicism and other aspects of "Theory," and uses a lot of the now familiar patter . . . without which it seems the business of modern criticism cannot be conducted. And like some New Historicists he seems to think that until the arrival of their own way of doing it all thinking about history had been "positivist" and "untheoretical." "Older historicisms found it simpler to pretend that their constructions were limpid, objective accounts of the past, unfiltered by the interests of the observer." Unsurprisingly, such names as R. G. Collingwood and W. B. Gallie (to name but two) are absent from the indexes of both these books; *The Idea of History* was published in 1946 and *Philosophy and the Historical Understanding* in 1964, presumably too early to be of interest to modern thinkers about historical explanation, who regard the writing of history with reference to the interests and presumptions of the observer as their own discovery, and sum up all former inquiries by reference to positivism and Ranke's remark about telling it as it really ("actually"? "essentially"?) was.[16]

Within this context—that of a problem in the history of the theory of history[17]—this book aims to rehabilitate one massively influential concept that runs the risk of elimination by default from its important position in education, public values, and culture. But as I have suggested above, my purpose is also to bring inside theory one part of the past that gives the idea of criticism a poetically luminous life, and in the process reveals its own conception of critical temporality. With this is mind, the initial concerns underpinning this study can now be set forth.

Definition, Disintegration, and Monopolization on the Modern Critical Scene: Four Aspects

"Study problems, not periods." This book is an essay on those aspects of criticism which deal with the problem of criticism, and it is therefore concerned not with every department of criticism's theory and practice but with the possibility, and the desirability in a "posttheoretical" world, of defining "criticism." The inquiry arises out of an attempt to take a number of traditionally separate problems and to see them as connected. Four concerns underpin this study:

1. The first is a question of history. "What do we read it for?" asks F. R. Leavis of the criticism of Samuel Johnson: "Not for enlightenment about the authors with whom it deals . . . and not for direct instruction in critical

thinking."[18] Modern critical assessments of the eighteenth-century critics—and of pre-twentieth-century critics more generally, perhaps—have tended to widen the gulf between the present of criticism and its critical past. In this a certain philosophy of history, itself a part of history, is inescapably implied. According to the terms of this philosophy, referring unself-consciously to the voices of the old critics whenever we are trying to contemplate art in the here and now in interesting ways is, of all uses of and approaches to the critical past, the *least* legitimate. Such critics may doubtless command the respect due to de facto dead authors notable for their representative or "transitional" ideas; they may sometimes look forward to later and livelier developments in critical thought by new critics in more prosperous communities of criticism such as our own; but their concepts and judgments are overtaken by history. This simplification rests on an inescapable paradox of historical representation: if the old critics are important enough to be worth recalling and recording, then their claims to value are not prima facie second-best to those of modern critics untested by time. Thus when critics of the past are not shaping interpretations or making judgments as such, but are articulating their comprehensive idea of criticism (as Pope does in his *Essay* of 1711), we want to know how far this idea can resolve our present crisis of definition, how far its past conception corresponds to, and is usefully different from, what we mean by "criticism" when we theorize about it today. We are interested in whether the past of criticism is able to yield something to the present beyond what the present is able to realize for itself. With certain exceptions,[19] answers to such questions have proved largely outside the range of options available to professional critical history.

2. A second concern is the status of radical theory and its ambition to stand comprehensively for the whole of criticism without a remainder. In the absence of an adequate sense of the historical diversity of criticism, it follows that much should now appear new and strange whose claim to novelty demands a sustaining historical comparison. The elevation of novelty above tradition has done much to support the optimistic confidence of cultural radicals of recent years. The move from "structuralism" to "poststructuralism," from "modernism" to "postmodernism," and latterly to the condition of "posthumanity" or the "post-postmodern" suggests that the essence of criticism is perceived to have changed over time. "The theory revolution has had real effects," write the general editors in their preface to the Longman Critical Readers series: "It has loosened the grip of traditional empiricist and romantic assumptions about language and literature."[20] But the evolving discovery of Theory's historical connections with Arnoldian values, with Leavisite or "New" criticism, and with the more recent manifestations of cultural thought may also indicate a degree of overstatement

in remarks of this kind. A tendency to load the terms of "debate" in favor of the most recent critical production suggests in addition a Bloomian "anxiety of influence" operating at the level of the critical text,[21] and thus a radical shift in the outward facades of criticism less considerable in its substance or depth. The rise of an "age of theory" has sought likewise not only to dissolve the idea of criticism but also to replace "literature" with the universal concept of the "text." And without literature there can logically be no *literary* criticism. Yet this is an area where quite ordinary distinctions can benefit from reiteration. Part of the function of this book is to identify aspects of the commonly known, of what "oft was thought," that run the risk of eradication from critical knowledge. The real existence of literature and the practical role of its critics would come into this class.

3. A third concern is the question of language. The issue here arises from the assumption that a new language for criticism is *in itself* a sufficient warrant for new critical thought; that the signifiers of criticism, like those of literature, are able to float free of their signifieds without consequence for changes in taste or the narratives of literary history. Many or all of the studies I have mentioned in my introductory comments have lamented the perfervid terminological chaos of modern criticism both before and after its commitments to Theory, and one might point to the irony of this condition in view of the intensified post-Saussurean emphasis on language.[22] But unless the vocabulary of the debates in and about criticism is agreed upon (or commonly comprehended), there is no knowing whether the pluralities of thought exist at a level able to make radical divisions between critics, and thus no assurance that any debate on radical grounds has been going on.[23] This uncertainty has consequences for relations between literary taste at the present time and the history of criticism. Critics have on the whole appeared to cling quite strongly to Renaissance and romantic cultural ideals. But it is not apparent that the literature and the criticism of the eighteenth century (the thought, tastes, and criteria of Johnson or Pope, for example, when compared with the influence of Renaissance and romantic models) have succeeded in shaping the terms of today's theory, or that profound changes in actual literary taste have in consequence occurred.[24] Where the logic of intersubjective assertion and refutation has broken down, the division between real and unreal forms of agreement between critics becomes increasingly hard to discern. Critics may have much in common but be unable to recognize the nature of their common ground.

4. A fourth concern is the defective social institution of literary criticism. This institution may be less divided than its appearance suggests (for reasons indicated above). But it is also at the same time more scattered and diverse a community, arguably, than would be implied by criticism's "poststructuralist" modes. In the very moment that criticism has expanded

into a postdisciplinary "general science," or universal humanity consisting of politics, economics, social history, psychology, anthropology, and linguistics, it seems to have withdrawn into a self-contained, specialized,[25] and even slightly paranoid, pugnacious or self-defensive world inconsistent with many critics' antihierarchical policy statements and out of kilter with a hostility to the "canon" of privileged texts. As critics like Frederick Crews, John Gross, and Bernard Bergonzi have lamented, criticism seems to have become a romanticized universe of "movement slogans" whose limits are defined by "research."[26] This squeezes out the larger community of the general reader, the creative writer whom the critic depends upon, the student of literature, and the student critic. It removes, in fact, the pillars supporting the whole situational network of criticism. And so critics are free to assert their professional identity on the narrowest of present-day terms—under the rubric of a revolutionary "antielitism," moreover. In this light, one must be impressed by W. W. Robson's strikingly unconventional (and to my mind truly "radical") perception that "[r]ecent attempts to make literary criticism more 'rigorous' have sometimes only succeeded in alienating it from many authors and readers" and by his personal ambition as a practicing modern critic and literary theorist: "to take conversation about prose and poetry out of the limited and specialised 'literary' or 'academic' world in which it so often takes place, and to turn it towards the broader world of thought which is shared by all reflective people, whoever and wherever they are."[27]

That these concerns are connected by the question of how to *define* "criticism" will become progressively visible in the course of this book. The definition of criticism requires explanation on two fronts: a conception of definition and a conception of criticism. Together these suggest limits of conceptual breadth and of depth. Moreover, a conception of definition assumes optimistically that the thing we wish to define really exists, and locates the problem of defining it—at the highest level of abstraction—within what Heidegger called the question of "Being." But the problem can also be narrowed down to certain deeply questionable preconceptions about the "Augustan" age of English literary criticism, to a critical-historical focus amenable to critical study, and to questions of literary quality. The importance of this focus is that no discovery anyone ever makes about the criticism of Pope today seems greatly to change the definition of criticism or even to complicate the question. Scholars of the history of criticism and critical theorists are often thought to be asking and answering fundamentally unconnected questions.

These problems have become increasingly apparent in the ways that I shall now try to set forth. Each chapter in the following discussion is meant as a piece in the puzzle that I hope by the end of this book to succeed in fitting together to make the picture complete. It is united by the argument that the move to dismantle criticism qua criticism is constructed on presupposings whose effect is part of the function of criticism and known to the present from the study of critical history—where and only where that study is wide and open enough to the aesthetic value of critical texts. The diagnostic phase of the study thus leads to a therapeutic one. Perhaps it sounds overly cynical or pessimistic to say this, and I certainly do not wish to restart or perpetuate the exhausted ideological conflict between protheory and antitheory views. I do not see how it is possible to dispense with theory if one is to generalize at all, or to criticize at all, and this book is a work of theory in precisely this sense. I completely agree with John M. Ellis in his claims for theory when he writes that "Theory exerts its pressure on the status quo by continual examination of the basis and rationale for the accepted activities of a field of study." Theory of this kind has the definitional value necessary to critical renewal:

> Inevitably, the results will in principle be quite unlike the usual deconstructive attitudes: they should not leave us with issues and activities more undefined than ever but instead introduce a clarification and differentiation of fundamentally different kinds of activities. The consequence of this kind of activity will generally be a pressure to rearrange priorities; by its very nature, then, theory is indeed disturbing.[28]

But this does not mean I wish to install a formal variety of New Humanism, or an ism of any kind, for that matter.[29] I am not a philosopher talking about criticism and seeking to strike an objective pose where mere literary critics have fumbled and failed. For reasons that will form part of my argument, I think on the contrary that this is a job that criticism must do for itself, using its own resources. This ought not to suggest that the aesthetic study of the nature of "artworks," on the one hand, and the "practice" of critical theory on the other, should not effect a closer rapprochement than they presently do. Cross-fertilization would instate a *critical* tension that is lacking in their estrangement; but one cannot learn how to swim before going into the water, and if my point of view tries to take what advantage it can of a philosophical perspective, it is nonetheless a specifically critical method that I favor. It is defined within terms of the topic it is trying to clarify. In what follows I shall keep the concrete example of critics and their works of criticism well to the fore.

Part I:
Logics of Definition

1
Defining Literature/Defining Criticism

> It is one of the maxims of civil law, that "definitions are hazardous." Things modified by human understanding, subject to varieties of complication, and changeable as experience advances knowledge, or accident influences caprice, are scarcely to be included in any standing form of expression, because they are always suffering some alteration of their state. Definition is, indeed, not the province of man; every thing is set above or below our faculties.
> —Samuel Johnson, *Rambler* 125

Paradoxes of Definition in Literature and Criticism

It is in the nature of the problem I have chosen to address that it should combine the seemingly obvious with the seemingly impossible, the unnecessary or gratuitous with the indispensable or compulsory. The value of trying to define criticism is of course greatly obscured by the obvious fact that no one has ever had any difficulty distinguishing a work of literary criticism from work of some other kind. While, doubtless, the cataloging of books for the library is a specialist skill that has to be learnt, it is not notoriously subject to "failure." The ambiguous cases would not be ambiguous cases unless the division between critical works and works of other kinds was otherwise clear; and clear this distinction certainly is, or certainly *seems*. A play by Shakespeare or Ibsen or Shaw is one thing; a work of criticism is unmistakably another. Marvell's *Horatian Ode* is a poem; Terry Eagleton's essay on *Macbeth* a critical work. It is when we attempt to say what the defining conditions for criticism are that we become conscious of the differences between different works of criticism and wonder how the same word can apply to them all. We may conclude the word serves little purpose and ought to be dropped, or we may take the path of invoking a narrow and esoteric idea of criticism. In questions of this kind we are looking at the various examples of criticism with an eye to their highest common factor, or lowest common denominator, the reality beneath or beyond the world of appearance. But how does one insure that all conceivable examples of the one *definiendum* are grasped at a level on which all their fundamentals are linked? Dictionaries get around the problem by defining words in terms of their sundry and several uses. The *OED* entry on "criticism" lists four; but we want to take hold of the concept behind the word.

It might be the norm, for example, to assume that critical works belong to the realm of prose; or that, while works of literature (and especially poems) appeal to feelings or emotions, works of criticism function according to argument, principle and reason, or that critical works are distinct from literary works on the grounds that they have a *mediate* purpose. But examples come instantly to mind of works we read for themselves and for what they tell us about literary works beyond themselves. They are auxiliary to them, but with value in their own right. Walcott's poetic and symbolic evocation of Caribbean life in *Omeros*, for example, is simultaneously a comment on Homer; Julian Barnes's novel *Flaubert's Parrot* illuminates Flaubert; Tom Stoppard's *Rosencrantz and Guildenstern Are Dead* stands in a critical relationship to Shakespeare's play. We sometimes refer to the "intertextual relations" of such works, or their translational value. They are good for something and good in themselves, and thus fall, in a sense, outside the conventions of criticism and, in a sense, within the idea. It is not that, with these examples in mind, or even with a hundred postmodernist novels before us, there is no prospect of using the term "criticism" normally. If these are "criticism," there is no arguing the fact on the basis of evidence. Someone unconvinced (if such there were) could not be convinced.

My argument in this book is that while propositions on the subject of criticism may assist the critical mind in its progress towards self-awareness, a mental vacuum cannot be filled by a finalist definition of criticism: for just as criticism is in part a thing of the mind, a thing in some sense created by thought, there is not the necessity to know or to say *everything* about it. Knowing the idea, I shall suggest, is acquired from inside its boundaries, so that the idea of criticism cannot be gathered *entirely* from the spectacle of its critical works, from its various theories or isms, or from the conventions of writing. For we are not seeking a creed, a philosophy, or a theory in defining criticism. We say: "We know a critical work when we see one," but what we see is a work we are in the process of thinking about in a certain way. If we try to construct a list of marginal and standard cases or to place critical and literary works on different sides of an imaginary fence, some prior conception has to govern what we put in each category of work. Literature and criticism do not come with their categories printed on them, and there is no special subject matter to which they hold the exclusive rights.

To illustrate this point, the present chapter will introduce and compare some representative recent attempts to define both "literature" and "criticism." The grounds for defining can then be judged in the light of the existing achievements in this field.

Defining Literature: Four Theories

To define "*literary* criticism" is to suppose that "literature," too, can be defined.[1] But criticism is also a kind of "literature" and has increasingly become so in the avant-garde manifestations of recent years. The trouble that arises out of this hypothesis is that the definition of "literature" is still an unsettled issue.[2] Both words are "vague terms" in the technical sense, and when they are used certain philosophical distinctions will need to apply.[3] I will distinguish between knowledge of two different kinds in this book: propositions about literary criticism evaluated according to aesthetic criteria and linguistic success (a definition, like anything else, can be beautiful or ugly, graceful or mean, inspiring or dull, plainly stated or subtly implied), and the knowledge of literary criticism that we presuppose according to our historical moment and the comprehension that this moment affords us.[4] As we will see, the resultant "definitions" are in neither case outside the problem they are trying to solve but rather are part of it.

The number of texts that engage with the nature of "literature," from Aristotle onwards, is of course immense. But a selection of the typical problems that arise in the definition of literature can be gathered in one or another way from four essays written from somewhat different perspectives within recent phases of the Anglo-American critical tradition; they are by René Wellek and Austin Warren, John M. Ellis, W. W. Robson, and Terry Eagleton, respectively.[5] I have chosen such critics for their methodological as well as ideological differences—these in addition to the distinctions in national traditions that they seem to display.

1. René Wellek's and Austin Warren's *Theory of Literature* (1949) is subtitled *A Seminal Study of the Nature and Function of Literature in All Its Contexts,* and their chapter entitled "The Nature of Literature" conveys an attitude to defining that opens up the concept to include "everything in print." In another light, they ask us to see "literature" as the tradition of "great books." But they soon show how both of these formulas for defining literature are inadequate. While the former seems unselective, the latter seems to leave too much out of account. Thus, they conclude that "The term 'literature' seems best if we limit it to the art of literature, that is, to imaginative literature" and go on to explain "the particular use made of language in literature": "Language is the material of literature as stone or

bronze is of sculpture, paints of pictures, or sounds of music."[6] In this way, the crux of the definition of literature offered by Wellek and Warren appears in the distinctions they find between the literary, the everyday, and the scientific uses of language. The language of literature, they suggest, differs from the language of science in that while the former is connotative, the latter is denotative, and in the language of literature "the sign itself, the sound symbolism of the word, is stressed." The pragmatic and expressive sides of language are ones "which scientific language will always want so far as possible to minimize." This principle that literature is to be defined according to the *kind* of language that is characteristic of it also informs Wellek's and Warren's distinction between literary language and "everyday language." And while this "everyday language," like the "scientific," overlaps with the literary to a certain extent ("Everyday language also has its expressive function"), it differs "quantitatively" from the everyday use. In literary language, "The resources of language are exploited much more deliberately and systematically" (23–24). Their argument is that language is more often like this *within* literature than outside it; and as becomes clear, the definition of literature that Wellek and Warren propose depends on satisfying certain *critical* principles or personal prescriptions that they hold in advance:

> We reject as poetry or label as mere rhetoric everything which persuades us to a definite outward action. Genuine poetry affects us more subtly. Art imposes some kind of framework which takes the statement of the work out of the world of reality. (24–25)

The center of literary art is here distinguished from the marginal examples on the grounds that it is "obviously [*sic*] to be found in the traditional genres of the lyric, the epic, the drama. In all of them, the reference is to a world of fiction, of imagination" (25). The fictive and the imaginative, then, are in this view linked to the "traditional" genres, all of which, we are told, are "obviously" at the center of literary art.

2. The logical flaws inherent in this approach are recognized in the definition of literature discussed in John M. Ellis's *The Theory of Literary Criticism* (1974). Ellis mentions the work of Wellek and Warren on the subject of literary definition only to dismiss it as "more a survey of previous answers to . . . [the question] than an attempt to solve it."[7] And he complains that

> Wellek and Warren build into the very structure of their book . . . a kind of distinction between literary and nonliterary approaches in their terms "intrinsic" and "extrinsic." Now these and comparable distinctions must beg

the question until we have a definition of literature that will allow us to give some substance to the notion of a treatment appropriate to literature, for the point at issue in disputes as to whether an approach is "literary" is precisely how we should understand "literary" treatment. (24 n)

Ellis argues that it is complacent to believe that we all instinctively know what we mean by "literature," even though we may be able to use the word instinctively. He locates the problem in the question "What is literature?" This question, he maintains, is a consequence of the referential theory of meaning. According to this theory we conceptualize the issue in terms of the attributes applicable to the referent of the term "literature" and go on—hopelessly, as it turns out—to seek an agreed equivalence for the term instead of concentrating on the circumstances in which we can agree that the term is appropriately used and can isolate the rules and conventions that govern its deployment. Thus, answers to the question "What is literature?" become of the same order as answers to the question "What is the temperature?" In reaching this point, Ellis rejects three different forms of attempt to define literature according to the characteristics that distinguish literary from nonliterary texts. These are:

       a. the "literary" ingredients
       b. the "literary" organization
       c. the "literary" authorship

The first, he suggests, is neither necessary nor sufficient to define literature. This is because it is usually based on attempts to find isolable features of "literary" language, but comes down to the identification of deviations from ordinary grammar and language (such as poetic license), which not all literary texts exploit. On the question of literary organization, too, there is nothing specific to literature that it is possible to separate out. Other kinds of linguistic performance are organized also. The third way of distinguishing "literary" texts—by postulating special authorship or pretextual authorial intent—must also fail: "[O]nly when we have decided that a text is 'literature' do we accept that its author is a poet." The notion of value does not solve the problem of definition, because the definition is then circular. Literary texts are those having literary value.

It is a consequence of this problem, Ellis argues, that we must look again at the question "What is literature?" The question is *mal posée,* because it yields not a definition of literature, but information *about* it. It leads to statements of literature's features held in common by the category rather than "the appropriate circumstances for the use of the word and the features of those circumstances that determine the willingness of the speakers of the language to use the word." This latter involves concentrating on instances of appropriate use whose aptness is less easily conceded. Ellis maintains that properties are not the relevant factor in definitions, and he pursues this argument by exploring analogically the attributes that we would have to identify to distinguish a "weed" in the garden. While we have no difficulty in using this word, and while weeds do—undoubtedly—exist: "Anyone who has tried to explain to his children what weeds are and has watched them then decimate his garden in the belief that they are helping him will know that it is incredibly difficult to do" (34, 37).

The concept "weed," Ellis suggests, "is evidently not taught by means of a catalogue of its empirical properties" (37). There is no particular size, no particular leaf, that defines a weed. A weed is simply a plant that we want removed. This definition rests on the social convention as to which plants are "not wanted." What matters is the way that society regards the plant. And the same goes for literature. What matters is not the intrinsic properties; it is whether the text has *use* as literature:

> Literary texts are not defined as those of a certain shape or structure, but as those pieces of language used in a certain kind of way by the community. They are used as literature. (42)

But what is this use? According to Ellis, literary texts should be defined "as those that are used by society in such a way that *the text is not taken as specifically relevant to the immediate context of its origin*" (44). What determines whether a text is used in this way by the community has nothing to do with whether any author or originator has *intended* it to be literature: "Many texts not so offered are included" (48). In this Ellis comes very close to suggesting that literature is a *social construct*.

3. In defining literature, Ellis moved from first principles to the occasional mention of works that could be literature but are not always thought about in that way (Gibbon for example). In the title essay to his *Definition of Literature and Other Essays* (1982), W. W. Robson was to rest his analysis more solidly on literary examples, and these supply (and are) the arguments about what literature may or may not be. Robson presents his more "ostensive" approach to the problem by posing a series of questions that each register the critic's wonderment or perplexity when faced with how to define. He seems reluctant to come down finally on one side or the other. Is this literature? Is that? What if we look at the Bible? Or Gibbon's *Decline and Fall of the Roman Empire*? Are they literature? Can literature be defined as fiction?[8] If so, what about all those works of fiction having their basis in fact, such as Tolstoy's *War and Peace*? Like Ellis, Robson takes his start from the chapter in Wellek and Warren, but he is less impatient with

their logic. Whereas Ellis ruled out Wellek's and Warren's attempt to define literature through literary language, Robson allows that linguists such as Jakobson did much useful work. There is some reason, if only some, to distinguish the poetic use of language from other uses. But, he says, "I doubt whether this approach is the right one for our purpose."[9]

One by one, Robson eliminates successive forms of descriptive definition of literature, moving finally to what he calls an *honorific* definition "more in keeping with normal usage." It is at this point that Robson's definition of literature, for all his differences in procedure, comes close to Ellis's. Taking the example of journalism, Robson writes:

> Journalism, however brilliant, does not survive its immediate occasion. If some journalism has become literature, this is because we read it although we are no longer interested in the immediate occasion. This transcendence of occasions seems to me a distinctive "note" of literature (in the honorific sense). (12–13)

Works that qualify as literature in the honorific sense transcend their occasion. But Robson goes on to explain that we cannot rely on the passage of time to make the selection. Works that have not stood the test of time, and are rejects, are still available to be read. Readers can still upgrade them into literature: "[E]ither . . . the honorific definition of literature is eroded, and we are back with descriptive definition; or the canon is enlarged, and the honorific sense of the word becomes so extended as to be meaningless" (14).

The trouble is, Robson argues, that it often looks as though most of the works that we have been taught to venerate as literature ("from the point of view of the great world") have been discarded. How many voluntary readers do some famous books really have? The perspective of the academic community is quite different. Academic experts encourage us to consider one forgotten work after another as worthy of consideration. This undermines the process of natural selection in literature: "But in the age of the Ph.D. industry is it possible to speak of a 'dead' author?" Forgotten and unfashionable works may often have a great deal to give us, albeit some works have been *justly* discarded:

> The most plausible reason for their failure to survive is that they only give us something which is better done by better men. They are not "originals," they lack the spiritual signature of a truly distinguished writer. This unique quality is one of the most important "notes" of literature; it is sometimes called textuality, and its unmistakable mark is the resistance of the texts that possess it to all kinds of paraphrase, synopsis, or translation. (14–15)

This both is and isn't, Robson argues, a matter of style: "That 'literature is the right use of language' seems to be true, but I do not see how we can tell when it is right irrespective of subject. Right for what?" (16).

But he concludes that this is the best *sort* of definition of literature: "It is not the subject, or the motive for writing, that makes a work literature." Robson uses the occasion of defining literature to make a personal case for a kind of literature that is too often ignored—"works that plain men enjoy, that we all enjoy, but which do not seem to be candidates for the great books paradigms of 'style'" (16). The examples he gives are *Ben Hur, Little Women,* and *King Solomon's Mines.* These works have stood the test of time better than Spenser's *Faerie Queene, Paradise Lost,* or Joyce's *Ulysses.* Only academic study of literature has really kept the latter group alive. "Most of the literature that has survived," Robson reminds us, "was 'what the public wanted'—Shakespeare's plays, or the novels of Dickens" (17). Robson distinguishes his definition of literature by claiming admission into the literary category of popular or what he calls "middlebrow" works.

4. The final essay on the definition of literature I will consider here is Terry Eagleton's "What Is Literature?," the introduction to the first edition of his widely used *Literary Theory* (1983). In some ways this is the most polemical of the pieces we have dealt with so far, but it is the most lively and engaging. Eagleton argues against the idea that literature is definable as fiction or imagination as distinct from fact, and he begins by assessing the claims of Russian formalist critics who sought to define literature in terms of a particular or peculiar use of language. Their position seems close both to Wellek's and Warren's and to Robson's account of the "right use of language": "[L]iterature was not pseudo-religion or psychology or sociology but a particular organisation of language." The view that Eagleton here summarizes was rejected earlier by Ellis on the grounds that literary and ordinary language are not demonstrably different except in the *exceptional* cases. The formalists, according to Eagleton, claimed that "What was specific to literary language, what distinguished it from other forms of discourse, was that it 'deformed' ordinary language in various ways."[10]

Eagleton rejects the idea of a fixed mode of expression from which literature is reputed to diverge, because he does not think there is any such thing as "ordinary language": Oxford philosophers and Glaswegian dockers are different in how their language is ordinary. However, he accepts the view advanced by Ellis that there is considerable overlap between "ordinary" and "literary language": "more metaphor in Manchester than there is in Marvell," as he catchily puts it. Whether the language is literary or not, he argues, depends on the *context*, on whether we encounter it in those things we call "literature," such as novels. Like Ellis, Eagleton questions the possibility of defining literature via the concept of inherent properties or intrinsic qualities, and he broadens the argument to embrace the question of how utterances are *read*. Thus, the drunk takes the sign on the underground "Dogs must be carried on the escalator" as a statement of general or cosmic significance: "By applying certain conventions of reading to its words, he prises them loose from their immediate context and generalizes them beyond their pragmatic purpose to something of wider and probably deeper import" (6–7).

This leads to the provisional conclusion that literature is "'non-pragmatic' discourse: unlike biology textbooks and notes to the milkman it serves no immediate practical purpose." Not that Eagleton thinks that *what* is said should be considered as unimportant; but literature cannot be objectively defined. It is how somebody *decides* to read something that seems to count the most. (Like Ellis and Robson, Eagleton cites the ambiguous example of Gibbon's *History*.) While it is possible to consider "literature" as a number of different ways in which people relate themselves to writing, it is at this point that a theoretical gap opens up between Eagleton, on the one hand, and Ellis and Robson, on the other. Eagleton's reasoning leads him to the view that there is "no 'essence' of literature whatsoever." Any bit of writing may be read "non-pragmatically," just as any writing may be read "poetically.'" Eagleton quotes Ellis's analogy of how one defines a garden weed, but carries the logic further. The position is one that Eagleton almost instantly qualifies, however, reminding us of the place of the value judgment, and of the *kind* of thing that literature is: "Nobody would bother to say that a bus ticket [Robson's example] was an example of inferior literature, but someone might well say that the poetry of Ernest Dowson was" (7–10).

Eagleton most clearly parts company with Ellis and Robson when he claims that just as anything can be literature, so anything can cease to be literature, including Shakespeare. While refusing to accept the idea that the study of literature is the study of a fixed, stable canon of respected works (something that was never actually an option in Robson's account), Eagleton does not say that the canon may be to *some* extent unfixed, but claims that the study of literature is now the study of an *entirely* unstable category. Eagleton's rationale for this switch (from one extremity to the other, as it were) is that value judgments change. Literature thus becomes a *construct:*

> [T]he so-called "literary canon," the unquestioned "great" tradition of the "national literature," has to be recognized as a *construct*, fashioned by particular people for particular reasons at a certain time. There is no such thing as a literary work or tradition which is valuable in *itself*. (11)[11]

But this canon, as Eagleton here implies, is something that *other people* construct— not me the writer or you the reader—and in this he looks forward to the theoretically possible situation of people valuing Shakespeare no more than they value graffiti today. Different historical periods "construct" the same writers in different ways (perhaps in entirely different ways) according to the values that preside in their personal and cultural present.[12] Because the same works are constructed differently in different periods, it follows that "All literary works . . . are 'rewritten', if only unconsciously, by the societies which read them; indeed there is no reading of a work which is not also a 're-writing'" (12). If there is irony in the fact that such an assertion should sustain the argument for instability in value judgments, Eagleton's point is not, finally, that such judgments are arbitrarily variable. They are controlled by structures of belief. It is the relation of critical ideas and responses to this social domain that Eagleton's discussion of the definition of literature ultimately seeks to explain.

Defining Criticism

The Question of Function

Discussions of the definition of "literature" can provide, then, no *conclusive* account of the concept "literature" in essence, extension, or shape; but by their appeal to language and genre, the concept of "social construction," and the "honorific" designation that signals a work's capacity to transcend its original occasion, such discussions afford important clues as to the parallel and connected problems of defining criticism. When we speak of "the literature of criticism" we thus raise two questions in one; and if we turn at this point from how "literature" is defined to accounts of the nature of "literary criticism," we will see that the essays, statements, and analyses resolve themselves into two broad groups: what criticism "is" and what the "function of criticism" is. The first is concerned with intrinsic properties of criticism, the second with extrinsic or relational ones. Reflection on "the function of criticism" has provided the definitional form and framework for important pronouncements by some of criticism's most important critics: "one could construct a brief history of the field," writes Imre Salusinszky, "simply by tracing the sequence of major essays bearing that title."[13] To the question "What is criticism *for?*" Matthew Arnold's answer was that this purpose is unequivocally moral:

> It is because criticism has so little kept in the pure intellectual sphere, has so little detached itself from practice, has been so directly polemical

and controversial, that it has so ill accomplished, in this country, its best spiritual work; which is to keep man from self-satisfaction which is retarding and vulgarising, to lead him towards perfection, by making his mind dwell upon what is excellent in itself, and the absolute beauty and fitness of things. A polemical practical criticism[14] makes men blind even to the ideal imperfection of their practice, makes them willingly assert its ideal perfection, in order the better to secure it against attack; and clearly this is narrowing and baneful for them. If they were reassured on the practical side, speculative considerations of ideal perfection they might be brought to entertain, and their spiritual horizon would thus gradually widen.[15]

As Arnold suggests, many important writers are remembered for their criticism over and above their creative works; but while "[t]he critical power is of a lower rank than the creative," not all epochs, as Arnold concedes, are equally rich in creation. Sometimes the genius of an age is the genius of criticism. The business of criticism is then "to see the object as in itself it really is":

Thus it tends, at last, to make an intellectual situation of which the creative power can profitably avail itself. It tends to establish an order of ideas, if not absolutely true, yet true by comparison with that which it displaces; to make the best ideas prevail. (318–19)

In Arnold's conception, criticism feeds the current of creative literature and supports the creative instinct. Where this critical buttress is absent (as in Arnold's opinion is the case with romantic poetry), the productions of literature and poetry seem "premature." If then as a first principle criticism's function is to underpin the emergent creative movements, in order to realize their nature, poets do not need to rely on a specifically academic form or tradition of critical thought. The relationship that Arnold has in mind is one where the poet lives in "a current of ideas in the highest degree animating and nourishing to the creative power" and where society is "in the fullest measure, permeated by fresh thought, intelligent and alive" (320). Arnold complains that the romantics "had their source in a great movement of feeling, not in a great movement of mind" (321). The times when ideas are channeled remorselessly into forms of practical and political action create for Arnold a peculiarly English condition, and this bears closely on the English conception of criticism's function:

It is noticeable that the word *curiosity*, which in other languages is used in a good sense, to mean, as a high and fine quality of man's nature, just this disinterested love of a free play of the mind on all subjects, for its own sake,—it is noticeable, I say, that this word has in our language no sense of the kind, no sense but rather a bad and disparaging one. But criticism, real criticism, is essentially the exercise of this very quality. It obeys an instinct prompting it to try to know the best that is known and thought in the world irrespectively of practice, politics, and everything of the kind; and to value knowledge and thought as they approach this best, without the intrusion of any other considerations whatever. (325)

But if Arnold confines the function of criticism in one way, he broadens it in another. This concept of the "best that is known and thought in the world" will not always be found in English literature or English criticism: "The English critic of literature . . . must dwell much on foreign thought." Criticism must be "sincere, simple, flexible, ardent, ever widening its knowledge" (336, 338).

The considerations that Arnold addressed in 1864 concerning the function of criticism were resurrected by T. S. Eliot in 1923 in his essay entitled "The Function of Criticism." Eliot here takes issue with Arnold on the question of whether criticism exists for purposes that are merely independent of literary needs. The critic's task, writes Eliot, "appears to be quite clearly cut out for him; and it ought to be comparatively easy to decide whether he performs it satisfactorily, and in general, what kinds of criticism are useful and what kinds otiose." One of Eliot's most famous claims for the function of criticism is that it should attempt to realize its common principles. Through these, he argues, personal eccentricities are checked and controlled: "The critic, one would suppose, if he is to justify his existence, should endeavour to discipline his personal prejudices and cranks—tares to which we are all subject—and compose his differences with as many of his fellows as possible, in the common pursuit of true judgement."[16]

The major objection that Eliot levels against Arnold concerns the relationship of the critical to the creative, in particular "the capital importance of criticism in the work of creation itself": "Probably ... the larger part of sifting, combining, constructing, expunging, correcting, testing: this frightful toil is as much critical as creative" (30). But Eliot may be nearer to Arnold than he is prepared to acknowledge at this point. As we have seen, Arnold wrote that criticism feeds the current of creative literature. The difference seems rather that Eliot was concerned with the combination of critical and creative qualities within the same creative mind; Arnold meanwhile was concerned with the intellectual context of which criticism is part and the way that the artist, to make new art, draws on this context. Eliot's distinction from Arnold seems greatest when he is arguing that criticism is not "autotelic" (i.e., it is about something other than itself), and he conveys the impression that Arnold had defined a far too insulated, far too self-contained role for literary criticism and had failed to realize criticism's relations to other things. As has often been pointed out, Eliot was forging a relationship between criticism and the creative that corresponds closely with the combination of critical and creative elements in his own work, in his poetry and in his prose, but his principles may also refer, in a more complex and subtle regard, to Eliot's own criticism in poetry. (Lines and passages from the *Four Quartets* on poetic creation have considerable importance here.)

Eliot explored the "function of criticism" further when he returned to it in 1956 in his essay "The Frontiers of Criticism." Here he wrote that thirty years before "I asserted that the essential function of literary criticism was 'the elucidation of works of art and the correction of taste,'" but "[t]hat phrase may sound somewhat pompous to our ears in 1956." "Perhaps," he added, "I could put it more simply, and more acceptably to the present age, by saying to 'promote the understanding and enjoyment of literature.'"[17] Echoes of Eliot's central theme have appeared in work by Yvor Winters,[18] by F. R. Leavis,[19] and most recently by Terry Eagleton, who took up the topic of criticism's function in a short but pungently argued book. In *The Function of Criticism: From the Spectator to Post-Structuralism*, Eagleton asks how modern criticism has become what it is. His answer was to outline the story of literary criticism from the eighteenth century to the present day, with a particular emphasis on the relationship of criticism to society. While in Addison's day the critic was the voice of the public, and shared in ideals of classical bourgeois culture, now, partly in response to the polarizing influences of the nineteenth century on social and political questions, the literary critic has assumed a professional, specialist, and socially alienated role. *The Function of Criticism* charts this development; but it also records something of Eagleton's personal frustration with the political and social impotence of modern criticism, including (perhaps) his own. Since radical political and social commitments have not been enough to enable critics to change society, Eagleton's advice to the modern critic is that his true role is, after all, traditional. It is in essence Addison's. But Eagleton is not seeking a return to eighteenth-century conceptions of criticism except in this sense. The modern critic, like the eighteenth-century one, becomes more, not less exclusively, the voice of his age. In these respects, Eagleton's theory of the function of criticism was created to fit the broadened definition of the "literary" set forth in the manifesto *Literary Theory*. In *The Function of Criticism* he wrote, "'English Literature' is now an inherited label for a field within which many diverse preoccupations congregate: semiotics, psychoanalysis, film studies, cultural theory, the representation of gender, popular writing, and of course the conventionally valued writings of the past."[20] "Conventionally" here, as Eagleton deploys the word, does the work of reordering the field.

The Question of Essence

In all such treatments of critical purpose, criticism's defining idea, fixed through the terms of its *use*, has pervaded many varieties of statement. Not all are quite so consciously or explicitly focused on the functional aspects of criticism as the essays of Arnold, Eliot, or Eagleton. Certain critics, such as I. A. Richards, have approached the definition of criticism by reference to the questions that criticism is characteristically concerned to answer:

> What gives the experience of reading a certain poem its value? How is this experience better than another? Why prefer this picture to that? In which ways should we listen to music so as to receive the most valuable moments? Why is one opinion about works of art not as good as another?[21]

For Northrop Frye, likewise, literary criticism can be defined as "the possibility of a synoptic view of the scope, theory, principles, and techniques of literary criticism," or by determining the reasons why "criticism has to exist" or defending "the right of criticism to exist" or deciding on what criticism "has to be based."[22] All these comments again serve to establish the essential nature of criticism in what might be called (somewhat paradoxically) *relational* terms. If Frye defines criticism, he defines it only contextually. The same contextual principle applies when critics isolate criticism according to the nature of the object to which it refers (that of a "discourse," which in the case of Barthes gave criticism "a great resemblance to . . . logic"). An attempt of this kind can be found in the following passage, again by Barthes, first published in 1963:

> Every novelist, every poet, whatever the detours literary theory may take, is presumed to speak of objects and phenomena, even if they are imaginary, exterior and anterior to language: the world exists and the writer speaks: that is literature. The object of criticism is very different; the object of criticism is not "the world" but a discourse, the discourse of someone else: criticism is a discourse upon a discourse; it is a second language, or a *metalanguage* (as the logicians would say), which operates on a first language (or *language object*). It follows that the critical language must deal with two kinds of relations: the relation of the critical language to the language of the author studied, and the relation of this language object to the world. It is the "friction" of these two languages which defines criticism. . . .[23]

Yet others have defined criticism by the kind or type of its "issues," by or through its content. Stein Haugom Olsen distinguished literary criticism from philosophy in these terms: "The issues of literary criticism concern aspects of literary works, and among these issues will be the handling of certain types of themes and concepts, but there is no accepted place for debate about the truth or falsity of general statements about human life or the human condition."[24]

But if at this juncture we leave the discussion of criticism's relational purpose and turn to its identity or being (its *esse* or essential), a wider range of statements, passages, essays, and analyses will come into play. These are, I suggest, generally obscured by traditionally highly regarded essays on the topic of critical function that chart the "history of the field"; but though they suggest the question in a different form, they are just as crucial to the problem of defining criticism. Turning to what criticism "is" brings us to a corpus of statements about criticism that must certainly include Oscar Wilde's claim (made via the persona of Ernest in "The Critic as Artist") that criticism "is" supremely a creative art:

> Why should it not be? . . . That is what the highest criticism really is, the record of one's soul. It is more fascinating than history, as it is concerned simply with oneself. It is more delightful than philosophy, as its subject is concrete and not abstract, real and not vague. It is the only civilized form of autobiography, as it deals not with events, but with the thoughts of one's life; not with life's physical accidents of deed or circumstance, but with the spiritual moods and imaginative passions of the mind.[25]

Here, by contrast, is Northrop Frye's more recently expressed counterassertion—that criticism is best described as a science:

> It seems absurd to say that criticism *may* be a scientific element in criticism when there are dozens of learned journals based on the assumption that there is, and hundreds of scholars engaged in a scientific procedure related to literary criticism. Evidence is examined scientifically; previous authorities are used scientifically; fields are investigated scientifically; texts are edited scientifically. Prosody is scientific in structure; so is phonetics, so is philology. Either literary criticism is scientific, or all of these highly trained and intelligent scholars are wasting their time on some kind of pseudo-science like phrenology.[26]

In their radically different ways, and while such statements address an identical question, they only further reveal the depth of the problem of defining criticism according to essence. Ellis, in an article of seminal importance on the topic entitled "The Logic of the Question 'What Is Criticism?,'" had written that questions of this kind may have "at least three logically distinct kinds of answers":

> Some answers will provide a definition which explains the literal meaning of a word or concept; others will provide statements of fact which give information about a concept or thing whose definition is already assumed; and still others will be normative statements which recommend a desired or preferred state of affairs for the thing under discussion.[27]

The examples that Ellis gives are:

(a) literary criticism is the interpretation and evaluation of literary texts;
(b) criticism is an ancient mode of discourse going back at least to the Greeks;
(c) criticism is essentially evaluative.

Ellis's point was that attempts at definition, being by definition mutually exclusive, always "compete with each other," and that the same may be true, where exclusivity is required, of normative statements on criticism. Such statements attempt to set criticism on "the right path." The question "What is criticism?" thus leads to our wanting "an intuitively satisfying, puzzle-solving answer which will take precedence over others" (19–20). In the first case, this has a pragmatic rather than a logical justification. Because the field of literary study contains no unique focus, the definitions of it are unsatisfying. Indeed, the concept of criticism, in Ellis's view, "is an inherently confused one, and conceptual analysis will only expose, not resolve[,] the confusion." In the second case (that of descriptive statements or statements of fact), the unfocused nature of the critical field is again revealed. This leads to a wish for normative statements that *"impose"* an order on the field: "What this means is that the third kind of statement beginning 'criticism is . . .' will necessarily involve us in a great many different kinds of prescriptions relating to many different kinds of aspects of the enterprise of criticism": "None of them will have unique, exclusive status, and so constitute the single central answer to the question 'What is criticism?' which the question always seems to seek" (23). The situation of the definer of criticism, Ellis believed, could not be comprehended unless he realized the pragmatic purpose of the definition he was trying to frame:

> Given this diversity, any critic who seizes on a particular normative recommendation and asserts that this is essentially what criticism is or does, implying that it is more important and central than any other possible norm, misconceives the situation unless he makes the primary focus of his recommendation a pragmatic matter; it then becomes a matter of arguing that in the present state of criticism it is more necessary to insist on this particular recommendation than any other. Now if this point is understood, it should

be possible to make a single normative assertion as to what criticism should try to do—now, in these circumstances. (24)

Philosophical Method and the Problem of Criticism: Collingwood on Definition

The implications of these claims for the definition of criticism will be more closely examined, and will need to be qualified somewhat, in the following chapter. First, however, it will be useful to set the problem of defining "criticism" within the context of the larger problem of conceptual categorization. It seems fundamental, in deciding between the kinds of definition that might be preferred, that we should know as far as we can, and at the earliest stage, what kind of concept criticism is. If the problems of defining criticism overlap with the problems of defining literature, on the one hand, they also, on the other, fall squarely within the scope of the laws governing the definition of "philosophical concepts" stated by R. G. Collingwood. In what remains of this chapter I will discuss the pertinence of Collingwood's *Essay on Philosophical Method* (1933) to the problem of defining criticism.

In his chapter "Definition and Description" Collingwood distinguishes the definition of the concepts of philosophical thought from those of mathematics, exact science, and empirical science, and he shows why, like the doctrines of classification and division, such concepts "have been framed rather with an eye to the peculiar structure of the scientific concept, and must be modified in certain ways before they can be applied to the philosophical."[28] Collingwood makes clear that he is discussing what is called "real, as opposed to verbal[,] definition: not the definition of words but the definition of concepts," and he begins by suggesting that the difficulty that people have found in defining philosophical concepts has led to "the tendency which exists at the present time to deny that philosophical concepts admit of definition" (93). There are two reasons for this. Either we make a circular definition by using in the definition the term we are trying to define. Or, using a different term, we substitute a different concept for the *definiendum*. Collingwood's point is that while this is true of definitions in mathematics, it does not apply to philosophical concepts. These require a somewhat different understanding of the word "define":

To define is literally to fix the limits of a plot of land or the like, to show where one thing begins and another ends, or in general to discriminate or distinguish. A person asked to define his position, in an argument, is being asked to remove ambiguities from a statement of it which, implicitly or explicitly, he is understood to have made, and thus make it clearer and more precise. A photographic image is said to be ill-defined when the degree of blurring is more than can reasonably be permitted. In these ordinary or common-sense uses of the word, it is implied that definition is a matter of degree: to define is not to make absolutely definite what was absolutely indefinite, but to make more definite what was to some extent definite already. (94)

Whereas in exact science, definitions define absolutely, so that a person possessing a definition "knows the essence of the concept perfectly" while a person who does not possess it "does not know that essence at all," in the definition of philosophical concepts there are degrees of knowing. Thus, no line can be drawn between the essence of a philosophical concept and its theorems, or between the essence and its properties. Here, a definition could be equated to an entire exposition of the concept, which is at once "a statement . . . of its essence, and of the properties regarded as the elements constituting that essence": "[T]he concept would remain undefined only in the sense that there would be no one phrase or sentence which could be taken out of its context and called the definition" (94–95).

Collingwood's second condition is that in defining philosophical concepts, unlike exact science, there need be no fundamental difference between knowing a concept and not knowing it. Defining a philosophical concept is in this aspect not the same in kind as defining a dodecahedron, "for there would be no occasion on which we were absolutely ignorant of any concept contained in its subject-matter." Nor would there be any possibility of the scientific type of definition, because "we could never come to a point at which our knowledge concerning the essence of a concept could be described as complete." This thinking derives from Collingwood's theory of the "scale of forms," "in which all ignorance is a lower or more rudimentary kind of knowledge, and the zero of absolute ignorance is never reached" (97). In philosophical study, correspondingly, "at each step we re-define our concept by way of recording our progress; and the process can only end when the definition states all that the concept contains" (97–98).

These, then, according to Collingwood, are the key distinctions between definitions of philosophical concepts and those in exact science; but there are nevertheless some similarities, Collingwood argues, both with the definitions of exact science and with those of an empirical science. The definition of philosophical concepts resembles that of exact science "in stating the concept's essence; and that, after all, is the essence of definition." The resemblance with empirical science lies in "stating an essence which is identified not with one selected part of the concept but with the concept as a whole" (98). In describing empirical concepts the exposition "cannot be accurately divided into exposition of essence (definition) and exposition of properties (theorems), because the logical connexions upon which that division rests are lacking" (98–99): "There is no one attribute of a comet or an elephant from which we can deduce all the rest. . . ." The exposition of a philosophical concept, Collingwood argues, resembles the empirical to the extent that it also aims at completeness and renounces "the attempt to select one element and call it essence, leaving the rest to be deduced from it" (99). The special feature of the definition of the philosophical concept was that while the philosophical exposition describes its subject matter, describing "in this case means not merely enumerating the items of which the subject-matter is composed but expounding them in such a way as to exhibit their connexions." The process Collingwood goes on to describe was cumulative rather than formally logical:

> To follow such an exposition means gradually building up in one's mind the conception which is being expounded; coming to know it better and better as each new point is made, and at each new point summing up the whole exposition to that point. The thought of the subject-matter is thus gradually becoming clearer and more complete. (100)

But in the way the concept is grasped there is also a qualitative development:

> [T]his is not a mere change in degree. It must be a change in kind also. The fresh points are not merely closer and closer approximations to the truth, like fresh decimal places; they are qualitatively new as well; and hence the phases through which the definition passes in its growth are not only new in degree, as we come to know the concept better, but new in kind, as we come to grasp fresh aspects of it. The various phases will therefore constitute a scale of forms, beginning with a rudimentary or minimum definition and adding qualitatively new determinations which gradually alter the original definition so as to make it a better and better statement of the concept's essence: a statement, at each step, complete as far as it goes, and expressing a real and necessary specification of the concept.
>
> To define a philosophical concept, therefore, it is necessary first to think of that concept as specifying itself in a form so rudimentary that anything less would fail to embody the concept at all. This will be the minimum specification of the concept, the lower end of the scale; and the first phase of the definition will consist in stating this. Later phases will modify this minimum definition by adding new determinations, each implied in what went before, but each introducing into it qualitative changes as well as additions and complications. Finally, a phase will be reached in which the definition contains, explicitly stated, all that can be found in the concept; the definition is now adequate to the thing defined and the process is as complete as we can make it. (100–101)

I shall return to Collingwood again in the course of this book, and in what follows I shall use this analysis as a touchstone or guide. It is a working alternative to the absolutist theories of definition that have tended to hold sway, and these latter have supported the claim, of which Eagleton's discussion of defining literature is one example, that what cannot be exactly or objectively defined cannot rightly exist. For we are now ready to consider the problems of defining criticism at closer quarters. First we will need to connect this theory of defining philosophical concepts more closely with the problem of defining criticism, and as for criticism today, we will need to consider the "overlap of classes" (in Collingwood's language) between academic and journalistic norms, and criticism's relation to other near-synonymous terms. But since we are interested in the implications this relation has for the historical conception of criticism as part of the whole of criticism, the status of critical histories—judged in narrativistic and literary terms—must then be discussed. As my argument runs its course, I shall, throughout, avoid making any personal move to complete (or finalize) the definition of criticism; but in order to fuse the components in the problem I am trying to outline, I shall appeal to what I shall call its "poetic idea," and commend the comparative precision that I think that this has. Here my historical case study will be the *Essay on Criticism* of Alexander Pope. In the discussion up to that point I shall construct a prefatory context of reflection for the *Essay* that includes criticism's pre- and posttheoretical determinants, and I shall suggest that Pope's is the kind of definition of criticism we must ultimately favor. But first we must consider some further examples of criticism's typical attempts to define itself.

2
On Definition and Debate

That part of my work on which I expect malignity most frequently to fasten, is the *Explanation;* in which I cannot hope to satisfy those, who are perhaps not inclined to be pleased, since I have not always been able to satisfy myself. To interpret a language by itself is very difficult; many words cannot be explained by synonimes, because the idea signified by them has not more than one appellation; nor by paraphrase, because simple ideas cannot be described. When the nature of things is unknown, or the notion unsettled and indefinite, and various in various minds, the words by which such notions are conveyed, or such things denoted, will be ambiguous and perplexed. And such is the fate of hapless lexicography, that not only darkness, but light, impedes and distresses it; things may be not only too little, but too much known, to be happily illustrated. To explain, requires the use of terms less abstruse than that which is to be explained, and such terms cannot always be found; for as nothing can be proved but by supposing something intuitively known, and evident without proof, so nothing can be defined but by the use of words too plain to admit of definition.

Other words there are, of which the sense is too subtle and evanescent to be fixed in a paraphrase. . . .
—Samuel Johnson, preface to *A Dictionary of the English Language*

CRITICISM. *n.s.* A standard of judging well. Remark; animadversion.
—Samuel Johnson, *A Dictionary of the English Language*

Uniqueness and Plurality in the Definition of Criticism

MOST OF WHAT PASSES FOR DEFINITIONS OF CRITICISM IS FRAMED IN PROPOSITIONAL terms. In whole passages, essays, or longer studies we tend to speak of theories or philosophies of criticism. Shorter statements of phrase or sentence length, particularly those governed by the verb "to be," suggest definitions. As we are variously told by critics writing over the last one hundred years,[1] criticism is:

1. the *exercise* of this very quality [a "disinterested love of a free play of the mind on all subjects, for its own sake"]. It obeys an instinct prompting it to try to know the best that is known and thought in the world, irrespectively of practice, politics, and everything of the kind (Matthew Arnold, 1864);[2]
2. *the record of one's soul* . . . the only civilized *form of autobiography* (Oscar Wilde, 1891);[3]
3. *the statement in language* of . . . [a] structure [of perceptions that do not accumulate as a mass]; it is *a development* of sensibility (T. S. Eliot, 1920);[4]
4. the *endeavour to discriminate* between experiences and to evaluate them (I. A. Richards, 1924);[5]
5. very largely, though not wholly, *an exercise in navigation* (I. A. Richards, 1929);[6]
6. the *condition* of discussing . . . [literature] relevantly at all (R. G. Cox, 1951);[7]
7. *a description and an evaluation of its object* (Cleanth Brooks, 1951);[8]
8. *a verbal imitation* of a human productive power which in itself does not speak. . . . If criticism is *a science*, it is clearly *a social science* (Northrop Frye, 1957);[9]
9. *discrimination, judgment*, and hence applies and implies criteria, principles, concepts, and thus a theory and aesthetic and ultimately a philosophy, a view of the world. . . . *a philosophy* and even *a form of theology*, an all-inclusive *system*, a world *hypothesis* (René Wellek, 1963);[10]
10. that *field of endeavor* which describes the relationships of texts to larger contexts of reality and value (E. D. Hirsch Jr., 1967);[11]
11. a *construction* of the intelligibility of our own time (Roland Barthes, 1963).[12]
12. a *principled activity* (M. C. Beardsley, 1970);[13]
13. the mimetic *duplication* of a conceptual action. . . . a criticism of consciousness (Georges Poulet, 1972);[14]
14. necessarily, *comparison*. . . . the act of preference, of the "placing" of one writer above another (George Steiner, 1972);[15]
15. *the art of knowing* the hidden roads that go from poem to poem (Harold Bloom, 1973);[16]
16. *the focal activity of a discourse* whose foremost general cultural function is the repression of politics (Francis Mulhern, 1979);[17]
17. ultimately *an exercise in persuasion* (John Carey, 1980);[18]
18. *a talent*, like any other talent (Clive James, 1980);[19]
19. *an academic thing,* located for the most part far away from the questions that trouble the reader of a daily newspaper. . . . *the present* in the course of its articulation, its struggles for definition (Edward Said, 1984);[20]

20. very largely *the art of putting questions . . . a life-choice* taken at the deepest level (H. A. Mason);[21]
21. *something* you do (or fail to do) (H. A. Mason);[22]
22. a hybrid or bastard *discourse,* or an arena of intermingling and jostling discourses (Chris Baldick, 1996).[23]

The logical problem raised by these statements is the problem of any substitution employing the present tense of the verb "to be." If A "is" A, the "definition" is simply circular. If, on the other hand, A "is" not A but B, the thing in question is not unique.[24] What kind of definition—if any—is then achieved by these statements? For if to define is not *just* to inform, we must not feel we have learnt anything *completely* new by them. They are not stipulations: the existence of criticism does not depend on what one or more of the statements has to say. But if the contents of the statements are already known when we read them, can they be *worth* the stating? To earn their keep as definitions, the statements must surely seem more than tawdry platitudes.[25]

A number of observations can now be made. First, there is a sense in which all these statements at once illuminate the possibility of defining criticism; and there is a sense in which they discourage or deny this possibility. The list is perhaps not endless (since the language holds a finite number of words); but what is immediately apparent is that we are not only in each case dealing with different things or propositions about criticism, but different kinds or orders of things or propositions. To say, for example, that criticism is a "hypothesis" (even a "world hypothesis") is not the same as to say it is a "talent." The one belongs to a group of words that includes the acts of surmising, imagining, conjecturing, and so forth; the other belongs to a group that might include skill or ability or allusion to other personal or internal faculties or attributes. The one draws attention to the logical affinities of criticism, its place next to philosophy or the law. The other alludes to its psychological or psychic origins as a facility, a knack or gift, something that is improved by practice, but "no methods teach." In the same way a "record" is not the same as a "science"—the one is a form of report or representation, the other a system of procedures by which something is examined or studied. One is a result; the other is the means for conducting the inquiries that lead to results. And so on.

But the crucial thing is that the different kinds of things or propositions are only *somewhat* different. The words have a family resemblance. This affinity depends on which conjunctions you happen to form from the list. Criticism as "evaluation" can without too much strain be said to possess a "system" (to evaluate can be "systematic"), and so is linked to the sense in which criticism is also a system. A verbal "imitation" may be otherwise described as a "discourse." Either can be an "activity." Few of the pairs we might choose (even such near antonyms as "art" and "science," for example) would be mutually exclusive. The problem of reconciling the statements seems, therefore, not insurmountable. One could say of the words used of criticism that they are as different and alike as those that Wittgenstein detected in language as a whole when he compared it to "a tool chest, containing a hammer, chisel, matches, nails, screws, glue": "It is not a chance that all these things have been put together—but there are important differences between the different tools—they are used in a family of ways—though nothing could be more different than glue and a chisel."[26] The likeness is not dependent on common attributes or identical properties, but a common relation to the same problem.

The second thing to be said of these statements is that they are all attempts at essentialist or foundationalist thinking about criticism. Each of the writers is implicitly claiming to have plumbed the mystery of criticism, its quiddity. In this, all the statements assume controversially that an essence of criticism exists somewhere out there in the world or behind or within the term. Each aspires to the irreducible essence of meaning dismissed by I. A. Richards as "the curious instinctive tendency to believe that a word has its own true or proper use, which . . . has its roots in magic."[27] What is offered is a didactic statement claiming correspondence: to adopt a formulation of Lamarque and Olsen, it is a pairing of one bit of language with another bit of language that stands for a bit of the world.

Thirdly, the statements are evaluations. They in each case register feelings about criticism, an attitude towards their object, and an implicit looking up to it or looking down upon it from some exterior viewpoint or perspective. They record admiration and deprecation. This makes them something less than disinterested spectatorial accounts (and "true" definitions in that sense). They are offered in contexts where listeners or readers are at risk of reaching one or another alternative conclusion. Lest we dismiss criticism as a wholly technical matter, we learn that it is a life choice ("taken at the deepest level"). Lest we think it is a matter of professional expertise and a particular course of training, we discover that it is a "talent." Should we be tempted to think it a chaos of uncoordinated and baseless opinion-mongering, we learn that it is a *principled* activity." The statements imply—in short—the existence both of a positive and a negative case, a determination to rescue criticism from common kinds of mistakes about it. The evocation of positives by negatives is in turn a very common form of defining criticism. Thus criticism may be defined as:

1. "[not] value-free" (Said);[28]
2. "not just an alternative approach to literature" (Cox);[29]

3. "not an 'homage' to the truth of the past or to the truth of 'others'" (Barthes);[30]
4. "not science" (Eliot);[31]
5. "not a passage from text to reader" (Terry Eagleton);[32]
6. "not cumulative" (Wendell V. Harris).[33]

And so on. Just as "[t]he negation provides a background against which the affirmation stands out in relief,"[34] so in statements of the form "criticism is . . ." such anticipations of what we *might* have thought are entertained only to be dismissed. Of the corresponding positive statements we may say what I. A. Richards said of critical statements (again using the verb "to be") when made about poetry:

> It is much harder to obtain statements about poetry, than expressions of feeling towards it and towards the author. Very many apparent statements turn out on examination to be only these disguised forms, indirect expressions, of Feeling, Tone, and Intention. Dr Bradley's remark that *Poetry is a spirit*, and Dr Mackail's that it is *a continuous substance or energy whose progress is immortal* are eminent examples. . . . [35]

The relationship of each of such general statements to the whole of the object towards which they express an attitude is captured by Morris Weitz: "Criticism of *Hamlet* includes many things; any claim about what is primary or relevant or necessary or sufficient in criticism, consequently, is not a true (or false) statement about its nature, but an expression of a preference on the part of the particular critic that he converts into an honorific redefinition of 'criticism.'"[36] Such statements belong to the essentially controversial context in which criticism as a whole is at any time redefined. But if in one sense this affinity corresponds with the widespread assumption that the fundamentals of criticism have in recent years given rise to vigorous debate, in another sense the different conceptions of the field that critics bring to their task must also suggest limits to the reality of this. It is part of the problem that criticism has with itself. Effective debate is denied if fundamentals go unshared. Let us follow this through.

Definitional Conditions for Critical Debate

The usual purpose of defining anything is to get a clearer idea of the thing in question fixed in our minds. The source of definitions, for any purposes—and certainly for the purposes of foreign learners of English words—is the dictionary. But little is gained by looking up "criticism" (or for that matter "literature") in an English dictionary. To define "literary criticism," in the ordinary sense of the term, might often come down to saying that it is the criticism of, or the commentary upon, literature, and this is not a great deal of help. When we look for a definition of criticism, we are seeking to have someone tease out the essence of criticism, the qualities that set it apart from other phenomena or concepts. We are wanting to have this essence distinguished from peripheral qualities that it might be easy for us to confuse with the essence. There is every reason to seek such essential qualities of criticism today when the world of criticism seems so disparate and divided.[37]

We have seen that in trying to say what criticism as a whole "is," it is natural to try to bring instances of it to mind. We may think of particular (written) works—an essay by David Lodge, say, or a critical classic like Johnson's *Preface to Shakespeare*, or Samuel Taylor Coleridge's *Biographia Literaria*. Once a mental list of such works has been made (and we might individually all draw up very different lists), we can begin by isolating common properties, qualities, or attributes by extracting from the individual instances of criticism those that are true, more or less, for criticism as a whole. We might, for example, say that criticism is criticism when a value judgment is made, or when a literary work is interpreted or explained. We might set a whole range of conditions, or settle on one—for example, that for a work to be criticism it must have a framework of theory.

The problem with this procedure originates with the initial selection of texts; these are subject to individual preference, opinion, or taste. As we have seen, some people do regard judgments, and judgments of value, as essential to criticism, and rule out works in which they do not appear. Others, equally strongly, assert that value judgments are peripheral, that criticism is not defined by the presence of the value judgment because of the importance of the interpretive, explicatory relationship between the critic and the text, and because all texts are equal. A definition will not arise from this procedure, because there is no guarantee that the person doing the defining is able to speak for the community of critics and readers at large. All that will arise will be propositions about criticism that may purport to sum criticism up, but actually reflect a very specific and personal set of ideals—those of the definer. Such propositions may lay claim to be true, but they have yet to be tested. There is no knowing whether any one of them is yet "the truth," the definition we seek. One can argue that the definition has to be accepted as true by every user of English, or at least by the community of those who deploy the word "criticism" in writing and speech with every expectation that they will be understood.

But one reason for having a definition of criticism is that it seems impossible to know how far the debates alleged to rage in criticism today are really happening; whether the critics locked in dispute are taking issue about the same things, and according to positions that conflict one with another. For debate exists only when participant A is asserting something that participant B is concerned to deny. Thus says someone: "That's not criticism—he doesn't declare if he actually likes the work." Someone else says: "That's not criticism—it's all generalized assertion; nothing is demonstrated or proved." One can conclude that such speakers are not engaged in debate, because they are working from different core conceptions of criticism. Sometimes, the difference may reveal beliefs that, though they seem to be based on the same perception, are diametrically opposed: "That's not criticism; it's only theory," says one. "But that's precisely why I like it," says the other; "Criticism *should be* theory." As John Searle has observed: "[A] fair amount—not all of course, but a fair amount—of what passes for passionate controversies and deeply held divisions within literary theory is in fact a matter of confusions having to do . . . not with competing answers to the same question, but with noncompeting answers to different questions, different questions that happen to be expressed in the same vocabulary. . . ."[38]

With a lack of competition on the *same* ground (according to an all-embracing definition), many of the more detailed conflicts within criticism are stripped of their meaning. The positions may often belong in different debates having their location within distinct "definitions"; and, perhaps, this may happen without the "debaters" realizing it. Clearly the differences that then occur are not disagreements that lead anywhere, any more than disagreements having their origin in disputes derived from efforts to describe the essential attributes of the color "yellow." They do not further thought about (or within) literary criticism. This is not because radically divided opinion upon such issues is not often encountered, but because the differences are not accommodated within a definition of criticism that is sufficiently *exclusive*. When the positions overlap, they create only a false consensus. When they do not overlap, the disagreements are then inevitable but not useful. They do not constitute a radical interrogation, because lying behind them is a fissiparous set of desiderata for literary criticism that are sometimes explicitly declared but may also signal different tacit assumptions.

The old divide—touched on in the last chapter—about whether criticism is ultimately an art or a science encapsulates this problem. The topic has characteristically aroused strong views asserted with the kind of oppositional energy that has come to express the outwardly confrontational attitudes of the modern critical scene. One notoriously aggressive definition of criticism by D. H. Lawrence—ostensibly on the criticism-is-not-science side of the case—illustrates very well both how general statements on the nature of criticism may seem to approach definition, but in fact hold only propositions, and how even the most passionate assertion of a particular position may very often be less exclusive of its opposing argument than the decisive tone and manner of the utterance might seem to permit. The passage has the advantage of bringing tacit understandings to the surface in explicit form:

> Literary criticism can be no more than a reasoned account of the feeling produced upon the critic by the book he is criticising. Criticism can never be a science: it is, in the first place, much too personal, and in the second, it is concerned with values that science ignores. The touchstone is emotion, not reason. We judge a work of art by its effect on our sincere and vital emotion, and nothing else. All the critical twiddle-twaddle about style and form, all this pseudo-scientific classifying and analysing of books in imitation-botanical fashion, is mere impertinence and mostly dull jargon.[39]

The statement is apparently uncompromising. Criticism is "no more than . . ."; it can "never be . . ."; there is such and such a quality "and nothing else." But Lawrence's complaint is not consistent. He says that criticism can be no more than a reasoned account of the feeling produced upon the critic by the book he is criticizing, but two sentences later the touchstone is emotion, "not reason." If Lawrence's imagined opponents insisted on the reinstatement of "reason," there might be little at all to argue about.[40] As it is, we do not know whether it is the idea of criticism as science or criticism as a degenerate pseudoscience that offends him. The position is an emotional one, not an analytic one. It is a definition of criticism only in Ellis's normative sense: there is no saying with Lawrence that criticism "can never be a science" unless we wish to make a point about what criticism ought to be like. (Were there not the perception that many instances were very much otherwise, there would be no need to set up the ideal and to state it so strongly).

As a definition of criticism, Lawrence's paragraph therefore falls foul of what has been called "the fallacy of the precarious margins": we seek distinction by locating the essence of the thing—in this case, criticism—in all those marginal examples of either criticism-as-art or criticism-as-science (or emotion and reason) which give the initial, superficial, and thus precarious appearance of not overlapping with each other. The margin is precarious, because on closer inspection the positions do indeed overlap (as Lawrence's do). This is because we are still seeking definition in terms of a category or a class, and tend to assume that criticism can be defined according to the attributes it shares with some other thing.

But the "debate" about criticism as art or science does not only fail to advance understanding of what criticism is; by simplifying art and science, it impedes understanding—as if such concepts were not themselves mysterious.[41] Criticism is fused with conceptions coarsened to the point that the most ordinary intelligence would find them inadequate. It is a commonplace of scientific thinking that reason is not the only or even main defining characteristic of such thinking, and that great leaps in science require the equivalent of imagination and feeling—the emotional charge that Lawrence is using to distinguish criticism from science. And art, it is often said, expresses truth. Isn't that an appeal to the idea of reason? Why then should criticism be the only ground on which science and art are differentiated if artists and scientists are clear they have so much in common?

In the act of categorizing criticism the problem of defining is referred to science and art, but it can only be solved by a further process of class referral to what we understand by these terms. But since "art" and "science" are large questions themselves—larger, conceivably, than the definition of criticism—they open out the problem rather than resolve it. And so, logically, the process goes on, fizzling out in pointless regression, and driven by the illusion that agreement on the attributes of literary criticism, its intrinsic properties, might one day be had. The process fosters a climate of "debate" by promoting a recurrence to extremes, but fails because we are still left with the need to define the host type in relation to criticism. This type, like science and art, is invariably left unanalyzed and unexplained.

There are, doubtless, similar reasons why attempts to define literature have sometimes resorted to the conclusion that it is a "social construction" (or "misconstruction"): "The category of literary texts," Ellis has written, "is not distinguished by defining characteristics but by the characteristic use to which those texts are put by the community."[42] Criticism, according to the same conception, has whatever meaning users of English acquiesce in when they deploy "criticism" as part of the language. There is no meaning (or definition) separate from the occasions within the language when the word is used. Such a conception removes the imperative to consider what essential attributes criticism might have, or any individual might arbitrarily choose, and instead focuses attention on the relationship between the word and its context of use. We are no longer seeking a definition that depends only on our identifying the boundaries of criticism, and counting some items in and some items out, as if the definition could be thought of as the sum of the unchangeable contents of a box labeled "literary criticism." The problem is that different people will have different ideas of what to include and what to leave out. At the same time, it follows from such ideas that pieces of language can be identified as criticism on the basis that that is how they are used, and that some evaluative distinction, at the social if not the individual level, still has to be made. But a definition of criticism cannot be simply a grouping of all those items which are good criticism and a rejection of those which are bad. The definition must get criticism itself into the net, including the bad, though some items will be so bad they are not criticism, as a boat may be so bad it is not a boat but a raft.

But in what sense is any work "used" as criticism by society? One answer to this question seems possible if we draw our inference from the works of those writers we agree to call "critics." There appears to be little mystery about who the critics are—Leavis, T. S. Eliot, Hillis Miller, say—and no one, presumably, unless they are exceptionally ignorant of the field, would deny the appellation of critic to these particular men. We may of course take issue with every word such critics wrote, and disagreements would be rife about where the criticism of each of these critics approaches its quintessence. We can say that "Leavis is completely wrong about Swift," or "Leavis is in error over the poetry of Pope," but in so saying we may at the same time register a sense in which being wrong in the sense Leavis is wrong is one of the ways that Leavis's writing has *use* as criticism—it is received as criticism by the community because it stimulates us to develop a clearer idea of what is right. How much we dislike the criticism, its standards, expression, or judgments is independent of whether we use it as such. The fact that some criticism seems used less than it should be, because for example it is written by critics who are long dead, neither strengthens nor invalidates this point.

And this idea of the definition of criticism as a social construct is surely the primary reason why it is possible to speak with perfect sense of literary criticism, and be understood to be making sense, when faced with utterances that have no formal correspondence one with another. They can therefore be long or short, can occur in letters, footnotes, or prefaces (like Johnson's), can consist of imaginary dialogues (like Henry James's or Oscar Wilde's)[43] or straightforward monologue. They can happen in prose (like Leavis's, Eliot's, or Hillis Miller's) or in poetry (like Pope's *Essay on Criticism* or Horace's *Ars Poetica*); can utilize argument sometimes, but sometimes need not; can include personal testimony or disinterested analysis, ample quotation or no quotation; can be angry or cool, supercilious or humble; and can be published as scholarly articles in learned journals, as student essays, or as newspaper reviews. Perhaps also, the utterances do not actually have to be written down (can a conversation constitute "criticism"?); nor, if the leading propositions of cultural studies are correct,[44] does the material of which they are the "literary criticism" have to conform to any particular definition of literature. There is no end to the forms it can take, because while there are characteristic forms *for* criticism (today, these would include the scholarly article, the prose essay, and the monograph), it is not usefully defined by its form.

And this is perhaps why the laws governing any definition of criticism must be fundamentally different from the laws governing what is commonly referred to, in the context of literary definition, as a *genre*. To be a sonnet, a poem has to have so many lines, and it was once believed that an epic was a poem of twelve or twenty-four books. Such features are guides to the intentions of sonneteers and heroic poets. We know they are intending to write sonnets and epics, because their works have that number of lines and that number of books. But while criticism too has characteristic forms, it is not isolable by them in the way that sonnets and epics, when added to other genres, *are* poetry (unreliably so, of course, since some epics are written in prose). We accept that a poetical work having fourteen lines may be meant as a sonnet and may meet the criteria for sonnet status. But we also accept that it may fail as poetry. So too, many would-be critical essays or monographs that succeed as essays and monographs by formal standards (or a publisher's specification) may fail as criticism.

But what succeeds as criticism—in that it is used as such by society—may by contrast constitute criticism in a merely figurative sense. Thus Matthew Arnold could write of poetry as "the criticism of life."[45] We commonly say that Donne's *Songs and Sonnets* are a "criticism" of the Elizabethan lyric, or that Wordsworth's *Lyrical Ballads* are a "criticism" of the eighteenth-century poetry of Thomas Gray. Wherever there is a distance between two comparable works that are different in some feature of form, content, or style, we identify an "implied criticism." Thus, Dryden's translation of Chaucer, say, is a "criticism" of the medieval poet, as in a related sense is Shakespeare's *Troilus and Cressida*. Many so-called modernist and postmodernist works are said to have broken down the distinction between their existence as works of original creation and the sense in which they are "criticisms" of a literary form. An interest is sometimes taken in past literature that is thought to be doing this. Sterne's *Tristram Shandy* can be taken as a "criticism" of the conventional narrative form of the novel.

This approach to the definition of criticism has the enormous attraction of opening the field, and liberates criticism from its formally academic contexts of use. But that it solves the problem of definition is far from clear—not least because, having once started on the path of designating this or that "criticism," the word moves by stages unchecked towards a figurative extreme, one that corresponds with the sense in which cultural studies regards all phenomena as "texts." From this we lose the respect in which any definition must isolate, condense, fix, or narrow down its subject from the vast array of possible candidates for inclusion within it. Nothing is finalized (or therefore in this sense defined) by the denial of intentionality—the fact that the reception of a piece as criticism by the community of users of English words does not have to depend on whether it was intended as criticism when it was made. Not only does this ignore a debate that the theory of criticism has not itself settled; it brushes aside the familiar fact of our ordinary moral lives, that good intentions are generally respected and taken into account (just as the intent behind any action when it is judged in the courts). We are again at an impasse.

Empirical and Transcendental Concepts of Criticism: The Logic of Circularity

To break out of this impasse, I would argue that we need to abandon the prescriptions that normally apply when we want something defined. The basic rule, we have seen, is that definitions should never be circular. According to the laws of formal logic, definitions that define in terms of themselves have failed as definitions. In the case of criticism (and this would be true, also, of other concepts of the same general category or type), I am going to suggest that a circular definition is impossible to evade. But this does not mean that a clearer idea of criticism cannot be had, or that the purpose of definition cannot be furthered. It does not mean that we should be obliged to resign ourselves to a summary of criticism as a mere chaos of fragmented perceptions, half-formed ideals, or momentary glimpses of truths within a mode that has no overall unity or coherence. I shall suggest that criticism is not impossible to define because it does not really exist, or because it exists but is not understood (by critics, readers of critics, or speakers of the English language), or because its essence is somehow ineffable, illusory, or inaccessibly secret. If its essence is secret, the secret is an open one. The gist of my argument is that a definition of criticism may be found in the same respect that Collingwood was able to discover an "idea of history" by means of the distinction between empirical concepts (which *require* dictionaries to define them) and transcendental concepts, which "are necessary to all thought." These latter need not be defined in the sense that a dictionary defines a word because we are all possessed of them "in so far as we think at all."[46]

The question is, how do we know that we are all possessed of an idea of criticism so far as we think at all? We ask the question "What is criticism?," surely, for the precise reason that we do not know, or do not know as well as we would like to know, what criticism is. An answer consistent with Collingwood's theory of the transcendental concept (itself derived from the analysis of Immanuel Kant)[47] is that in the very act of bringing the identity of criticism to mind, we are creating an instance of it. The idea of criticism, I suggest, is an emergent property of our experience in critical practice. Further definition is then not only superfluous; it cannot in any case be achieved. To put the matter in another way: the definition of criticism is itself an intrinsic problem of criticism. It is raised as a problem by the critical process it is trying to pin down. Criticizing anything is one of the ways we are able to think about it, and this is because thinking critically is necessary to thinking. Thinking, to be thinking, is necessarily critical. The posing of the question "What is criticism?" is then an implied component in any process that is critical. What criticism "is" is not an *answer* to any question regarding its nature, since its definition includes the question. Its definition is subject matter to itself.

We cannot, in other words, draw out of our collective understanding of criticism a stateable definition that corresponds with the sort of final definition appropriate to an empirical concept (teacups and bald-headed stationmasters are Collingwood's examples of these). It is useless to try to define criticism in terms of the attributes that supposedly attach to a category or class, and we have seen that most general statements about criticism are not definitions but propositions. And while there seems the potential for a working agreement about "what criticism is" based on the use of utterances and texts as criticism, so that our meaning is that of a "social construct," a criterion of use (that is, a concept of criticism) is still required to enable us to say whether it is indeed as criticism that these utterances and texts are used.

In any ordinary understanding of the word "define," the search for a definition of criticism as a social construct is doomed to failure, because it cannot supply us with a sufficiently *enclosed* formulation of the kind we require when we open a dictionary to determine the meaning of a word. Nevertheless, arising from this preliminary discussion, there are two propositions—both too evidently disputable to be regarded as "absolute presuppositions" in the Collingwoodian sense—that we may extract if we wish to encourage a definition of criticism that is sufficiently essentialist in nature. One might be that criticism is essentially without form because it is essentially mental, an idea in the mind, and it is only when we begin to seek definition in terms of examples of criticism as talk or writing that we are in danger of making the kind of mistake that sometimes occurs when painted canvases are taken for art, or the organization of sounds is used as a basis for defining music.

The second proposition is one that I have already outlined: that criticism is only criticism when its own nature (and definition) is up for inspection. It is criticism only when its intrinsic status, attitudes, principles, and even existence are being questioned and put to the test. This is only to make a similar point to that which has already been made by the critic W. W. Robson:

> Criticism is much criticised. But this logically establishes its title to exist. Criticism never decides anything.[48]

The impossibility of having a finalizing, excerptible definition of criticism complies with this verdict. The definition of criticism, as Collingwood described the philosophy of history, can never be expressed "in the form of a completed doctrine."[49] The doctrine can never be completed, because the instances that the doctrine must summarize, contain, or account for are like those of literature—they are forever in flux. Old work dies and is forgotten. New work cannot be anticipated, but room has to be made for it in any statement that aspires to define criticism. A watertight doctrine or definition must be too narrow to be true. The definition of criticism is thus established not by pinpointing or fixing criticism at any particular moment. *It arises as we go along.* Whether it arises at all, of course, depends on the nature of the occasion and on our recognition that that is the kind of occasion it is.

3

Criticism, Function, Category, Complement

Ordinary and Proper Meanings of Criticism

I HAVE ARGUED FOR REASONS THAT I HOPE ARE BY NOW CLEAR THAT NONE OF THE statements examined so far in this book could ever *finally* define criticism. My initial concern (in part 1) has been to apply to the problem of criticism some of the difficulties identified in such essays as W. W. Robson's "The Definition of Literature": to consider, as preparatory to bringing Pope's *Essay* under the defining aspect, rather "what *kind* of definition is most likely to be useful."[1] But this statement in turn presupposes (as I have done) that one or another "kind" of definition of the thing in question is at least possible. Throughout this exploration, our central problem—the situation that makes evaluating definitions of criticism at once so necessary and yet so elusive—will be obvious to any reader of modern literary criticism. It is that the pervasive idiom of one "kind" of criticism—the poststructuralist— makes discussing the issue *except* in poststructuralist terms appear simply absurd, a naive and ignorant faux pas. This central problem is not open to solution, but is a risk going with acceptance that the word "criticism" is part of the currently usable nonspecialist vocabulary of English and that the existence of "poststructuralist criticism" is one comprehensible instance of use. But we have seen that what counts as a definition of criticism can be examined. It is open to inspection in two possible ways. The first is the clearing away of all those statements, formulations, approaches, and so forth that prima facie do not comply with the conditions we decide should govern the definition of something. I have in mind here all the kinds of utterances on criticism that easily pass for definitive remarks, and give us some of the satisfactions we associate with definitions (finality, comprehensiveness etc.), but do not do the job that we are asking definitions to do—because it is in their nature as utterances not to. Outlining the problem in broadly twentieth-century terms, and by reference to attempted definitions of criticism drawn from the literature of criticism of later years, has been the business of part 1 of this study.

A further stage—analyzing the relations between "criticism proper" and other concepts that are commonly merged or confused with it, as a presiding social category or some constituent element or internal subdivision—will form part 2 of this book, and is foreshadowed in the context and purpose of this concluding chapter of part 1. For it would not be enough to say (with John M. Ellis, for example) that the concept of criticism is "an inherently confused one" where "conceptual analysis will only expose, not resolve[,] the confusion."[2] If the concept is confused, and the confusions are exposed, the user would be better armed to evade them and usage would become clearer. The exposure of confusions is a stage in their elimination. If, however, the confusions are inherent in the sense that it is impossible to have criticism without them, then we would have to say that criticism was another name for confusion. When we use the word "criticism" it would be a sense of confusion we would call up.

The best we might do, then, in seeking "criticism proper" would be to seek a working definition of criticism, a definition in use. We are not concerned to boil down "criticism" to some core meaning that nobody uses and that could not be useful. We are interested in "criticism" in its ordinary acceptation, as deployed by speakers and writers of the English language who expect to be understood in conversations and writing containing the word. As I have suggested above, we are not interested in its status as a technical term, as when, for example, we encounter for the first time the term *différance*, or "signification" in transliterated structuralist criticism, or "base" and "superstructure" in Marxist criticism, and want the meaning explained. Our problem is that while "criticism" is a word in common usage, the usage is equivocal or ambiguous. There are different usages that do not always announce themselves as different. In this situation, our aim cannot be to fix on a central usage at the expense of all the ways that the word "criticism" is used, and to leave these out of account, to kill them off. It must be to keep these uses in play, as part of the totality of meaning, but to recognize their distinctness. The meaning of any word, as Collingwood pointed out in seeking to define "art," is constantly sliding off in any number of different directions:

> The proper meaning of a word . . . is never something upon which the word sits perched like a gull on a stone; it is something over which the word hovers like a gull over a ship's stern. Trying to fix the proper meaning in our minds is like coaxing the gull to settle in the rigging, with the rule that the gull must be alive when it settles: one must not shoot it and tie it there.[3]

Collingwood went on to suggest that the way to this "proper meaning" was not to ask what we mean, but "'What are we trying to mean?'": "And this involves the question 'What is preventing us from meaning what we are trying to mean?'" (7). To use the word "criticism"—according to this formula—is thus constantly to do battle with a barrage of distractions, wandering meanings that are all the time tending to divert us from meaning what we are trying to mean. What we are trying to mean by "criticism" is obstructed and impeded by all the adjoining concepts jostling for attention. Thus, criticism may not be the same thing as, say, history. But we can have historical criticism, and the historical study of criticism, where criticism is understood as a branch of the study of history. Likewise, criticism may differ from biography (many, though not all, biographies are about writers). And there is then the question of whether biography is necessary or sufficient for criticism, or even desirable within it (many New Critical "anti-intentionalists" and Foucaultian abolitionists[4] have argued for an outright ban). Similar rules apply to the position of psychology, ethics, autobiography, philosophy, linguistics, cultural studies, art in general, science in general, and so on. The problem also refers to criticism's relation to such interdisciplinary concepts as theory or interpretation, and to the object of the kind of criticism we call literary criticism, literature itself. It was the confusion inherent in this last concept, which critics have themselves sought to resolve, that led I. A. Richards to explain why criticism also appeared confused:

> If the definition of a poem is a matter of so much difficulty and complexity, the discussion of the principles by which poetry should be judged may be expected to be confused. Critics have as yet hardly begun to ask themselves what they are doing or under what conditions they work.[5]

But although it is not a purpose of this study to produce a *new* definition of criticism, we do not have to *start* from the position that criticism cannot be defined, that a definition is impossible. If we assume that criticism is impossible to define, then we are forced into a logical track that insists that it is so *completely* ambiguous, and means so many different things to so many different people, that the concept has effectively collapsed. This part-nihilistic, part-pluralistic dead end—sometimes known as "postmodernism"—is exceptionally common in criticism; but it is usually adopted prematurely in reaction to some form of inadequate definition (or contested proposition), or a definition of a certain form where no obvious substitute form springs to mind on the same occasion.

This is, I would argue, an unwarrantably extreme position, though it may result, understandably, from bewilderment at the sheer number of general statements on the nature of criticism that seem to contradict each other, and is a natural reaction to the polarized voices of modern criticism, languages seemingly constructed to undermine the existence of common understanding and speech. A distinction can, however, be drawn between cases of this kind and the famous occasion of F. R. Leavis's protest against attempts by philosophical thinkers to pin down criticism explicitly to certain principles and theories. Leavis felt that such thinkers had missed the essence of criticism; that criticism had to be "defined" (he uses the word only in quotation marks) in the form of an implication based on a specific practice. Leavis's "definition of criticism" was implicit in (and a tacit inference derived from) how he went about criticizing the authors and works that he did:

> I stand, then, by my account of *Four Quartets*. I stand also by my contention that "English" should be a liaison-centre, and that, in the "co-presence" needed to make it that, no discipline of thought is more important than the philosophical to that quite different one, the essence of which I have tried in my book, with inevitable clumsiness, to "define." I hoped to get accepted among members of a small philosophical élite that the "defining" can't be done with philosophical cogency. That, of course, involves some such avowal as the following. I should have been encouraged if Tanner could have been brought to see that it is not mere "serendipity" in me to insist on recommending "English" students to read Polanyi's essay, "The Logic of Tacit Inference."[6]

Without having to accept that Leavis's personal practice as a critic does, in fact, define criticism (an inference that many would now regard as outrageous), one need not assume that the most tenable definition of criticism must equate to a formal proposition. If the criticism we are interested in is the criticism of literature, and if literature is widely regarded as a channel for suggestion, intuition, and evocation, the probabilities might conceivably point in a decidedly different direction. But then defining literature seems part of the problem of defining criticism, and there is no taking for granted that literature is defined in this way. The "theorization" of criticism, as we have seen, has ensured that.

But to return to why anyone would want a definition of criticism (of any kind) and who would want it. A definition of criticism would be useful in any attempt to understand what it is that we think we are doing at a time when the remnants of the *communis criticorum* give the appearance of unprecedented disagreement about this. The search for a definition of criticism is one of the ways that the subject investigates itself, renews itself by reminding itself, and reinstates its bounds and limits as they have become overgrown and subject to dispute. Many or most new students of English literature find it impossible to discover what is supposed to be happening when reading a work of criticism, and thus to determine what, as critics, they themselves should be doing.[7] And then there are the writers of all the works of literature themselves. Does criticism still have something to do with them? A definition might reveal this. Here, once again, I do not assume that the kind of definition likely to be thought of help requires the nature of criticism to be simply spelt out, as a creed, or dogma or checklist (for the reasons suggested above). I merely presuppose that it will always be useful to know more about the kind of problem the defining of criticism is, and that it is a problem. If criticism proves incapable of giving an account of itself to people outside criticism (reflective people in general, physicists, historians, new students of literature, or whomever), then such people should know that, and should be privy to the reasons. Individuals can then decide for themselves how seriously or lightly they think criticism needs to be taken, and whether it can be taken seriously at all. This is a major consideration—given the quantity of human time that is currently devoted to criticism's study and the general conviction that the study of criticism constitutes a "field." Where then are the fences? Or are the divisions only internal?

One curiosity of the inquiry so far is its circular form: it has to be criticism which conducts the search to define criticism. Another is that the idea of criticism, in common with the Collingwoodian definition of art (like that of all philosophical concepts), has to be already there in our heads. The definition, once encountered, then "rings true" as we say. The assumption of this book is that we all do know what criticism is, precisely enough, and that when we use the word we do not *mean* to invoke a confusion, much less a nonentity, nonexistent until it is defined. Nor is the difficulty that of a foreign language term. Our problem is not the absence of facts: all the facts about criticism that we need already lie open before us (in all the "texts," ancient and modern, that we call "criticism"); nor is it that we do not know what we are trying to say: our problem is that we can't quite put what we know into words. And that is the essence of the difference between the "proper meaning" of criticism whose conditions for definition are open to inquiries of this kind and the nature of a technical term. No simple act of translation will do. The problem will not be solved by a paraphrase.

Three Limits of Definition

I will therefore conclude part 1 of this study by recalling three ways in which criticism tries for, in a sense achieves, and in a sense evades definition. It is not completely defined by statements of the following very common kinds: (1) accounts of its function; (2) accounts of its categories and types; (3) statements of the form: "Criticism is . . . ."

We can now recapitulate these in order, and in more detail.

The Function of Criticism

We have seen that to speak of the "function of criticism" implies an awareness, within the elements of the situation of criticism, of a distinction between means and ends. We may think of how criticism is a means to an end if we think of the sense in which it assists a reader in gaining a clearer idea of a literary text, explanatory or interpretive. But theories of the function of criticism differ widely in their conceptions of the ends that criticism should have. A scrapbook of extracts taken from the writings of critics on criticism over the last hundred or so years would probably have to include the following diverse, if not plain contrary, convictions. All represent answers of some kind to the implied question: "What is the critic (or criticism) *for?*":

1. "to try to know the best that is known and thought in the world, irrespectively of practice, politics, and everything of the kind . . . ." (Matthew Arnold, "The Function of Criticism at the Present Time," 1864)[8]
2. "to make a beginning for that more free speculative treatment of things. . . ." (Matthew Arnold)[9]
3. "the elucidation of works of art and the correction of taste." (T. S. Eliot, "The Function of Criticism," 1923)[10]
4. "to forerun composition, to serve as a gunsight. . . ." (Ezra Pound, "Date Line," 1934)[11]
5. "Excernment. The general ordering and weeding out of what has actually been performed. The elimination of repetitions." (Ezra Pound)[12]
6. "The business of the literary critic is to attain a peculiar completeness of response and to observe a peculiarly strict relevance in developing his response into commentary; he must be on his guard against abstracting improperly from what is in front of him and against any premature or irrelevant generalizing—of it or from it." (F. R. Leavis, *The Common Pursuit*, 1952)[13]
7. "The role of the contemporary critic is to resist that dominance [of mass-media commodification of the public sphere] by re-connecting the symbolic to the political, engaging through both discourse and practice with the process by which repressed needs, interests and desires may assume the cultural forms which could weld them into a collective political force." (Terry Eagleton, *The Function of Criticism*, 1984)[14]

But all these statements have in common the view that criticism, whatever else it may be, is definable as a means. When we use the word "criticism" in this functionalist theory what we mean to say is that criticism is the thing (the means) that leads to or produces another (quite different) thing (a completeness of response, a clear experience in the mind of the reader, a more civilized and sensitive society, a politically conscious and literate population, and so on and so forth), and is then left behind when its purpose is served. The function of criticism, like a function in mathematics, is to constitute the value on which criticism's own value depends. T. S. Eliot is adopting a functionalist theory when he writes that criticism "must always profess an end in view."[15]

We can try to suggest that criticism is "defined by its function."[16] But for this to be true we would have to be sure that the end of criticism (a better society, clearer ideas in the reader's mind, etc.) was only achieved when criticism provided the means; when criticism and only criticism was the special kind of activity proper to the realization of these things. And it is clearly an activity of no such a kind, any more than "a vehicle for getting from A to B" defines a car by its function when there is always the possibility of going by train. Not only are the ends proposed for criticism very different indeed, but the achievement of ends by means allows for the possibility of different means. Thus "a clearer idea of the poem (say) in the reader's mind" need not entail the reader having benefited at any point from a critical exposition of the poem: it might, for example, be the effect of the same person reading the poem again in a completely different, refreshed frame of mind, or coming back to the poem after having read other poems or other poets. Likewise, criticism is not the exclusive means by which it is possible to achieve the end of enhancing the political consciousness of society. Literature itself can do that, as the poetry of Dryden, Shelley, Wordsworth, and Bob Dylan have all at different times shown. So can political speeches. We can, of course, say that achieving ends of this kind is one of the ways in which poems and political speeches may function *as* criticism: they are "criticism" *in that respect*. But criticism is defined by its function in this regard only when other factors in the situation are fixed.

Criticism by Category and Type

The basis of this approach to defining is to see criticism as the sum of its divisible parts, as a composite of its differentiae, as the logicians might say. In this event criticism exists as a kind of protean being—or a monster with many heads. Again, by turning to the criticism of the last hundred or so years we can see that there are various ways in which this creature divides. It is possible, for example, to specify, adjectivally, different "types" or "categories" of critic, as T. S. Eliot does in his essay "To Criticize the Critic" (1961):

> First of all among those types of critics other than mine, I should put down the Professional Critic—the writer whose literary criticism is his chief, perhaps his only title to fame. . . .
> Second, I name the Critic with Gusto. This critic is not called to the seat of judgment; he is rather the advocate of the authors whose work he expounds, authors who are sometimes the forgotten or unduly despised. . . .
> Third, the Academic and the Theoretical. I mention these two together, as they can overlap; but this category is perhaps too comprehensive, since it ranges from the purely scholarly . . . to the philosophical critic. . . .[17]

Here the effort is to define criticism by drawing defining lines between its family varieties. A slightly different technique was used by Ezra Pound in "Date Line" (1934). Here the critic tries to pin down criticism in terms of divisions corresponding to genres, or formal types of expression, within criticism itself. The result is a kind of menu—the same dish with different flavors and fillings:

> Criticism has at least the following categories, differing greatly in the volume of their verbal manifestation, and not equally zoned.
>   1. Criticism by discussion, extending from mere yatter . . . up to the clearly defined record of procedures. . . .
>   2. Criticism by translation.
>   3. Criticism by exercise in the style of a given period . . . .
>   4. Criticism via music, meaning definitely the setting of a poet's words. . . .
> This is the most intense form of criticism save:
>   5. Criticism in new composition.[18]

Such setting forth of criticism in, as it were, its component parts is not confined to creative writers: such writers might have special reasons to want to keep criticism in its place. There are, for example, the rubrics used by the scholar and aesthetician Northrop Frye in his magnum opus, the *Anatomy of Criticism* (1957). Frye seeks here what he hopes will be "a comprehensive view of criticism,"[19] and this he does by reference to immense general categories that go by the names of "Historical Criticism," "Ethical Criticism," "Archetypal Criticism," "Rhetorical Criticism," and so on. Much subsequent critical scholasticism has followed similar lines. A more recent version of this practice of critical typing can be found in the semihistorical, semidoctrinal divisions one finds in almost all modern introductions to literary theory designed for newcomers to the "field" of critical studies: Russian formalism, structuralism, poststructuralism, feminism, and so forth.[20] Such studies reflect two important trends in the implicit definition of criticism: (1) the "category-mistake" in which criticism has come to be seen as entirely defined in terms of its theories, and (2) the success of an essentially descriptivist, nonevaluative typology as a suitable medium for the introductory discussion of criticism.

In each of these cases criticism can be seen as the total of a sort of addition sum: X (= criticism) = $a+b+c+d$ and so forth, where a, b, c, and so on, correspond with "professional" and "academic," say, in Eliot's breakdown, "X by discussion" and "X by translation" in Pound's, or "historical" and "ethical" in Frye's. The "critic proper" is thus the additive result of, say, the "professional," the "academic," and the rest, while "criticism proper" may be regarded as the gathering of a number of subdivisions, or "approaches"—liberal humanist, Marxist, feminist, structuralist, poststructuralist, and so on—whichever the individual writer on criticism happens to choose as the appropriate set. Totting up the elements then gives you criticism.

The problem here is this: while the differentiae of the definition are specified, the genus is not. It is not to define criticism to say—in effect—that it is that which has "discussion," "translation," "an exercise in style," "music," and "new composition" as its types, because the genus (the general class of things to which all these attach) is missing. Moreover, to continue in this somewhat harshly logical vein, the differentiae are all shared with concepts other than criticism. They are accidental, not essential, attributes of the concept's referents; they are symptoms, not part of the defining criterion. Thus, it is not only possible to have a "professional" cricketer, an "academic" administrator (to again use T. S. Eliot's breakdown), where the attributes can be linked with perfect sense to referents that have nothing whatsoever to do with what we are trying to mean when we use the word "criticism": the *same* combination of attributes applicable to "criticism" could apply equally to the definition of "art."

The consequence is an array, not a totality. We are made aware of the attributes that go to compose criticism, but not the unique, irreplicable sense in which they are related to make criticism something distinct, a concept in its own right. The approach to defining criticism satisfies the analytic aspect of a definition—that it should enhance our insight into the components of a concept. But it also works to deny the respect in which to define something is to achieve a focus, a condensation, a confirmation that the totality is only the sum of the attributes specified and nothing else. If criticism is to be defined by the identification and naming of differentiae minus a genus, the division must take place without a remainder. But the elements into which criticism is divided here give no guarantee that this is the case. They can come together to make something more than criticism, or something less. Pound's "at least" seems to recognize this.

A similar problem has to be confronted in accounts of critical writing containing the formulation "The critic as . . . " or "Criticism as . . . ," e.g.:

"The Critic as Artist" (Oscar Wilde) or "Criticism as Language" (Roland Barthes). Such accounts may be seen as trying to move criticism's definition in one preferred direction or another. Their possibilities have no end. In this respect they share the character of statements of the form "Criticism is...."

Criticism is ...

Statements of the form "criticism is ... " are, as we have seen, exceptionally frequent in the literature of criticism and provide an account of criticism in what is probably the most commonly accepted definitional format: "Hypocrisy is the tribute that vice pays to virtue"; "Love is ... "; "Happiness is ... ," and so on. We may think of these statements, in the case of criticism, as straight answers to the kind of straight question that has often been posed of art, of poetry, of literature, and of criticism itself: the question "What is ... ?" Unlike statements on the function of criticism considered above, the genus of the definition is perfectly explicit in this case. The grammar of the answer is controlled by the grammar of the question. It rests on the verb "to be." And so, amongst many other examples, we have been able to juxtapose remarks such as T. S. Eliot's that criticism "is a development of sensibility";[21] Northrop Frye's that "criticism is a science";[22] Harold Bloom's that "Criticism is the art of knowing the hidden roads that go from poem to poem";[23] and Clive James's that "Criticism is simply a talent."[24] Such remarks are like epigrams, apothegms, bons mots, or aperçus. They sound an oracular note that is perfectly designed to create the impression that it is possible to clear up the mystery of criticism's essential identity once and for all. "Criticism in short," writes Edward W. Said, "is always situated; it is skeptical, secular, reflectively open to its own failings."[25] Pith is everything in such comments. They do not lack the focus, the condensing power, we demand of the definition. But the nature of such statements, as John M. Ellis has discussed in his essay "The Logic of the Question: 'What is Criticism?,'" is that they are normative. They are nondefining in not excluding the truth of other, different statements of the same kind—as the above very various and sometimes directly contrary examples will show. This is because they are not truly "once and for all" definitions of criticism so much as propositions, statements of personal conviction about what criticism is. As we have seen in the previous chapter, they reflect what the person forming the definition thinks that criticism ought to be like, or would be like if only order could be imposed on the concept's confusion. They are more expressive of an unfulfilled wish or hope on the part of the speaker than a description, the irrepressible craving for clarity and conviction in a context whose laws do not seem to allow it. In that they may be the *reverse* of the critical case—antidefinitions.

The Durability of Terms

So there is much in the literature of criticism that serves a day-to-day definitional need—to explain, to inspire, to amplify, to justify; nothing in what we have seen supplies more than three different kinds of pseudodefinition: the functionalist, the typological, and the normative. The identification of these inadequate definitions *as* inadequate is the first step in the direction of making the concept clearer than it would otherwise appear (by removing one element—the prima facie element—of the confusion). In consequence, we may ask whether "definitions" attracting the adjectives "functionalist," "typological," and "normative" can really be definitions, since toleration of other definitional types seems (by qualifying the noun) to cancel the "definition." But if this is a step in the direction of clarity, the situation we find still seems little different from the one characterized by I. A. Richards over fifty years ago in his chapter "The Chaos of Critical Theories":

> A few conjectures, a supply of admonitions, many acute isolated observations, some brilliant guesses, much oratory and applied poetry, inexhaustible confusion, a sufficiency of dogma, no small stock of prejudices, whimsies and crotchets, a profusion of mysticism, a little genuine speculation, sundry stray inspirations, pregnant hints and random *aperçus;* of such as these, it may be said without exaggeration, is extant critical theory composed.[26]

The cases we have considered so far fail as definitions, in the one strict sense noted above, but it is *only* in this sense of a finalizing definition of criticism that the concept appears indefinable. We may therefore conclude that failures of these kinds are among the only useful definitional kinds that the concept will bear—the only kinds we might need. The extent to which finalizing definitions of words are necessary to us has been set forth by Wittgenstein in his *Blue Book*. There is the way that philosophers talk about words and the way that words are actually used:

> For remember that in general we don't use language according to strict rules—it hasn't been taught to us by means of strict rules, either. *We*, in our discussions on the other hand, constantly compare language with a calculus proceeding according to exact rules.
> This is a very one-sided way of looking at language. In practice we

very rarely use language as such a calculus. For not only do we not think of the rules of usage—of definitions, etc.—while using language, but when we are asked to give such rules, in most cases we aren't able to do so. We are unable clearly to circumscribe the concepts we use; not because we don't know their real definition, but because there is no real "definition" to them. To suppose that there *must* be would be like supposing that whenever children play with a ball they play a game according to strict rules.[27]

We use the word "criticism" and we know well enough, in Collingwood's terms, what we are "trying to mean." We know as well as we can expect to know. In Wittgensteinian terms, we recognize the *useful* imprecision of language. If some words do have precise definition, others do not, and "criticism" is arguably of this kind. Our conception of "criticism," we could say, while not *in itself* confused, nor nonexistent, is only approximately represented in language, and these approximations are helpful. They allow for expansion. The precise meaning such representations have, where a precise meaning is wanted, is the meaning we *choose* to give them on any occasion of use. If we want to use the term in a precise way we can. We can draw the defining line as we speak: "By this I mean criticism, not mere appreciation"; or "I am talking to you about criticism, now, not just subjective gush"; or "What I am saying applies to criticism, not theory"; or "When I say criticism I *mean* theory." Moreover, "criticism" seems to be one of those terms which perpetually *invite* such redefinition. We like to think of it as something able to be reshaped by the appearance of new examples of the kind; or as T. S. Eliot put it: "[A]n important work of literary criticism can alter and expand the content of the term 'literary criticism' itself."[28] Granted that we still have to have some antecedent idea of what this "kind" is if we are to recognize what content is to be expanded (and this we have, in virtue of the fact that we do not have to explain the term to have others understand it); yet there is clearly a point when isolating the idea of criticism in verbal form will cease to have use. Our definition will then be too tight. H. A. Mason has noted the sense in which "The difficulty in defining criticism is on all fours with that felt in trying to define poetry."[29] The concept of criticism is neither nonexistent nor confused; but its formulation in language is never uncontested, its useful "definition" never final. The conflicting testimony is part of the value of the term; and this is why "criticism" can and does continue in use. Current ideological and dialectical standoffs concerning the idioms of critical discourse neither negate the concept nor erase the term from the usable vocabulary of English.

Part II:
Whole and Part in the Description of Literary Criticism

4

"Outside the Academic Fold":
Radical Theory and the Modern "Men of Letters"

> Most Criticks, fond of some subservient Art,
> Still make the *Whole* depend upon a *Part*
> —Alexander Pope, *An Essay on Criticism*

> most of the really interesting criticism to-day is the work of men of letters who have found their way into universities, and of scholars whose critical activity has been first exercised in the classroom. And nowadays, when serious literary journalism is an inadequate, as well as precarious[,] means of support for all but a very few, this is as it must be. Only, it means that the critic to-day may have a somewhat different contact with the world, and be writing for a somewhat different audience from that of his predecessors.
> —T. S. Eliot, "The Frontiers of Criticism"

> criticism . . . is an academic thing, located for the most part far away from the questions that trouble the reader of a daily newspaper.
> —Edward W. Said

> There is a simple point to be made about literary criticism. It is that literary theory is not, and does not aim to be, "criticism"; and in fact criticism, which flourished so brilliantly in the era of Eliot and Leavis, of Empson and Donald Davie, has now largely gone out, except perforce on the part of reviewers.
> —P. N. Furbank, *TLS* review of Ford Madox Ford

POLEMICAL REPRESENTATIONS OF THEORY AND THEORISTS

W<small>E COME IN THE SECOND PART OF THIS BOOK TO THE SOCIOLOGY AND VOCABULARY</small> of the current position-taking that has shaped the definition of criticism. Think of literary criticism as a single whole composed of subordinate parts.

What are these parts? And what happens if, for example, literary theory and the practice of literary journalism, say, are added together and their constituents then combined? Does literary criticism result? If so, what elements of the mix are left out of account and what remain within the compound? Defining criticism—and, for that matter, the identity of its substructural species—may very often entail drawing a line between one thing and others that are like it, or with which it is commonly confused; and we have seen that an important feature of any definition is thus its ability successfully to demarcate the concept at issue from distinct but adjacent concepts. The process of defining will then have two identifiable features: (1) the exposure of superficial resemblances for the falsities they are, and (2) the diagnosis of hidden affinities that on first glance were not detectable but on examination are actually there. This is the case if we try to isolate "literary criticism proper" by uniting any one of its various institutional forms or symptoms—such as literary journalism—with the symptomatic practices of criticism that have become the province of the modern university academic. The latter will most often include the kind of thinking and writing that goes under the very broad and approximate heading of radical literary theory. Where, if anywhere, do we draw the line between these two? And how does that help us to decide where "literary criticism" stands, or whether it is a distinct concept at all?

In his 1991 afterword to *The Rise and Fall of the Man of Letters* (1969) John Gross describes a conflict arising between two classes or communities of criticism in terms of the contrast between the great tradition of English reviewing and Literary Theory. The concept of the man of letters that was born in the eighteenth and flourished in the nineteenth and early twentieth centuries is now, he says, approaching extinction; and this is because literary criticism has over recent years increasingly turned its back on literature. Instead it has transferred its allegiance to the university institution itself, and to the formalisms of a new kind of self-sustaining professional activity that privileges criticism over literature. Criticism is now that which is written by academics for academics. Thus it has lost contact both with its proper object of attention (literature) and with its audience (the people everywhere who read literature and wish to discuss their reading). And so criticism has abandoned its raison d'être, and has reduced the circle of its concerns.

For this reduction in criticism's effective role as criticism Gross blames "theory":

> [A] great deal of critical theory is devoted not so much to illuminating literature as to undermining it, robbing it of its autonomy. In the kingdom of theory the author's role is reduced to that of a meeting-point of external forces; the text itself is no longer "the privileged container of meaning";

reading a poem or novel for its own sake becomes a mere naive prologue to the serious business of analysis. Everything is up for interpretive grabs.[1]

Without specifically indicting Theory, John Newton writes similarly in the *Cambridge Quarterly* that the university system has taken over criticism only to ensure its silent extermination:

> If it weren't that the universities have already more or less defeated literary criticism, or at any rate have claimed and taken possession of the words and quietly killed their meaning, I might have been trying to argue ... that they are among its natural enemies. But possession of the words "literary criticism" does not now seem to be the universities'. .... So I think the words can't any longer be used seriously.[2]

Be that as it may, criticism outside the universities has not stopped in its tracks with the advent of Theory. It is not likely to do so as long as there are authors willing to publish books, readers willing to read them, and a public mechanism for disseminating opinion about them. Regardless of the critical quality of the great mass of reviews, the sense in which daily, weekly, or periodical reviews of newly appearing literary works for the press are "criticism" is the only meaning of the term for the many nonuniversity readers with no professional vested interest in Theory or salaried dependence upon it. It is a crucial meaning for the authors of the works, anxious to know how their writings are received, and whether they will sell, and a meaning that provides the important sense whereby criticism acts in partnership with a community of aesthetic interests to include the creative writer. Such criticism entails an important element of risk: it must grapple as best it can with the literature appearing now, with the immediacy of the contemporary scene. It must initiate the judgments that cooler and more leisured reflection, academic scholarship, and the passage of time will go on to confirm or deny. It must go out on a limb.

This therefore continues to raise the possibility of "a serious critic operating outside the academic fold,"[3] as it does the related possibility that the definition of criticism, when seen from sufficiently far away, might have to include understandings that transcend the current formalisms of university literary studies. Here the traditions of what may at this stage be roughly termed critical journalism would appear to offer a fundamental challenge to Theory's occupation of criticism and its "undermining" of literature.

But how then do literary journalism and Theory differ—if both are in some sense "criticism"? My answer is that they differ in appearance fundamentally, but in reality superficially. The grounds of the apparent distinction can be found in the statements each gives of the elements of the situation of criticism. For most journalistic critics (as we might somewhat haphazardly call them), this situation is defined by the following suppositions:

1. The Author: That there are such persons as authors, that authors are individually responsible in some ways for the books they write, that they have feelings, hold views, and opinions, and that these feelings, views, and opinions may be contained in the books and be of theoretical and practical interest to others able to read and understand them.
2. The Audience: That there is such a thing as a wide audience for literary works and that the members of this audience are capable of being engaged in discussion about the literary works and have very roughly common expectations with regard to literary satisfactions and standards.
3. Books: That books exist as sufficiently independent, freestanding entities not to mean entirely and completely what any reader of those books may want them to mean; conversely that the effect of any book on an audience of readers may differ discernibly and discussably from the effect that the author of the book intended that the book should have.
4. The World: That authors, audience, and books all, in some sense, exist in the world and are all concerned, at some level and in some particular way with the real.

Theory, in the congregate mass of poststructuralist theory, is thought to have questioned all of these assumptions in one or another way.[4] They are seen as illusions and fictions, as the bones of pervasive myths that require exposure, deconstruction, or disposal. The reasons for taking exception to them fall into two groups: first, that they are not articulated and thus go unexamined—so that simple exposure to the light would cause them to crumble; second, that they are wrong or simply naive assumptions, based on an ideological mistake. Theory, allegedly, seeks to abolish the idea of the author, the distinctness of "literature," and the relation of books to life, preferring a stance that is socially constructed, textually promiscuous in focus, and "self-reflexive." Whereas the above suppositions do not appear to say anything new, or anything that everybody does not already know, the putative purpose of Theory, its *conditio sine qua non*, is to uncover what has never been thought before. Its speciality is what few, outside universities, could possibly think. This aim is fundamental. But the tenacity with which literary journalism has adhered to its system of beliefs, implicitly or explicitly, and has gone on regardless in its own conventional practice (reviewing, judging, recommending, preferring, damning, praising—along with the usual bitching and posing) has effectively resisted Theory's claim to occupation of the whole critical domain, the whole meaning of the term "criticism." In the same way, the premises of literary journalism remain largely unscathed by the Theory Explosion.

Identity, Difference, and the Communities of Critical Practice

But I do not think that literary journalism can be opposed to literary theory in so simple a way. Too much in their respective value systems seems held in common or relies on their juncture. It is often maintained—as negative criticism of literary journalism—that criticism of this form tends to commercialize and thus to degrade the sanctity of the literary experience. A commodity itself, literary journalism commodifies art, and barbarously exalts the criterion of easy, unearned pleasure: that quality in works of literature that can be instantaneously enjoyed. By celebrating what sells, such criticism demotes more serious and challenging literature with something of genuine importance to say, the sort that is in need of critical explanation in addition to critical recommendation. From the creator's viewpoint, criticism of this kind may also be seen as peevishly severe, niggardly, and peremptorily judgmental, even cruel, part of a dog-eat-dog world in which individual privacy is ruthlessly invaded and finer sensibilities are ignored. In his book *Criticism* (1987), Hans Keller seems particularly to have in mind the type of adverse press musicians and musical performances have to endure when he launches his attack on criticism as one of the "phoney" professions whose members specialize in the licensed application of malice. Such critics are a channel for the killer instinct, an uncontainable and unregulated urge to destroy:

> Like the rest of humanity, the critic doesn't quite know what to do with his aggression, but unlike most of the rest, he—like the soldier, the hangman, and the vet—is invested with the authority to kill if necessary; moreover, it is left to him to decide when it is necessary, and since he harbours this need to kill, the necessity often arises.[5]

If it is in the nature of critical reviews to be pithy and short (few reviewers write without some kind of editorially imposed word limit), the weapon of destruction is only that much sharper and more lethal.

But if critical journalism is committed to a view of artistic material as a form of commercial commodity, the end result of a system of production, this exactly corresponds with primary commitments of postmaterialist theory and of those who mediate it. Such theory holds precisely to the view that literature—with everything else that it is—is a commodity:

> Literature may be an artefact, a product of social consciousness, a world vision; but it is also an *industry*. Books are not just structures of meaning, they are also commodities produced by publishers and sold on the market at a profit. Drama is not just a collection of literary texts; it is a capitalist

business which employs certain men (authors, directors, actors, stagehands) to produce a commodity to be consumed by an audience at a profit. Critics are not just analysts of texts; they are also (usually) academics hired by the state to prepare students ideologically for their functions within capitalist society. Writers are not just transposers of trans-individual mental structures, they are also workers hired by publishing houses to produce commodities which will sell.[6]

The role of critical journalism within such a scheme might conceivably be to oil the capitalist-productive wheels, to cooperate with the system in which the literary product is launched on consumers. The criticism may be seen simultaneously as an advertising tool and as an aid to consumer selection. In just the same way, such literary journalism as appears typically in the *Guardian* or the *Sunday Times* caters to parts of a market that in other corners is served by the channels of critical opinion on popular music *(NME)*, or by the comparative criticism of new and secondhand cars *(What Car?)*. Here the material published is ambiguously a critique of the product and also advertising copy. There is a rhetorical continuity with popular culture. Moreover, if much literary journalism exists as a disposable commodity (on the newsstand today, in the dustbin tomorrow), this might be thought to correspond with the way that Theory opposes the notion of artistic works enjoying the status of classics, and all efforts at constructing critical opinions apt to endure with the works. I am thinking here of all the would-be "lasting" judgments that presume (wrongly in Theory's view) to assert the sense in which values are eternal.

One analogy between this built-in obsolescence in critical opinion and literary ephemerality is with the position of popular fiction, or "pulp." This is conventionally prized by Theory on the grounds of the ideological need to affirm the textual equality of proletarian literature and the canonical classics. Popular literature that lasts ("folk" lyrics of the medieval period, Shakespeare, Dickens, etc.) presents a more complex case. Is the criticism which treats such literature favorably recouping the popular values that have ensured its appeal from one generation to the next? Or is it colluding reprehensibly with the taste of an approved canon? I do not believe we yet have an answer.

At any rate, the test of durability offers a very inadequate rule for drawing the line between Theory and literary journalism. There are at least two reasons why. One is the tendency of particular theories within the general domain of Theory to obey the law of the consumer durable and to wear out quickly with the passage of time. What is new one day becomes boring and commonplace the next. It is then supplanted by later models in the same line of historical product development. A second reason is suggested by the occasions when literary reviewing originally done for the periodical or broadsheet press is then subsequently collected and reprinted in book form. Here the classic example is Sainte-Beuve. Sainte-Beuve is mentioned by Eliot as the author of two important books, but also as the critic "the bulk of whose work consists of volume after volume of collected essays which had previously appeared week after week in the *feuilleton* of a newspaper."[7] Other instances might include Stendhal, Henry James, and the literary reviewing of Johnson and of Arnold. The essays of all these writers have survived the test of time and have been absorbed into the history and theory of criticism; they have become both the literature of criticism and part of literature itself. Examples current today would have to include John Carey's volume of literary reviews for the *Sunday Times*, published in hardback form as *Original Copy*,[8] and Clive James's collection of essays reprinted, in part, from the *London Review of Books*. (This is available in paperback form as *From the Land of Shadows*.) The writers—one inside, one outside the academic fold—are modern (if somewhat diminished) incarnations of the "heroes" of Gross's tradition. It remains to be seen if they will last.

But if the essays and reviews of these writers are not journalism, it is perhaps difficult to say what is. At the same time, the identity of such essays *as* journalism—they were written for an immediate editorial deadline—does not reliably define them. They start life as ephemera (as everything in a newspaper is ephemerally destined as wrapping for the next helping of fish and chips, or for lining the cupboards in the kitchen). They were not meant to last, but for some reason they did. (We have in this case to ignore the presumed shift in intention, which corresponds with the author's or publisher's decision—made, one assumes, with the live author's consent—to work the essays up into nondisposable books designed for the shelves of a library. The implication of which is that the criticism now really is worth something, and so worth preservation, in its own right, long after the initial purpose has been served.) A kind of double standard applies here. Journalism, to achieve a critical status, has to transcend the circumstances of production and origin that made it the kind of criticism it is. But in becoming "criticism," does it then it cease to be "journalism"? Does excellent journalism remain always "good of its kind," and thus limited critically? Yes and no.

The fact is it is impossible to define literary journalism by its intrinsic attributes alone. No one says: "I am now writing journalism and therefore insist that what I write should be received and judged in a certain way; that this or that allowance should or should not be made for it." A critical writer may to some extent choose where to publish his or her work; but no writer has that kind of control. The literary journalist does not define the type of his or her utterance in the way that the writer of a sonnet defines his intentions in a poem of a certain form having so many lines. Whatever identity is accorded to literary journalism, and whenever the phrase "literary journalism" is used by speakers of English trying to convey some meaning by it, it is accorded in recognition of its extrinsic relations—the readership at which the criticism is aimed, the "somewhat different contact with the world" of which T. S. Eliot speaks. This may be different for readers of papers than for readers of books. The literary professional is not its primary addressee but a motley and assorted public. Such criticism must therefore entertain; it must amuse; it must seem of the world, not of the library. There must be no whiff of the pedant. The critic must know how to carry it to prince and peasant. The corollary of this ambition is sometimes an acid skepticism about the value of Theory and the closed and closeted world from which it seems to arise. Some of the tartest comments by John Carey or Clive James on the current scene appear in their reviews of books having theoretical ambitions. Just as the media can serve as the object of theoretical study (cultural analyses of television etc. à la Fiske),[9] so Theory itself, we here see, is the object of not always the most flattering critical attention in the literary press. Thus Carey's judgment on David Lodge's ill-fated efforts to practice theory in *Working with Structuralism* are seen as rather like "Surviving with Sciatica."[10]

To take another example: in Clive James's collection, mentioned above, there are several occasions on which the business of the professional reviewer (working outside the academic fold and pissing in) allows some severely abrasive reflections on the nature of academic criticism and on the risibility of its current fashions. On why, for example, in the eyes of the critic-as-man-of-the-world, the academic methods of criticism can be dismissed as a joke:

> A good critic is always an ordinary reader in the first instance. A bad critic, not being that, is usually obliged to come up with an angle in order to stay in business. If he contented himself with saying what he found to be true, he would sound platitudinous to everybody else, like that guileless American professor of drama who discovered Jimmy Porter's monologue to be composed of both long and short sentences. So he relies on his mode or method to produce impressive results on his behalf. Structuralism, in this regard, is the greatest invention since pig Latin. It can make any idiot sound unfathomable.[11]

Later, in the same review, James writes of "live criticism, which finds its consistency in its own vitality, and not in relation to a supposedly logical framework," and asserts (with Lawrence) that "Criticism is not a science. . . . Criticism is simply a talent, like any other talent" (204–5). Theory and journalism are not completely at odds here. Theory is the object, the material, for literary-journalistic derision in the same way that fascination with the victims is necessary to any satirist and something without which the satire cannot rise to its heights: this Pope found in his richly evocative glorification of fools in *The Dunciad*, and Erasmus in *The Praise of Folly*. A comparison can be drawn with the fixations of the popular press with crime, catastrophe, sexual peccadilloes, and moral outrage in ordinary nonliterary life. Much of the literary journalism of Clive James is satirical in much this way. It serves as a platform for the comic wit that makes it possible to laugh not only at Theory but also at typical examples of popular literary pulp, high on the best-selling lists despite the reviewers. Such relations are more symbiotic and collusive, or perhaps incestuous, than they are competitive. But they are not without ironies, as we are now to discover.

"GRUB STREET AND THE IVORY TOWER": CRITICAL INSTITUTIONS AND THE COMMUNITIES OF SOCIAL VALUATION

Analysts of modern radical Theory have often commented on the sense in which works of theory pronounce the death of the author, the invalidity of authorial intention as an interpretive tool, and the exclusively readerly construction of textual meaning, but have authors whose names appear, like any others', on the covers of their books, invariably have perfectly discernible intentions, a highly conscious sense of what they are meaning to say, and very specifically articulated designs on the reader.[12] Thus Antony Easthope, for example, in his *British Post-Structuralism since 1968* sets out to "argue through and illustrate a theoretical assertion"; Terry Eagleton, likewise, in the preface to his *Literary Theory* says he has "argued through a particular *case*." Among continental theorists we find Julia Kristeva writing of her own essays in the preface to *Desire in Language* that "their aim does not presuppose the writer's neutrality but, on the contrary, her involvement. . . ." Jacques Derrida, in the first chapter of his *Of Grammatology*, defines the nature of his "Program."[13] What we have is a sequence of essentially *personal* hypotheses.[14]

To this can be added the fact that many established theorists, without any perceptible sense that it may be inconsistent to do so, operate in precisely the forms—including the form of the literary review—from which it has been possible to derive the above "journalistic" presuppositions. The review, so called, is both an academic and a journalistic genre. The journalist and the academic theorist, moreover, are not necessarily different people: many salaried university academics eminent as theorists have been recruited to the task of reviewing, as Gross notes, and one might almost go so far as to say that Theory has strengthened rather than weakened the respect in which an author can be seen as the type of textual progenitor that Theory consigns to an empty space: Gross's "meeting point of external forces." One of the most striking features of any standard account of Theory is the incidence of *names:* Benjamin, Showalter, Jameson, Fish, Kristeva, Barthes, Eagleton, Althusser, Belsey, etc., etc.

From the vantage point of the theorist, the role of contemporary guru seems quite unproblematic. The recent career of Jacques Derrida amply demonstrates that it is perfectly possible for a theorist committed to the negation of writerly authority to generate an academic personality cult— this in consequence of the perfectly ordinary authorship of written writings and the perfectly ordinary effect of the content of the written writings on readers who read them. Many theorists are highly conscious of their own and other theorists' authorial individuality, the import of their pronouncements, and the responsibility to be taken for them. Critical humility does not seem to figure significantly in the manners of either camp. Both seem capable of allowing criticism to degenerate into two fairly indistinguishable varieties of vast ego trip; and it is possible that our feelings as readers of the criticism are somewhat ambiguous about this. With respect to journalistic criticism H. A. Mason speculates that we like it that way:

> Don't we . . . prefer the critics in our newspapers to prefer themselves to the works they are pretending to pass judgment on? Do not these self-lovers increase the circulation of the *Observer,* of the *Sunday Times,* of the *New Statesman* and of the *Spectator?* We enjoy the exhibition of pride and vanity.[15]

The crucial ground for the comparison between literary journalism and critical theory is the role of critical evaluation. This bears with especial importance on how Theory and literary journalism alike instantiate values that may be defined as nonelitist, popular, "low" or "middlebrow." (The two communities are alike in making some version of this claim and defend themselves in relation to its strength: both set themselves against an "establishment" whose elitist values each locates at the other's door.) Theory, it is sometimes said, has challenged the essentially judgmental definition of literary criticism and has replaced this with a conception of criticism in which its nature is to interpret texts and not to judge them, to "read" meaning rather than to pronounce on its value, or the value of its originator, the author. Indeed, one ambition of Theory may have been to evacuate criticism of questions of value. In so doing, the claim to be operating on behalf of the nonelite world is widely canvassed by theorists. This is expressed both in the methodology of criticism and in the choice of objects of critical attention. Just as cultural studies seeks to eschew exclusive attention to the written ("highbrow") literature of a culture, preferring rather to examine "texts" (written, nonwritten, etc.), so poststructuralist materialist Theory seeks to be insurrectionary, rescuing marginalized proletarian values from the falsifying overlay of bourgeois-liberal-humanist credos—of which the very idea of a literature may have been one. In this view, literary journalism may be regarded as having conspired with bourgeois-liberal-humanist tradition. Such journalism upholds and mediates the very exclusivities that Theory wishes to destroy.

There are two ironies here. One is the fact that Theory's revolt against bourgeois-liberal-humanist values is itself expressing a value—a decidedly negative valuation of a body of literature and a body of criticism. A second is that the claim to have blown to bits the myths of bourgeois-liberal-humanist thought does not sit easily with the exceptionally specialized critical manners of Theory and tolerance for a terminology that studiedly disavows continuity with the language used in everyday intelligent exchange. The irony of the elitism of Theory is seen to be sharpest when set against the efforts of higher journalism to address the reading public at large, to stimulate general debate, and to engage in the "popular" cultivation of critical ideas. To the extent that such "mediation" resembles Addison's ambition to improve the taste of the eighteenth-century reader, it is open to the charge of condescension, of speaking from high to low, of taking on "superior" airs and graces. It pre-supposes that taste is in need of improvement. But here we can say that if the battle to appropriate the term "literary criticism" has meant that Theory has sought freshly to deny value to the assumptions of the "journalistic," it has done so by working in cooperation with a very traditional set of reservations about any criticism outside the university fold. We have seen, however, that it is often in secret alliance with such criticism and subject therefore to the same doubts and concerns.

"Journalist," "journalistic," remain terms of abuse. Their use as a slur or a smear goes with an attitude of snootiness towards the popular and ephemeral in literary art; it damns the popular pleasure that literature can give and the channels of communication about it. From the perspective of high and serious scholarship (with which Theory assumes an association) literary journalism may be seen as a shorthand term for work having merely a pretense to criticism, as "would-be" criticism, essentially superficial and unserious. The sense in which the advent of Theory has been to discover a further form for this traditional distaste, a profound (but we have seen ironic) revulsion against the popular, has been described by John Carey in his postscript to *The Intellectuals and the Masses* (1992):

> "Theory" (which, it is no surprise to find, often makes obeisance to Nietzsche) teaches that art and literature are "self-referential" or "self-reflexive"—that is, they have no relevance at all to the real world or to the life

> ordinary people lead. This viewpoint is . . . perfectly in accord with the Bloomsbury aesthetes' horror of the "photographic" realism that the "gross herd" clamours for. . . .[16]

The trouble with such a comment—its weakness as an antielitist critique of Theory written from the viewpoint of a critic who has been careful to cultivate an audience for criticism "outside the academic fold"—is that it does nothing to qualify the crudity of the form of the realism whose justified popularity it defends against the reaction of Bloomsbury horror. Too little is done with the term "realism" to suggest why it is wrong to consider the herd as gross.

Theory and journalism (to the extent we have been able to explore them here) thus cannot comprehensively define criticism, independently or when added together; because of the kind of categories that these are and their own want of secure identity. They are both ways in which criticism is successfully spoken of, and they exist as convenient if ambiguous differentiae within a larger idea of criticism whose genus is indeterminate. But both are rooted in the social description of criticism and the "conflict" between them—such as it is—is social before it is intellectual, attitudinal rather than conceptual. The divisions are in turn those of gesture, fashion, posture, and contemporary situation. Both are caught up in the swirl of their respective institutionalization (the rise of the universities, the power of the press, the demands of the book trade, etc., etc.). Their attributes are in this way a function of habitat and mores, a version of the old quarrels between highbrow and lowbrow that Leonard Woolf satirized in "Hunting the Highbrow,"[17] where he identified the different anthropological types—*altifrons aestheticus, pseudaltifrons aestheticus,* etc.—that peopled the literary jungle of his times. Such types are not extinct, but in modern British culture they are more likely to be tracked down in the undergrowth of Hamstead or the BBC studios (in the case of *pseudaltifrons aestheticus*) or the departmental graduate seminar (in the case of *pseudaltifrons intellectualis*). The numbers of both species have grown enormously since Woolf's day, and they remain quarrelsome. Their study belongs more to social psychology, group dynamics, or behaviorism than to criticism.

There is no essential conflict; nor are the claims to antielitism made by the rival critical communities especially profound, since both operate within the value systems of their respective professional norms. Journalese or structuralese makes no serious difference. What we see are the elements of a contemporary *querelle*. This may be every bit as heated as the one Pope sought to cool in his *Essay on Criticism*, but there is no "debate proper" of the kind I have discussed in chapter 3, since the positions articulated are not exclusive. The common ground we find applies to the working suppositions of literary journalism from which we began. We can now recollect what these are: (1) the Author (the person responsible for writing the book the audience will read), (2) the Audience (the group of people the author seeks to communicate with via the pages of the published work printed in a language they can understand), (3) Books (the containers of the imaginative and other messages and material that the audience encounters in written form and that convey certain meanings), and (4) the World (the point of experiential reference for the author in creating the literary work, the term of comparison for the critic in discussing its character and for the members of the audience addressed by the critic of the work and its author alike). We have seen that Theory has not in practice disintegrated these concepts, but has relied on them implicitly to extend its own agenda. It could do nothing else.

5

Criticism, Valuation, and Useful Purpose

> At once the *Source*, and *End*, and *Test* of *Art*.
> —Alexander Pope, *An Essay on Criticism*

> For there is no question that the instalment of the "value-question" at the heart of critical enquiry is a rampantly ideological gesture. The ideological unity between the old-fashioned school of "appreciation," and the anti-academicist school of "relevance," is nowhere more clearly revealed than in the priority they assign to problems of value, on which all else is made to turn.
> —Terry Eagleton, *Criticism and Ideology*

> We cannot possibly understand what is written or said unless we understand its interest and importance for the writer or speaker; which affects inevitably its interest and importance for us. Evaluation, in this sense, and interpretation are the same.
> —Geoffrey Strickland, *Structuralism or Criticism? Thoughts on How We Read*

Valuation and Criticism

THE TOPIC OF THIS CHAPTER EMERGES NATURALLY FROM OUR CRITIQUE OF THE struggle between Theory and literary journalism for criticism's heart and soul. This is the theme of critical "evaluation." Evaluation is instinctive to literary journalism and problematic to "Theory," and again, points to a source of what is commonly seen as a form of contemporary "debate." Defining, and attempting to answer, "the question of value" is embraced by the larger problem of criticism's definition. As we can see, many critics have cast their views on valuation, or evaluation (a term sometimes used interchangeably with it),[1] in a general statement on the nature and function of criticism. "Criticism," writes I. A. Richards, "is the endeavour to discriminate between experiences and to evaluate them."[2] For F. R. Leavis (one of the single most controversial critics operating within the sphere of debate about criticism and value), "You can't discuss 'valuation' intelligently except in a general account of the nature of criticism."[3] Other major critics in the past have seen the various operations contained in the valuing or evaluation of literature as an unavoidable concomitant of criticism's essential nature. "Judgement is forced upon us by experience," writes Samuel Johnson: "He that reads many books must compare one opinion or one style with another; and when he compares, must necessarily distinguish, reject, and prefer."[4]

Such views are supported by the analyses of modern aestheticians such as E. D. Hirsch, who writes in post-Kantian terms of the necessity of valuation in literary judgments and that "value judgments are ... inherent in literary description."[5] Terry Eagleton meanwhile has pointed to the respect in which all statements, even those that seem to convey simple matters of fact, can be construed as "value-judgements":[6] it is sometimes said that the critic "cannot but evaluate"[7] or even that "to exist is to evaluate."[8] Proscribing valuation—in the sense of banning the right to prefer—may in its turn be portrayed as simply stupid or dull, as Robert Graves famously relates:

> "I understand, Mr Graves, that the essays which you write for your English tutor are, shall I say, a trifle temperamental. It appears, indeed, that you prefer some authors to others."[9]

It is in the nature of the situation of criticism that we should not expect that the arguments used to defend or promote evaluative criticism will be counteracted in any especially coherent way by the arguments used to insist that criticism is (or should be) value-neutral. Similarly, it is in the nature of the situation of criticism that the valuation of literary works should not be seen as the essence of criticism's definition. Critical valuation is attacked and disputed on all sorts of grounds, sometimes by the same critics who at other moments give the appearance of finding it inevitable, a necessary feature of all statements. It is for this reason sometimes hard to discern whether objectors to evaluative criticism object absolutely to the fact that criticism may evaluate; or whether they are merely repudiating some of the kinds of evaluation it is possible to find in certain evaluative critics they disdain—Johnson, Arnold, or Leavis, for example.[10] There may be only a pragmatic objection (itself an expression of an evaluator's instinct) against the style conferred on criticism generally by critics they disagree with or dislike on other grounds. Antievaluative sentiment can be part of a war on some of the more outspoken or dogmatic evaluations within critical tradition; ones that are perceived to evaluate unfairly, or grossly, or where critics allow their personal feelings to run riot. The letters of D. H.

Lawrence quoted earlier contain much personal evaluation of this kind—"I hate Strindberg"; "I like Wells"; "I don't like Dostoievsky";[11] and so forth. One response to such statements is part of the ethical case against evaluation and is that the critic is telling us more about himself than we want to know.

On another level, valuation in criticism may be rejected for what seem to be more fundamental reasons—as, for example, those given by critics like Frye or Barthes who hold that criticism should be (and really at bottom is) a science, and therefore only concerned with the objective treatment of objectively verifiable phenomena within a formal system.[12] Here too, personal feelings of the kind that Lawrence expresses do not or should not come into the picture. Another significant strand of antievaluative sentiment can be discovered among those who find evaluation in its discriminatory aspect unacceptable on political or social grounds, or ideologically taboo. Evaluative criticism may in this context appear to abuse equal rights—the right of all works to be considered without preference or privilege. The very setting up to judge of literary texts at all may inspire what I. A. Richards has called "hatred of 'superior persons.'"[13]

The complicating factor in all these forms of objection is that none of them is simply antievaluative. Even the fundamentalist rejection of all discriminatory practice proves to be a valuing of sorts—in this case a committedly positive valuing of certain social principles and ideals that could be debated quite coherently even if literature, literary criticism, and literary theory did not exist. A second complicating factor is that some of the antievaluative arguments would seem well designed to cancel others out. This is true of the charge that evaluative criticism (being invariably the product of personal evaluation) shares the flaws of any subjectivist perspective. Such a complaint sits strangely beside the kind of argument against evaluation made by John Carey that "Nowadays almost no one believes in the possibility of objective or 'correct' literary judgments any longer."[14] It is as if critics making value judgments on literary works were laboring under the false impression that their valuations were indeed "correct," that objectivity in evaluative criticism was normally something they did expect to achieve, and that people once generally believed they achieved. It is typical of the confused nature of the debate on value that the position open to criticism by the opposite side in the question seems obviously objectionable or crass. This consistently tends to drive the debate about evaluative criticism to overstatements—to misunderstandings that seem to sacrifice all to delight in disputation. If criticism as a whole may be defined by the arguments for and against valuation, then a survey of these arguments can only reinforce the respect in which the concept of criticism seems hopelessly elusive and confused.

The "Debate" on Value

What we need to do, I would therefore suggest, is to press harder in the direction of resolving such misunderstandings as can be simply resolved, and to examine by the same means some of the divisions founded on misconceived concepts of evaluative or nonevaluative criticism. Who the "evaluative critics" are seems surprisingly uncontroversial. We do, however, need to know more clearly what is going on behind and within the phrase and whether it is usable in discussions of criticism, if only the better to decide whether the critics we confidently call "evaluative" are justly so described. This process is severely hampered by at least three different and distinct emphases inherent in the way the discussion of valuation and criticism has tended to relate the concepts concerned.

1. Valuation may be seen as a presence or absence in criticism's content. This is suggested (prepositionally) in the idiom of the title to F. R. Leavis's essay "Valuation *in* Criticism," or W. W. Robson's "Evaluative Criticism and Criticism *without* Evaluation."
2. It may be seen as an indication of criticism's capacity for value registration (where criticism is the means or tool to record the value of literary work: various doctrines of appreciation adopt this view).
3. It may be regarded as an account of the capacity to confer value. In this case, the suggestion is not that valuation resides within criticism, as an intrinsic property of some kind, or that it records value, but that criticism operates the concept of value to enable its construction or creation in other concepts.

Many writers with left-wing commitments relate valuation to criticism in terms of (3). Here is Widdowson: "[A]ny critic . . . must begin to suspect and analyse the received tradition of 'great' literary works. . . . ; to scrutinize the premises on which 'Criticism' has operated; and to ask how far 'Criticism' has itself *created* 'Literature' by way of its pre-selections, evaluations and tacit assumptions as to what constitutes 'literary value.'"[15]

This position is sometimes seen as part of an argument for the wholesale dissolution of literature. "To put it bluntly," writes Widdowson, "the question 'Is there Literature?' is now replacing 'What is Literature?' as the crucial question for radical critics." And he adds: "[T]he question of 'literary value' . . . can only be considered in the context of such a debate" (139). Critics who write in these terms sometimes urge that the idea of literature (as constituted by bourgeois criticism) is replaced by the more general and embracing idea of "the text," or perhaps that of the "signifying practice." But if the answer to the question "Is there Literature?" is in fact "no" (as it often is), then such a conclusion is logically difficult to square with any ambition to modify a specifically "literary" criticism or to advance a specifically "literary" theory, because you cannot change "literary criticism" or "literary theory" without retaining "literature" as a concept. If, however, we start with criticism as a form for registering rather than conferring value (in the second of three ways noted above), then literature will exist independently of its constitution by criticism—that is, whether criticism is there or not. The existence of a "theory of literature" and a "criticism of literature" becomes less problematic.

It seems difficult to find a "question of value" within differences of this kind—or, for that matter, in the kind of problem created by the assumption that evaluative judgments of literary works are meant to be true ("certain" in the sense that Carey is suggesting when he uses the words "objective" and "correct"). Objectors naturally complain that evaluative judgments cannot satisfy the demand for truth, since they cannot rule out other judgments; and since no judgment is not open to challenge, no judgment can be right. There is no right. All readings are misreadings. Yet critical discourse mingles subjectivism and objectivism in all sorts of ways, and there is an obvious difference between personally valuing a work of literature and the self-deception to which one would have to fall victim to think one's judgment of that work uniquely correct—the one and only true judgment. We can despair of the fallibility of value judgments; but rejecting evaluative criticism on this ground may neglect somewhat the fact that such value judgments do not have to make infallibility claims, and may not normally do so. Unless they are very naive, critics regularly expect that the valuations they place on literary works are ones with which other critics may not agree. The argument in any case comes full circle: "A doubt that doubted everything," wrote Wittgenstein, "would not be a doubt."[16] The belief that certainty is the mistaken assumption of critical evaluators must itself be judged alongside the fact that while no judgments may be provably true, some, though they may be never "unquestioned," are more possibly true than others, and some are probably true. When a judgment of value about a literary work is called into question, there may be no good basis for doubt.[17]

A no less awkwardly debatable approach to the issue besets the topic of explicit versus implicit valuations. Part of the negative reaction to value judgments in criticism is founded on a sense of the insidiousness of hidden or covert valuations of things not sufficiently made explicit by a critical text—concealed ideologies and so forth. The principal source of this reaction would seem, however, to be those particularly concerned to bring out the importance of just this sense in which evaluative estimates may be inferred. It has arisen through implicit value theorists committed to an anti-intentionalist point of view. Just as criticism is "as natural as breathing"—an action of the involuntary muscular system—so there is a sense in which valuations that are not intended can also be construed alongside the reception of those that are. Barbara Herrnstein Smith touches on this aspect of valuation in relation to the appearance of Shakespeare's *Sonnets:*

> But, before we come to their "reputation" . . . we should acknowledge an intermediary history of valuings . . . the simple fact that they were found to be, for whatever motives, ah! *publishable;* worth the printing and presumably, for some purchasers, worth the price; and even . . . worth the keeping. Each of these acts—publishing, printing, purchasing, and preserving—is an implicit act of evaluation, though we may think it necessary to distinguish *them*, with their mixed motives, from real literary evaluation, the assessment of intrinsic worth.[18]

In recent years, considerable value has been attached to the kinds of valuation that can be construed but are not intended, particularly by analyses sympathetic to a Freudian perspective. The pervasiveness of valuations of this kind has been illustrated by Terry Eagleton's example of an apparent contrast between statements of fact like "This cathedral was built in 1612" and statements of value such as "This cathedral is a magnificent specimen of baroque architecture." Eagleton suggests that the factual statement could after all function as a value judgment and that that is what it implicitly or unconsciously is: "Statements of fact are after all *statements*, which presumes a number of questionable judgements: that those statements are worth making, perhaps more worth making than certain others, that I am the sort of person entitled to make them and perhaps able to guarantee their truth, that you are the kind of person worth making them to, that something useful is accomplished by making them, and so on."[19]

But if the revelation of covert ideological (or value) frameworks can be used at one moment to expose the sense in which statements intended as fact are functioning unintentionally as vehicles of value, it is hard to see how diagnosing such judgments forms part of the case against valuation. The evaluative implications of a piece of criticism are in truth sometimes under the critic's control and sometimes not. Criticism is always a mixture of implication and explication—in all sorts of proportions; and both are open to be misunderstood. An exceptionally common kind of statement in literary criticism is implicit only so far as to suggest how a work or author may appear to the critic good or bad, liked or not liked, without the use of so many words. Thus when Thomas Rymer calls "the tragical part" of Shakespeare's *Othello* "a Bloody Farce, without salt or savour,"[20] he does not have to say he dislikes the work he is judging or that it is bad. It would not add to the clarity of the statement if he did. The evaluation is no less forceful or personal as judgment than any of the explicit likes and dislikes expressed in D. H. Lawrence's letters. The situation is the same when Leavis notoriously pronounces Shelley's poetry "unreadable," and where he yokes a palpable distaste for the poetry to a sense of the grounds on which it is based.[21] There is no "pure" value statement about Shelley or about Shakespeare. Other critical inferences are more deeply embedded in their textual material. Their meanings and intentions have to be discerned by interpreting the critical text. But this is not to suggest that the meanings are not meant.

In none of these cases is it possible to restrict the issue of evaluative judgment to the analysis of the single statement of sentence length: "*Othello* is . . . ," "Shelley's poetry is. . . . " and so on. As we have seen, judgments of value come in all conceptual sizes, and in every textual dimension. On many or most occasions whole paragraphs and whole essays make what we call "the judgment." Indeed, a lengthy piece of critical discourse is sometimes necessary for the critic to develop a complex position that is adequately balanced and fair. Dryden's famous "statement" on Shakespeare in his "Essay on Dramatic Poesy" contains positive and negative observations to both of which the critic has made a commitment, and this is the sense in which Dryden's evaluative stance on Shakespeare is "judicial."[22] Aesthetic inquiry into the question of value is always simplified when its central examples are represented as judgments only in summary form, void of supporting context. When the larger structure is left out of account, along with all the other single statements of response, explanation, analysis, interpretation, qualification, and so forth, the quality of evaluative judgments tends to seem more assertive, generalized, and unsubstantiated than it really is.[23]

Value, Politics, and the Law

The political incorrectness of "judgment" has of course done much to suggest the uncompromisingly opposing nature of the positions entailed in "the question of value," and to ensure that attitudes to evaluative criticism are imbued with the general politics of opinion formation and opinion denial. Antijudgmental conceptions can sometimes therefore seem justified by political ideals—revolutionary or democratic. The latter, like the former, leads to a somewhat fragile analogy for literary evaluation. For example, in a real political democracy that respects majority and minority opinions within a state, issues will in the end be brought to the vote. But an evaluative judgment by a literary critic almost always has more shades of gray than a vote. Popular taste can be only uncertainly equated with a show of hands. There may be certain exceptions, such as statistically based audience research for radio or TV. But critical opinion cannot in the ordinary sense be counted.

Similar dissatisfactions may be aroused by an analogy between literary judgment and judgment in law—one whose degree of inaptness is obscured to some extent by the fact that works of literary art do sometimes go on trial and critical issues (such as those of sexual morality and public obscenity) do sometimes come to court. The parallel is, however, in all sorts of ways imperfect and inexact. One of the elements of the situation that differs (as Hans Keller points out in his comments on the critical reception of music) is that the critic of the work of art or its reader does not complain to the offender on trial but about him: "In courts of law all over the civilized world, severe precautions are taken for the listening object of criticism, the defendant in a criminal case, to have the opportunity, if not indeed the duty, to answer back; but the object, or the author of the object, of unfavourable music criticism is *a priori* condemned to listen in silence to what ought to have been addressed to him, rather than to others, in the first place."[24]

As judges in the courts frequently opine, popular opinion, the majority verdict outside the court, does not always function in the interests of justice. But in many respects the situation of the critic of art or the critic of literature differs in its relations from that of the judge within the judicial system—if only because the application of the rules of law to a legal judgment forms an inadequate comparison with the critic's dependence on criteria. It is, however, fair to suspect that emotions generated by one side in the comparison are liable to infect emotions present on the other. Hence the antiauthoritarianism that sometimes attaches to arguments against critical evaluation. Attitudes are charged by views that have their origin in contexts that are at least partially unrelated.

Value, Marginality, and Canon Formation

In this case, it is usually the doctrine of evaluation itself (and not—ostensibly—the false consequence of valuing) that is open to attack. Such attitudes frequently underlie those aspects of attempts to debate value which relate to the phenomenon of canon formation. In this, the next department of the general question to be touched on here, preference for an elite group of works or authors seems to ignore or suppress a body of marginalized texts, much as a tyrant seems to suppress a rebellious and restless social group. The equivalent of this group is the noncanonical literature excluded by the institution of evaluative criticism. This may range from women's writing, soap operas, and black writing to nonliterary matter of all kinds, including advertisements and other manifestations of popular culture. The problem that arises here is that in order to regard these examples as marginalized works, it is necessary to adopt a fairly static view of the value attaching to texts within the canon and of the necessarily authoritarian origins of canon formation. The consequence for attacks on the canon is that the selected works set aside as privileged members of the elite group are regarded as part of a sealed system. Anticanonical opinion somewhat ironically requires that traditional perceptions be kept intact. It must be assumed (and not independently judged) that all soap operas are inferior to the poetry of Pope; that popular fictions are never a livelier read than a nineteenth-century novel. Without such prior graduations the concept of canon-as-value dissolves and the case for the textually marginalized disappears with it. This is because the "radical" argument can only have logical force if something of agreed value exists for the marginal items to be marginalized by—even if the nature of criticism seems unlikely to assure such agreement. There is little allowance for the fact that "great" literary works are commonly hated for reasons that are unconnected with the fact that they form part of a canon.

Anticanonical writing can therefore thwart debate about individual works rather than excite it. In an exchange with Peter Fuller in the *New Left Review* Terry Eagleton says that "at any given point the literary canon contains an enormous amount of rubbish"[25] and invokes Wordsworth's poems celebrating capital punishment. In so doing, Eagleton places a value on certain literary works (a low one). But in order to dispute the value attached to these works in the form the critic defines it we would have to say we thought capital punishment a good idea. The low valuation does not expect to be contradicted except by those whose views are beyond the pale of serious consideration, and it is thus made safe. Yet this reluctance to opening up the discussion of individual works or authors when attacking the canon-as-value does not mean that some selectiveness is not freely admissible—even among and between the noncanonical works that form an alternative canon of "minority writing." The term generally excludes the manuals used to repair the car, the minutes of board meetings, or *The Tibetan Book of the Dead*.

In practice, again, it proves extremely difficult to resolve the opposed attitudes into the two mutually exclusive positions necessary to constitute a debate on evaluative criticism. To disrupt a canon, you have to "value" the claims of the new against the claims of the old. Popular literature or culture must sometimes be "preferred" to the traditional variety. Challenges to the canon are misnamed if they are seen as "antievaluative," since they clearly promote values—specifically those of an egalitarian social or political philosophy committed to the rejection of discriminatory practice in criticism and the overthrow of a privileged textual practice in literature. If cultural or radical critics sometimes deny the special status of literature and insist that everything is a text, they still have to choose what texts it is worth doing cultural and radical analyses of: a "signifying practice" depends on someone finding it significant.[26] At the same time the proposition of no-value theory that anything can have value somewhat takes the edge off the suggestion that literature is one thing that cannot. That a radical position is available on the question of value seems for all these reasons deeply unclear.

Useful Purpose

The usefulness of the phrase "evaluative criticism" must therefore be called into question—on the one hand, because of the widespread view (at least in academic circles) that the according of value to anything is no longer the essence of what critics do (except perhaps in their unconscious constructions of literature as value); on the other hand, because valuing in criticism is seen as inevitable, an inescapable consequence of any utterance about anything. Theoretical problems attach to both of these options. The first presents the difficulty of envisaging a nonevaluative criticism and defining its nature. The second leads to tautology. If "we can't but evaluate," then nonevaluative utterances would fail to exist and would thus have to be excluded from the category of criticism. Moreover, if every act or non-act, every utterance or nonutterance is unavoidably a consequence of choice (to choose to speak or be silent, whether to get up in the morning, etc.), and therefore is—in that unrestricted sense—a value judgment, then nothing is a value judgment. From this rationale we have no description of the form of valuing relevant to the situation of criticism. Yet something definite is presumably meant when Johnson, Arnold, Leavis, and others are distinguished as "evaluative critics"—something more than the suggestion that their criticism reaches awkward or unpopular conclusions about authors and works, or that their writings belong to a mode or genre of evaluative work somewhat resembling in form (and existing contrastively alongside) Marxist or feminist criticism. Can it be merely the "image," "voice," and "flavor" that Herrnstein Smith refers to when she cites Northrop Frye's characterization of their "debaucheries of judiciousness"?[27] Such terms seem too vague to convey their essential nature as valuers.

To fix what we mean to say when we use the phrase "evaluative criticism," I am therefore going to suggest that we once again abandon the generic definition with its emphasis on textual features, and fall back on a test of identity that emerges from the elements of criticism's situation—the critic, the work he/she is criticizing, the reader of the criticism, and the world in which all these elements live. The essential feature of this test may be seen as the concept of "useful purpose." The evaluative quality of criticism is determined solely in terms of the relationship useful to the purposes of all the relevant parties. From this I do not mean to say that the reader's interest has to be the same as the critic's, or that it must become so. Carey's suggestion that "All literary criticism is ultimately an exercise in persuasion"[28] seems to impute to critics a will—exerted through the making of value judgments—to have others reach the same conclusions as themselves. But this cannot be taken for granted. Differences of critical opinion are often relished by those who hold them. The whole modern critical scene is proof positive that the satisfactions of "persuasion" may be very limited indeed. But the disinclination to find critical evaluations persuasive is no embargo on finding them useful. A reader may be amused to discover that Samuel Johnson thought *Tristram Shandy* "did not last"[29]—particularly in the light of the vast modern scholarly industry devoted to Sterne. And if Lawrence's "I hate Strindberg" tells us nothing about Strindberg except the fact that he is hated by Lawrence, this does not have to be an uninteresting or useless fact. No antievaluative critic of criticism would want to be shielded from such views. Even attempts at persuasion do not have to succeed. The defenders of a critical proposition and the objectors to it must become increasingly specific as the argument proceeds, and the fact that there is never a perfect agreement does not mean the debate is invalid or uninfluential.

But it has to be recognized that this is the kind of occasion where values are at stake.[30] Some of the confusion that arises with the concept of evaluative criticism arises because no understanding about useful purpose is established, or because it breaks down. What seems to be necessary for the phrase "evaluative criticism" to be used with the precision required for it to be used intelligibly is reference to any situation where particular instances of criticism secure agreements that a statement on the value of a literary work is what the reader expects the critic to supply at that point. Once the agreement dissolves, the critic and the reader are at cross-purposes. The critic may then seem overbearingly judgmental or uselessly noncommittal. The ensuing difficulty will not be resolved by debating "the question of value," nor by pretending that people are not commonly interested in the valuations of others. As the present discussion has tried to suggest, the problem will expand in dimension.

The same criterion of "useful purpose" can also be used to distinguish "nonevaluative" criticism. Within the paradigm of a logical analysis, the concept of "nonevaluative" criticism appears excluded by the success of the proposition that valuation is necessary; but this is—as we have seen—at the expense of tautology. In practice no tautology is ordinarily perceived when we call criticism "evaluative." The need for agreement about useful purpose brings within limits of relevance the uncontained range of senses in every possible context that are truistically valuations of some kind. In circumstances where the reader intuits that the making and reception of value judgments is not the kind of relationship the critic is seeking with the reader, and the reader comprehends the usefulness to her of the fact that it is not, perfect sense is made of the "nonevaluative" appellation. In these conditions, an overriding interest in other kinds of information defines the relationship. This is the reason that "literary history" may be "criticism" but may also raise and satisfy the expectations of "literary history"; and why it is perfectly intelligible to talk about "statements of fact" in order to distinguish them from "statements of value." Even when the statements in literary histories seem rich in appreciation or depreciation, it is still the historical relations of the text or author we are primarily interested in. We accept unproblematically the sense in which evaluative selections have to be made before history can be written at all. "When was this work composed—exactly?" "How does it draw on the conventions of the time?" "What effect did contemporary forms have on this or that author's directions as a writer?" And so on. These are the reasons we pick up the book. It is not in the least meaningless to call this "criticism," and if literary history were described as a type of criticism no confusion would arise. But the dichotomy between criticism with and criticism without evaluation is not entirely false. The distinction becomes problematic when overdetermined by the divisions of contesting critical schools, cultural gestalts, or diverse theoretical kinds. In the two chapters that follow we can turn to a further dichotomy arising from the terms of criticism's modern institutional life: that between "Theory" and "Judgment." To explore these notions will be to use the mediating language of criticism to move between questions of conceptual content and questions of vocabulary. And to reconstruct criticism after theory in its continuum with criticism before is to dwell—once again, I suggest—on these elementary units of sense.

6
Criticism and the Meanings of "Theory"

> And I will venture to lay it down, as the first Maxim and Cornerstone of this our Art; that whoever would excel therein, must studiously avoid, detest, and turn his head from all the ideas, ways and workings of that pestilent Foe to Wit, and Destroyer of fine Figures, which is known by the name of *Common Sense*. His business must be to contract the true *Goût de travers;* and to acquire a most happy, uncommon, unaccountable Way of Thinking.
> —Alexander Pope, "Peri Bathous"

> Minim professes great admiration of the wisdom and munificence by which the academies of the continent were raised, and often wishes for some standard of taste, for some tribunal, to which merit may appeal from caprice, prejudice, and malignity.
> —Samuel Johnson, *Idler* 61

THE RHETORICS OF MEDIATION: CRITICISM AND THE THEORY GUIDES

THE TENDENCY OF "CRITICISM" TO TRANSFORM ITS CONSTITUENTS BY A CIRCULAR process into the presiding categories for comprehending criticism is further suggested, on the heels of this discussion of value, by the relationship between "criticism" and "theory." Here the most pressing problem is the experience that any commentator on the subject of "theory" must at some stage face—that the relevant field of inquiry is constituted by certain kinds of texts and not by others. For if "theory" is now considered a creative form, as Geoffrey Hartman reminds us,[1] the literature of theory seems predicated to exclude a wide range of what is to be found in the vast world of imaginative literature and of poetry. Are George Eliot's chapters on the Jews in *Daniel Deronda* not theory? Is Lucretius's *De rerum natura* not theory? When Theseus at the conclusion of Chaucer's *Knight's Tale* provides the appropriate Boethian consolation, is he not theorizing? In each case: "If not, why not?" What excludes these instances as material exhibits in the definition of theory's current use? Perhaps a temporarily plausible answer might be that we are only concerned to define theory that takes literature and criticism as its object. But this begs the question of what, specifically, literature and criticism are, and how they might be separated out. Earlier discussion has shown that experience of attempts to define literature and criticism will suggest that even if these concepts *could* be isolated, "theory" in the au courant sense does not seem to evince much respect for such notionally theoretical works as Sidney's and Shelley's "Defences" of poetry, Tolstoy's essay on the nature of art, Dryden on the art of verse translation, or Ted Hughes on poetical diction. There might be past works of criticism and theory that serve as exceptions to the rule, but such texts do not seem to figure prominently in the discussions and "debates" about "theory" that currently take place.[2] They do not fire our contemporary vision of the term. This is only to say that the questions surrounding the meanings of theory are not in the ordinary sense open questions. To introduce such texts into a conversation about theory would be regarded as seriously missing the point. We would be making not a logical but a social mistake, like eating peas with one's knife.

A further characteristic of the situation that confronts anyone seeking to interrogate theory comes oddly with the restrictions mentioned above. This is the pressure to say *something* about it regardless of the number of times its presiding importance to literary study is questioned or rebuked—"The Band Plays On," as Raymond Tallis has remarked.[3] Such a moral or professional obligation must override any distaste felt for the body of writing that conventionally occupies the genre of theory. Commentary is undoubtedly controlled to some extent by a certain "bandwagon" effect, the intellectual fashions that boost or depress other literary or aesthetic forms; but John Holloway cannot be the only recent academic commentator to confess that his reading in a particular branch of twentieth-century theory was not performed from a strong natural attraction to the field, a tenderness for the work he found it necessary to comment upon:

> The body of work that I hope to take stock of is large. I had better say frankly that I have read in this field (not, doubtless, as extensively as I might) more because there is widespread interest in it and it has become influential, than because I have found it exceptionally congenial.[4]

Could exposition of any other subject in the literary or critical sphere be introduced with quite such self-sacrificing respect for what has mattered to *other* people? It is therefore at the risk of seeming insincere (or being drawn to the subject only because its material has been found "influential"), that one embarks on discussion of the way that theory is defined. But this risk has to be taken if one is to inquire into the nature of theory's relations with "criticism." Two circumstances would seem to require this.

The first is the apriorism I mentioned in chapter 1; the fact that much theorization of theory is written from a point in close proximity to the cause and purpose of the theory being commented upon and is in some respects not differentiated from it. (Terry Eagleton's *Literary Theory* is of this kind).[5] Granted (with Pope), we cannot but regard our writers' (or our theorists') ends; but there comes a time when it is also necessary to view the achievements of theorists in a more distant light, by surveying the whole. Writing on theory that neglected to do this would lack the requisite *salt* to be taken seriously by a disinterested observer.

The second circumstance more especially justifies this phase of the discussion. This is the difference between the intractable and impenetrable obscurities that the advent of post-Saussurean theory has seemed to many to leave in its wake and the list of resolvable problems—the needless ambiguities that do not have to be left lying around forever among the debris after the "theory explosion."

In the first case, it may be that no progress can be made: we might have to admit that understanding has taken a backward step, and "the most evident truths are so obscured that they can no longer be perceived, and the most familiar propositions so disguised that they cannot be known."[6] In the latter event, more optimistically, the issues are ones that discussion and analysis can take practical measures to address, even if further talk about theory can make only a small addition to clearing the ground. But to do so the conversation must avoid the vast abstractionism to which its subject matter has been found fatally prone. It must first seek clarity on the simple level. At the risk of seeming petty, we need to deduce what writers devoted to rendering theory for public consumption think they are saying from the words they use when they talk about it, and from the idioms and structures in which this talk is conceived. We need to get as precise an account of it as we can. How, then, is "criticism's" relation to "theory" translated into terms the consumers of theory will understand and apply?

In the publishing boom in "theory guides," introductions, anthologies, commentaries, and "readers" intended for beginners, there is much of substance to support the view that we now live in an "age of theory."[7] The structure and context of this embankment of volumes is uncannily stable—a fact that suggests an unusual stability in the idea of criticism (and the idea of criticism's relation to theory). But this settled and expanding condition in the affairs of theory (quite the opposite of a crisis) is constantly undermined by shifts in what is meant or intended or supposed when the idea of theory is spoken about, and when understandings are put into words. I do not mean the normal semantic evolution taking place over hundreds of years (from Samuel Johnson's "theory" = "speculation, not practice" to the twentieth century's "theory in praxis"). With "theory," we are talking of a mental thing that appears as if through a fog at dusk. But some allowance has to be made at this point. Critical terms may seem legitimately vague. They are tools to think with as well as meanings to think about, and we would not want or expect a dictionary-type (verbal) definition in order to pin them down. All critical terminology is in some sense malleable and fluid. New words come in, while common, older words (such as "theory") take on new meanings. One of the generally acknowledged functions of criticism is to redefine this language, and thus criticism itself. But all this adds greatly to the belief that the concept of criticism is inherently inchoate and confused, a terrain unnegotiable without the help of a dictionary of literary or critical terms and specialist assistance from professional, qualified sources. Since we cannot even get hold of the words that criticism adopts to convey its notions, the idea of criticism must always seem to evade us. It must always seem lost in the desolation of the field.

Much usage across the range of the language, as I have suggested in chapter 3, is *usefully* imprecise. Particular terms always have a number of jobs to do. Pre- and post-Saussurean critics have always recognized that the door has to be kept open for changes in the relation between language and meaning, for adjustments in the "fit" between words and the extension of the concepts they serve. But other "types of ambiguity" do not qualify for this kind of extenuation. They may be too casual (where the writer does not know what he or she is meaning to say); they may also be too calculated (where the writer is putting a "spin" on the meaning of a term while seeming to use it in a generally received sense that only a naive and uninformed person would find open to objection). The latter tactic is always useful if one wishes to exploit the shades of language to suggest the acceptability and orthodox nature of propositions otherwise subject to more rigorous challenge than the writer might wish. This may be one of the ways, to recur to Ben Jonson's phrase, that critics addressing the question of theory "make more faults than they mend."[8]

THEORY IN CRITICISM AND CRITICISM IN THEORY

When he was asked by the Committee on the Research Activities of the MLA to write a piece on theory for an introduction to scholarship, Paul de Man confessed that "the main theoretical interest of literary theory consists in the impossibility of its definition";[9] and in the sense that usages of theory cannot be brought within a single system, this is surely the case. But to recognize this is also to recognize that there has to be *some* precision in the use of a word, and the common perception that criticism in the wake of theory is full of arcane and exorbitant ideas and impenetrable expressions does not seem a sufficient excuse to set the effort of definition aside in despair. The most important difficulties in the definition of theory are, after all, ones that it may be important to *"stoop to . . . understand"* (Pope's *Essay on Criticism*, line 67).

The problem in brief is this: there are two meanings of theory, but they are sometimes treated as one. This difficulty is not mitigated by the radical indeterminacy of modern theoretical prose, in which certain very different meanings of theory are concealed symptomatically in the play between transitive and intransitive uses of the verb "to theorize." Intransitively speaking, I theorize "about" something in the sense that I "think about" or reflect upon it, the consequence of which (if all goes according to plan) being "an explanatory generalization inductively arrived at."[10] Freadman and Miller in their book *Re-Thinking Theory* suggest that "it is important to distinguish between theorizing about an object and merely offering other and more informal accounts of it,"[11] and it would be consistent with this conception of theory to say that Samuel Johnson, in the famous passage from his *Preface to Shakespeare*, is theorizing "about" the dramatic unities of time and place, that Matthew Arnold is theorizing "about" the function of literary criticism in his essay of that title, or that Sir Philip Sidney is theorizing "about" the whole idea of poetry in his "Apology" or his "Defence." But the verb "to theorize" can also be transitively put to use, and this is the common usage of writers in the poststructuralist mode. I now no longer theorize "about" something but theorize the something itself—a text, a critical position or opinion, and so on—as a direct object. "In poststructural criticism," writes M. H. Abrams: "what is called 'theory' has come to be foregrounded as the central and dominant issue, so that it becomes incumbent on every critic to 'theorize' his or her position and practice."[12]

The change is a change in the whole of the implied situation of theory. The one usage of the verb refers to the content of the theorizing (what it is about); the other refers to its complement (that which is affected directly by it). The one registers theory's capacity to reflect reality by constructing explanatory systems about it; the other, theory's capacity to change (to "radicalize") that reality, to consider it in the light of a theory drawn not from the thing itself (the opinion, the work) but from an antecedent political, social, and linguistic perspective of inclusive authority and truth. Grammatically speaking, we may say that Theory turns from a "countable" to an "uncountable" or "mass" noun, from "a" theory "of" to Theory. It loses the indefinite article and gains a capital "T."[13]

Most recent attempts to systematize the meanings of theory have tended to concentrate on this latter usage as the one most urgently in *need* of defining, yet hardest of all to pin down. Of these, some seek to provide a definition in the sense of an essentialist account of Theory—that is, to construct hypotheses as to its genus. W. J. T. Mitchell writes,

> Theory is . . . ocular, spatial, and graphocentric. . . . Theory . . . repeats within itself the oppositions that distinguish it from nontheory. . . . Theory is monotheistic. . . . Theory is . . . to thought what power is to politics. . . .[14]

Others offer an ostensive tour around the boundaries of the concept's differentiae; they give examples of the sorts of "things" (works of criticism, essays, didactic treatises, etc.) that normally qualify as Theory without the principle of selection or single criterion of relevance that points to what can be included within the term's current spread and what has to be left out. This sometimes leads to the definition of Theory as a list—a cumulative index of types of writing whose relation to the term "theory" is different on every occasion. Raman Selden, in the introduction to *The Cambridge History of Literary Criticism: From Formalism to Poststructuralism*, writes of the successive types of allusion, reference, and connotation that connect the various meanings of the word to the word itself:

> First, it alludes to the scientific ambition to master and define a conceptual field. Secondly, the term is used to refer to those critical discourses which aim to disrupt such mastery, truth-seeking and systematic closure. . . . Thirdly, "theory" may connote a poetics or aesthetics concerned not with interpretation of texts but with theorizing discourse in general.[15]

For Paul de Man, theory is defined as an "either/or," an emergent entity discernible either through a choice of "approach" ("Literary theory can be said to come into being when the approach to literary texts is no longer based on non-linguistic, that is to say historical and aesthetic, considerations. . . .") or through an "object of discussion" ("when the object of discussion is no longer the meaning or the value but the modalities of production and of reception of meaning and of value prior to their establishment . . .). These alternatives give rise to theory as "an autonomous discipline of critical investigation" precisely concerned with investigating "its possibility and its status" ("its"—one has to understand from the circular turn of this sentence—being the possibility and status of "the modalities of production and of reception of meaning and of value prior to their establishment").[16]

An important aspect of such accounts of "theory" is the practice of definition by negatives. Thus Jonathan Culler can assert that "The writings to which this term alludes do not find their justification in the improvement of interpretations." Theory is not so much a discipline as the nickname for a nameless "domain."[17] According to Eagleton, meanwhile, "literary theory is less an object of intellectual enquiry in its own right than a particular perspective in which to view the history of our times." Yet while a perspective on history, it is not to be defined by its methods of inquiry about literature—even (somewhat curiously, perhaps) if it is *literary* theory we are thinking about:

> There are two familiar ways in which any theory can provide itself with a distinct purpose and identity. Either it can define itself in terms of its particular *methods* of enquiry; or it can define itself in terms of the particular *object* that is being enquired into. Any attempt to define literary theory in terms of a distinctive method is doomed to failure. . . . [18]

Theory, now, is "concerned *not* with interpretation of texts"; is "a domain as yet *un*named"; is "*not* 'philosophy' in the current sense," and "its most interesting works do *not* explicitly address literature." "Literary theory," in Eagleton's opinion, is "a *non*-subject" (all my italics).[19] Thus conceived, theory (or Theory) is indeed an object strange and high, and it would seem to follow that, rather like the abstractions captured poetically in Marvell's poem "The Definition of Love," definitions of theory will often appear begotten by despair upon impossibility (or like the famous definition of a net as a series of holes joined together by pieces of string). Moreover, while some allowance may be made for the informalities and lapses of discursive prose, the terminology is exceptionally—as we say—"undecided." Since critics are not always referring clearly to the same thing, one cannot feel confident that theory in any new, fundamentally revised sense of the word is yet satisfactorily "defined." We read at random of "literary theory," "critical theory," or just "theory," in the case of the unqualified noun. "Theory" and "criticism" may be near synonyms or virtual antonyms. We sometimes encounter talk of "critics," sometimes "theorists," and sometimes "critics and theorists"; and as indicated above, writers "on" theory, and the constructors "of" theory, tend not to be sharply discriminated: theorists on theory are commonly its most enthusiastic proponents or advocates. Commentators like David Lodge may discuss "the importance of theory in contemporary criticism, and its ambiguous status —both part of and larger than literary studies,"[20] as if its place within "study" or "studies" (criticism in its specific educational and professional scholarly context) were the primary issue for theory, and this context the primary mode in which criticism exists, and as if theory in relation to criticism other than the "contemporary" variety were hardly an issue at all.

Other writers think of the relation between "theory" and "criticism" in terms of a contrast between "theory" and "critical practice," as if criticism were in essence a question of "practice" and existed mainly minus the theory—as "practical criticism" perhaps. Christopher Ricks notes that Geoffrey Hartman thinks that "the *only* alternative to theory is 'practical criticism'"[21]—a false dichotomy surely. Yet others, now perhaps in the ascendant, think of "theory" and "practice" conjoined. K. M. Newton writes in the introduction to his "Reader" in *Twentieth-Century Literary Theory* of "new forms of approach in which practice and theory are intermingled."[22] "[T]he proper relation between theory and practice," write Brooker and Widdowson, "is a dialectical one in which they test and transform each other."[23] The "especially Marxist" genesis of this conjunction is explained by Raymond Williams. "Theory" is one of Williams's "Keywords":

> In our own time, one use of **theory** is sharply distinguished from *speculation*, and, even more strongly, one use of **theoretical** from the relevant sense of *speculative*. . . . This depends on an important development of the sense of **theory** . . . which is in effect "a scheme of ideas which explains practice." . . . The specialized modern sense comes from a development in German, c. 1840, in origin late Hegelian but now especially Marxist, where *praxis* is *practice* informed by **theory** and also, though less emphatically, **theory** informed by *practice*. . . . The distinction or opposition between **theory** and *practice* can then be surpassed. This view has strong and weak forms, over a range from informed and conscious practice to the recent **theoretical practice** which, in most of its examples, is predominantly **theoretical** and, as its critics now say, **theoreticist.** (Williams's emphases)[24]

But it is hard to say what this "theoretical practice" is, since critics are radically undecided on theory's true relation to criticism. Within the terms of this present conjunction—the relation between theory and criticism that is the "central issue" for Brooker and Widdowson[25]—there is a generous range of opinion. Some think of criticism and theory in a state of conceptual coexistence: theory has grown out of criticism but now strikes independent root, "a distinct subject in its own right" in the words of Jefferson and Robey.[26] Others seem to have in mind a relationship where one concept *composes* the other, where, for example, "theory" is a part of the whole of criticism—one of the matters that a "critical consciousness" larger than theory, and working from outside theory, has as its business on which to reflect. "[W]e distinguish theory from critical consciousness," writes Edward Said, "by saying that the latter is a sort of spatial sense, a sort of measuring faculty for locating or situating theory."[27] In this conception, we might imagine that when all the separate "theories" situated within "criticism" are added together they will accumulate to form an identity of indiscernibles with "criticism." This seems to be the understanding communicated by the "theory guides," but it is also more generally current among commentators upon theory. Jonathan Culler writes of criticism as a "field" constituted by theories:

> Once upon a time it might have been possible to think of criticism as a single activity practiced with different emphases. The acrimony of recent debate suggests the contrary: the field of criticism is contentiously constituted by apparently incompatible activities . . . structuralism, reader-response criticism, deconstruction. . . . [28]

Looked at from the other direction, criticism is reduced from its role as an embracing concept to something conceptually less than Theory; it is contained *by* and subsumed *within* Theory's greater interdisciplinary breadth and sophistication of method. We could see "criticism" here as one of the several "objects" of Theory—part of its conceptual content, as "theory" in the former examples was one of the "objects" of "criticism." If theory at one moment exists under the aspect of criticism, criticism at another moment is under the aspect of Theory. Patrick Parrinder has written that "Theory tends to regard criticism (in the sense of the study of specific texts) as an activity properly subordinated to its own stronger and wider concerns."[29] This goes closely with the idea that Theory is to be seen as an originating, shaping force from which all criticism begins, an ultimate cause. "Contemporary critical theory," write Rice and Waugh, "sees itself as existing at the heart of the critical enterprise, insisting that there is no critical act that can transcend theory."[30] According to Brooker and Widdowson: "All criticism . . . is dependent on theory."[31] The nature of this tree-structure of concepts is described by Terry Eagleton as follows:

> First, there is the meta-theory; then the literary theory it takes as its object of enquiry; then literary criticism, which much literary theory reflects on; then literature, the object of critical investigation.[32]

What is at one moment a vertical hierarchy may at the next be a rule of temporal salience. Here Theory is seen to transcend "criticism" at some point in the fairly recent past: "It is this theoretical 'anti-humanism,'" writes Raman Selden, "which marks a real break with the era of 'criticism.'"[33] Another way of articulating this proposition is to see Theory as defined by a kind or type of criticism among many kinds or types of criticism having specific sources in earlier theory and from which superior historical authority it derives a privileged, supervenient status: "I use it loosely," says Helen Taylor, "to describe that body of critical work which has drawn on post-Saussurean, Marxist and feminist thought since the late 1960s."[34]

Finally, there is the model of "interdependent equivalence" or the complementarity of "criticism" and "theory." This is perhaps more often expressed as a wished-for ideal rather than a proposition about the reality of the current situation. According to Patrick Parrinder, "The relationship between theory and criticism should not be one of master and slave but a two-way process, in which not only does theory question criticism but criticism questions theory."[35] Edward Said writes that "it is the critic's job to provide resistances to theory."[36] The disparities identified in the relations between the concepts can be plotted as a kind of power struggle between two ideas locked in competition for the upper hand, a battle comparable with that of the Soul and the Body in another of Marvell's poems.[37]

The Logic of Theory in Practice

While this struggle is unresolved, a more settled, definitive view of theory and criticism—one where theory emerges out of criticism and can withstand criticism—seems fairly unlikely, as does a more considered meaning for the concept of "practicing theory" or the somewhat posher "theory in praxis." The problem with "practicing theory" that I have in mind stems from the fact that the theory most people are interested in practicing is confessedly a "practice" in its own right. It is the all-embracing Theory that (ex hypothesi) already authorizes and explains anything we seek to apply it to, and in so doing might be thought to remove the point of the practice on which we are about to embark. In order to be "applicable," theory has to exist in a world where there is something we want explained that has *not* grown out of it.[38] How to "apply" Theory creates a difficulty, therefore, and may necessitate refurbishing the earlier meaning of "theory"—now by all accounts superseded—as a tool for interpreting works of literature and art. "We need initially to make a distinction" write Freadman and Miller, "that is anathema to many avant-garde literary theorists: the distinction between a theory and its object":

> The theory itself will consist of a set of claims or principles in respect of some object or phenomenon; and the objects or phenomena may be widely varying in nature. In this instance, however, the object of theorising is literature. It is in our view imperative to resist the temptation—and indeed the tendency—to collapse the distinction between object and theory. Theories or quasi-theories may strongly condition conceptions of their objects, but they cannot literally construct those objects or entirely determine our conceptions of them. Were they able so to construct and determine, we would be unable to apprehend, or even to posit the existence, of the object;

and it would follow from this that theorising would literally be inconceivable since there would be nothing to *theorise* about. Quite simply, a theory is a theory of something.[39]

There are, we can recall, two systems of thought (two "paradigm-situations") which should not be confused. One is where a man or a woman is regarding an object (let us call it a work of art) and is doing the best they can to represent what they see or hear by reference to various principles or criteria that account for its properties in generalized form (let us call this a theory of art). The other is where a man or a woman reiterates, analogizes, or illustrates a particular body of ideas that he or she takes to be of unique force and authority, and where the presence or effect of an autonomous work of art may be merely instrumental to this. In the one case, the theory is applied to what it is a theory "of." In the other, all that can be applied in practice are the various "*theories* of" language, style, fictional representation, textual ideology, knowledge, social and historical constitutiveness, and so forth. These "countable" theories are those which the essays and books of Theory in the "uncountable" "mass" sense *incidentally* comprise, and it is these and not the "mass" type of Theory that we "apply." Will this do as practicing Theory? If we accept with several of the critics examined above that there has been a revolution in the meaning of Theory—and one meaning replaces the other—then no. For the reasons given, Theory in the "mass" cannot be practiced if by "practice" we mean "apply." If, however, we assume the meaning of theory to be in reality unchanged, and we are speaking with Freadman and Miller of theories distinct from their objects, then practicing theory may occur in this sense. But we still have to note a collapse in this meaning's distinction from Theory with a capital "T." The crux of the problem may be represented as follows. There are two propositions:

1. that critical theory and literature have become one;
2. that critical theory can be "applied."

But if theory $= x$ and the thing to which it is applied $= y$, then if (1) is true, (2) must be false. It is simply that if x is the same as y, then x and y are identical; and if x and y are identical, x cannot be applied to y without some change in y's definition. There are then three possibilities. One *either* rejects the proposition that theory and literature are identical, *or* one dispenses with the idea that theory can be applied to literature, *or* one admits the currency of different definitions of theory used opportunistically. But whichever option is chosen, the same definition of theory will not serve both propositions at once. The meaning of "practice" has to be changed.

The further suggestion that theory can be "tested" by practice seems now merely odd. Can this be intended? True, to transfer to criticism what is said of both life and art in the language of Henry James's *The Tragic Muse:* "[T]he point of an experiment is that it shall succeed." One may therefore have some sympathy with Howard Felperin's attempt to prepare the ground for his "poststructuralist reading" of Shakespeare's *Sonnets* by asking: "[I]s there any text, or group of texts, in the literary canon that so readily lends itself to exploration of the negativities, absences, and indeterminacies of textuality itself."[40]

And it may seem overharsh to condemn practicing theory in this sense on the grounds somewhat scathingly stated by John Harwood: that "the better understanding [of literary texts] invariably turns out to be that which justifies the application of the theory."[41] But to say baldly (as do Brooker and Widdowson, for example) that "theory and practice . . . test and transform each other"[42] is surely to place the works of art so far outside the dialectical circle they are irrelevant to it. It is in *literature*, after all, that a theory about literature is put into practice. Wordsworth puts his theory of poetical diction into practice in the *Lyrical Ballads* (or rather notoriously fails to); James his theory of fiction in his novels; Hopkins his theory of sprung rhythm in his poems. "Practice" cannot test and transform theory (or *be* transformed or tested by it), because "practice" is what you do when you apply the theory, and you apply the theory to the *works*. Practice is the means, literature the object of the theory. Without belaboring the point: the formula confuses two things that we always *already* know are distinguished.

7
Criticism, Interpretation, and Judgment

> Does a man have to be a critic in order to write "Shakespeare criticism"? I might well sound merely sarcastic when I ask the question, and merely sarcastic again when I follow it up with even such unoriginal reflections on the nature of criticism as the following: that a critic is rare and is so, in the first place perhaps, because he is a man of strong, vivid and delicate feeling with an exceptional capacity for being clear and honest about his feelings; that this is so because only the response to a work of art of such a person can be sure to reach another person's true inner response and thereby illuminate and extend or change it.
> —J. M. Newton, *"Scrutiny's* Failure with Shakespeare"

> Criticism is not advocacy.... Judicial, it should be.... And Judgments depend on laws, on established laws.
> —Gerard Manley Hopkins, *Journals*

CRITICISM AND THE LIMITS OF INTERPRETATION

INTERPRETATION FOLLOWS FROM THE MEDIATE ROLE TRADITIONALLY ACCORDED TO criticism, the convention that criticism is the *handmaid of the muse* (*An Essay on Criticism*, line 102). Be that as it may, the driving force of interpretation—"interpretosis" as Raymond Tallis has scathingly called it[1]—has been to *escape* the shackles of the critical past. Because in this light Theory is thought to give rise to meanings that no previous critic could have imagined before, an interpretation has value in eluding an untutored audience, and may often be counterintuitive, cutting "against the grain" of mere common sense or the standards of a "common reader." Such a definition of critical activity does much to meet the needs of a post-romantic criterion of creative originality dialectically pitted against the appeal to Pope's "What oft was *Thought*" (*An Essay on Criticism*, line 298); but it also finds a role in the more mundane context of professional scholarship. In simulating conditions we associate with the prestige discoveries of a specialist science, the criterion of novelty is brought powerfully to the fore.

Some critical books of interpretation, like those of Theory, have attempted to perform their function by seeming to re-create their "object" of criticism. Geoffrey Hartman's reading of Jacques Derrida's *Glas*, itself an interpretive play on the philosophy of Hegel, is among those modern works of interpretation which cast Theory itself in the role of the literary text.[2] As James M. Heath and Michael Payne have observed of this general tendency, "Literary theory, hermeneutics, or critical theory examines the art of interpretation itself and, in so doing, often replaces the literary text with a critical text that becomes the focal point of the study."[3] But in highlighting the function of "interpretation" *within* "criticism" here, this legitimate part of criticism must not be seen to subvert the concept's scope—while the latter, more comprehensive term is misnamed, unanalyzed, and misunderstood. F. E. Sparshott has rightly suggested that interpretation is "indisputably a prime task of criticism,"[4] while P. D. Juhl, in his comprehensive study,[5] has brought the interpretive task further to the fore. But some controlling sense of the limits of "interpretation," vis-à-vis "criticism," seems also to be required.[6]

In the recent series of "Tanner Lectures" published under the editorship of Stefan Collini as *Interpretation and Overinterpretation*, a case is developed against the overinterpretation of literary texts on the grounds of "unlimited semiosis."[7] Umberto Eco fears that the inexhaustible meanings of a text will sooner or later collide and the problematically "true" interpretation will be obscured. With special reference to the recent workings out of interpretation through deconstructive criticism, this particular resonance of the "Tanner Lectures" echoes the arguments of Susan Sontag's famous essay in *Against Interpretation* of 1964;[8] but it defines the problem in a less root-and-branch way. It is concerned not so much with the place of interpretation in the totality of criticism, but with what E. D. Hirsch in his focus on evidence and intention has called "*validity* in interpretation."[9] Sontag had referred to interpretation as "the intellect's revenge on art," by which the meanings are squeezed out and the husk is discarded, eclipsing the tradition of *appreciation* in criticism—the celebration of art, its elevation. But whereas Sontag was concerned with the aspects of criticism that interpretation left out, Eco and his disputants are primarily exercised by *how much* interpretation, the limits beyond which interpretations give way—as if the extracted meanings could be solely conceived in the terms we use to speak of rival propositions in philosophical debate.

But this procedure appears to leave too largely unqualified the prior assumption that criticism "is" interpretation, a concept that plays out its role when engaged with the entirety of the text, the complete work of art, the "organic whole" of romantic literary theory. The prestige of interpretation has been heightened at different times by the dedication of Renaissance hermeneutics to the Word of God, by the application of Freudian psychology to literary criticism, and by the "verbal icon" of the American "New Criticism." But the inference must in each case be that it is the whole text that is our *primary* or even our *single* concern as literary critics. The difficulty of such an inference must always be the critical question of where the "text" under interpretation merges into its context or rises from it, as works of literature indeterminantly do. Critics might reasonably disagree about what "a" work is—one of the poems from Hughes's *Crow* or all of them? One item from a sonnet sequence or the whole sequence? The collection of short stories or each story in turn?

Leonard Cohen's "Suzanne Takes You Down" (1968) randomly exemplifies the sort of task the interpreter of modern poetry may typically face:

> Suzanne takes you down
> to her place near the river,
> you can hear the boats go by
> you can stay the night beside her.
> And you know that she's half-crazy
> but that's why you want to be there
> and she feeds you tea and oranges
> that come all the way from China.
> Just when you mean to tell her
> that you have no gifts to give her,
> she gets you on her wave-length
> and she lets the river answer
> that you've always been her lover.
>   And you want to travel with her,
>   you want to travel blind
>   and you know that she can trust you
>   because you've touched her perfect body
>   with your mind.
>
> Jesus was a sailor
> when he walked upon the water
> and he spent a long time watching
> from a lonely wooden tower. . . . [10]

In his essay "On Liberty of Interpreting," W. W. Robson has discussed the difference between the meaning of a *word* and the meaning of a literary *work*, and has asked whether a work of literature such as a novel or a poem can have meaning in the sense of a word. The two expressions, he suggests, have a different force. In this connection "Questions about the meaning of 'To his Coy Mistress', or any other literary work, are not to be taken as questions about the meaning of this or that word or sentence or passage."[11]

The problem in the case of Cohen's work is similarly one of resemblance—*Ähnlichheit* in Wittgensteinian terms—on different levels. The critical interpreter of "Suzanne Takes You Down" must not only know what the word "river" means, or what a "tower" is (as questions that could be answered by a nonliterary critic); he or she must also feel the symbolic value of these things in their context, and read off the equivalences between the images and the latent meanings when we bring our imaginations to bear. Put crudely, we enter the play of meanings, trying, with each successive sally, the "fit" of one or another interpretive frame. The work of interpreting comes to an end when, having found the best correspondence, we give the most plausible description of what the poem is "about." And to appeal to "aboutness" is to make a statement composed of relatively unambiguous answers to the various separate questions raised by the puzzle: Who is Suzanne? Why is Jesus is a sailor? Who is supposed to be speaking the voices in different stanzas? And is there any particular significance in the tea and oranges that Suzanne feeds to all and sundry when she takes them down (as preparatory to a sinister narcotic or sexual experience, for example)? Interpretation overcomes the poet's resistance to spelling these things out, and works with our ordinary pleasure in discovering nonobvious meaning—even where the satisfactions are the arithmetical pleasures of putting two and two together toward a "solution." It is easy to see the appeal of this search for possible meanings to examiners setting literary examinations for students in universities and schools. For all its invitation to free association, degrees of correctness seem to apply; when criticism is defined as interpretation, it takes its place with other kinds of deductive test. Gerald Graff has written of "the sheer determination to rationalize that seems to be built into the dynamics of the explication industry."[12]

But the inference that the practice of interpretation leads to a more objectively measurable form of critical success is, I would argue, unsound. It may be taken to be a recent "discovery" of modern critical thought about itself, inaccessible to naive readers in darker ages, that no single interpretation can settle the meaning of a poem, or silence other attempts that lead to different or conflicting meanings. But this appeal to a straw tradition assumes that past critical communities ever did think in this way. The point of what is now termed "undecidability," the condition of infinite deferral associated with relativistic theories of criticism and their legitimation of endless interpretation, was put long ago with reference to conjectural criticism by Samuel Johnson:

> That a conjectural critick should often be mistaken, cannot be wonderful, either to others or himself, if it be considered, that in his art there is no system, no principal and axiomatical truth that regulates subordinate positions His

chance of errour is renewed at every attempt; an oblique view of the passage, a slight misapprehension of phrase, a casual inattention to the parts connected, is sufficient to make him not only fail, but fail ridiculously; and when he succeeds best, he produces perhaps but one reading of many probable, and he that suggests another will always be able to dispute his claims.[13]

Sontag complained that some works are created consciously in order to invite multiple interpretations. If therefore our idea of texts is specialized or selective in some way, then our idea of criticism will be too. If the text is a conundrum, or enigma (e.g., Shakespeare's *Hamlet* or Blake's "The Sick Rose"), then interpretation may seem an indispensable tool; and there are times when texts propose themselves as problems requiring solution, or codes to be cracked. Many of Donne's poems challenge the reader to trace associations between ideas "yoked by violence together," while allegorical works, like Spenser's *Faerie Queene*, imply the necessity for interpretive treatment at greater length (combining discrete interpretive acts). In his essay "The Frontiers of Criticism," T. S. Eliot described a kind of interpretive conspiracy between creator and interpreter that was not part of the creator's conscious, or at least stated, intentions:

> [A]fter the production of my play *The Cocktail Party*, my mail was swollen for months with letters offering surprising solutions of what the writers believed to be the riddle of the play's meaning. And it was evident that the writers did not resent the puzzle they thought I had set them—they liked it. Indeed, though they were unconscious of the fact, they invented the puzzle for the pleasure of the solution.[14]

But if this interpretive function were found actually sufficient to exhaust "criticism," criticizing works that are not palpably enigmatic, allegorical, symbolic, or otherwise problematic in this way (Ben Jonson's poem "On the Death on His First Sonne," for example?) must be excluded—not because establishing "the meaning" does not present problems of a profound kind for the critic, but because the interpretation must be unproductive of any substitute versions of meaning, as when a photograph replaces to the point of obliteration the memorized image of a scene imprinted on the mind. A *statement* of meaning must in this case seem inescapably reductive. Thus the point of grasping the "meaning" in the context of literary criticism is not to elicit "statements," but to find out why a poem is valued, or in what chambers of the modern psyche it continues to vibrate. Critics do not always *have* to be interested in stated meanings to function as critics. Can we say, for example, that the following printed utterance is necessarily excluded from the writing by Samuel Johnson we bring into our minds when we describe his achievement, in the language we use when we expect to be understood, as that of a "critic"?: "[I]f my sensations could add anything to the general suffrage, I might relate, that I was many years ago so shocked by Cordelia's death, that I know not whether I ever endured to read again the last scenes of the play till I undertook to revise them as an editor."[15]

Johnson's emotional reaction to his text is quite different from any successful interpretation of a *work* of literature, and the meanings yielded by the text at this point are not the consequence of a strictly hermeneutic procedure. What he says is heartfelt; and though we may assume that contact with the play has occurred on a number of earlier occasions, it comes on the instant. The words register not a "reading" but are quite obviously a response, restrained though emotive. The only critical tool that Johnson uses is the capacity to react as he does, as an unrealized potential. The critical framework is at the same time that of the moral and human self, and the question of resemblance, the problem of the "fit" between interpretation and work, momentarily disappears from the equation. The text, in this case a play containing the death of a female character for whom sympathy has been poignantly and powerfully aroused, has invaded the subjectivity of Johnson, removing the critic from his position of external intellectual control, so that Johnson's own "sensations" are now the "object" of the criticism. This is not an argument "against interpretation," but to say that the potential to extract "meanings" (the concern with "validity," "intention," or "overinterpretation") does not exceed in importance the capacity for tears or the critic's susceptibility to pain. In this event, we do not read the criticism for the meaning of the work, but to learn how other humans have felt. This is normal, and it is part of criticism. Annette Barnes, in her book *On Interpretation,* writes of "interpretive criticism" but would not need to unless the existence of criticism of other kinds was implicitly acknowledged.[16] In the act of interpreting we abandon the option that criticism theoretically permits of allowing the text to "speak for itself." This seems to challenge the raison d'être of criticism, as Pope realized in his satiric exhortation to the critics of his day:

> Leave not a foot of verse, a foot of stone,
> A page, a Grave, that they can call their own. . . .
> (*The Dunciad*, book 4, lines 127–28) [17]

Interpretation, then, overrides or preempts criticism when it decodes the unitary text *before* the approach to it (which might be thought the deciding factor with regard to the unity) has yet begun. And since the implied norm is the whole text, which is a priori, the many different ways that the critic comprehends an age or an oeuvre, a line, a scene, an item of vocabulary, or plays between texts of different kinds and different ages, take second place. Moreover, the paradigm of interpretive criticism seems to centralize the "confrontation model of criticism."[18] This privileges one of the essential resources necessary to the critic, the rational, at the expense of a willingness to share the emotions released by critical contact with the work. It grounds the identity of criticism in its application, as a tool, constraining the sense in which criticism may be imagined as like other things that are not used in the ordinary way we use a tool. We say we use language, and in a sense we do. But language is also of the matter that makes us us.

The Idea of Judgment and the Scope of Criticism

In moving from interpretation to judgment, we turn from a definitional constituent of criticism relatively congenial to Theory to one antagonistic to it. Raymond Williams is one recent critic who regrets the close association of criticism with "judgment" and with a process that is too generalized for criticism in what he considers to be its essentially concrete form: "when what always needs to be understood is the specificity of the response, which is not an abstract 'judgment' but even where including, as often necessarily, positive or negative responses, a definite practice, in active and complex relations with its whole situation and context."[19]

The comment goes with Williams's words in praise of "practicing theory" quoted above. But in opposing the "abstract" to the "active and complex," Williams is making substantially the same distinction as had been made by F. R. Leavis in a famous passage on two decisively different ways of being "judicial" in criticism:

> Words in poetry invite us, not to "think about" and judge but to "feel into" or "become"—to realize a complex experience that is given in the words. They demand, not merely a fuller-bodied response, but a completer responsiveness—a kind of responsiveness that is incompatible with the judicial, one-eye-on-the-standard approach. . . . The critic—the reader of poetry—is indeed concerned with evaluation, but to figure him as measuring with a norm which he brings up to the object and applies from the outside is to misrepresent the process. The critic's aim is, first, to realize as sensitively and completely as possible this or that which claims his attention; and a certain valuing is implicit in the realizing. As he matures in experience of the new thing he asks, explicitly and implicitly: "Where does this come? How does it stand in relation to . . . ? How relatively important does it seem?" And the organization into which it settles as a constituent in becoming "placed" is an organization of similarly "placed" things, things that have found their bearings with regard to one another, and not a theoretical system or system determined by abstract considerations. . . . The business of the literary critic is to attain a peculiar completeness of re-

sponse and to observe a peculiarly strict relevance in developing his response into commentary; he must be on his guard against abstracting improperly from what is in front of him and against any premature generalizing—of it or from it. His first concern is to enter into possession of the given poem (let us say) in its concrete fulness, and his constant concern is never to lose his completeness of possession, but rather to increase it. In making value-judgements (and judgements as to significance), implicitly or explicitly, he does so out of that completeness of possession and with that fulness of response.[20]

For Leavis—who is no more in favor of abstraction removed from "the real terms of response"—there are narrow and more comprehensive meanings of "judgment." For Williams, "judgment" cannot be the wide thing that Leavis thinks that it is, but merely one of a "succession of abstractions of . . . [criticism's] real terms of response," alongside "*taste, cultivation, discrimination, sensibility; disinterested, qualified, rigorous* and so on."[21] As in the discussion of critical value, judicial criticism (the "standard of judging well," in Johnson's dictionary definition) gives place to criticism of other kinds, and in this (if we compare the opinions quoted above) it is clear that the thinking of Williams has largely prevailed. Thus "judgment" has fallen into disrepute among most prominent critical theorists.

But the judgments of actual criticism themselves vary in all sorts of ways. Stein Haugom Olsen, in his essay "Value-Judgements in Criticism,"[22] has differentiated three distinct types of "value-judgement" in literary criticism—the "local" (concerned with "diction . . . use of words and phrases"), the "regional" ("dependent for its meaning and point on an interpretative argument"), and the "global," where the "object of evaluation is the whole literary work." This is not an exhaustive account of all the types of judgment that criticism contains and is not intended to be. Here, for example, is Wordsworth passing judgment on the decline evident to him in the whole latter age of poetry up to his own time:

> The earliest poets of all nations generally wrote from passion excited by real events; they wrote naturally, and as men: feeling powerfully as they did, their language was daring, and figurative. In succeeding times, Poets, and Men ambitious of the fame of Poets, perceiving the influence of such language, and desirous of producing the same effect without being animated by the same passion, set themselves to a mechanical adoption of these figures of speech. . . . Poets . . . who had before contented themselves for the most part with misapplying only expressions which at first had been dictated by real passion, carried the abuse still further, and introduced phrases composed apparently in the spirit of the original figurative language of passion, yet altogether of their own invention, and characterised by various degrees of wanton deviation from good sense and nature.[23]

The vast historical sweep of this statement stands at one end of the range. Other judgments are period-specific. They apply to chronological subdivisions within this larger span. Thus we can have Eagleton's embracing (and equivocally negative) assessment of the whole eighteenth century as a time when "the neo-classical notions of Reason, Nature, order and propriety . . . were key concepts" and "Literature was not a matter of 'felt experience', 'personal response', or 'imaginative uniqueness.'"[24] Further judgments focus on single authors. Dryden, we have seen, declared that Shakespeare "was the man who of all modern, and perhaps ancient poets, had the largest and most comprehensive soul,"[25] while Leavis himself once claimed that Shelley's poetry was "almost unreadable."[26] Judgments may take as their objects generic types or components of literary works, or they may arise as synoptic accounts of whole individual works or whole oeuvres. And they may be devoted to assessing genres embedded within particular periods—such as Leavis's comment that "the fine flower of modern poetry" is "not so much bad as dead."[27]

Another source of variety, as I have suggested above, is the emotional participation of the critic in the judgment he advances, from Johnson's exceptionally detached-sounding "The tragedy of Lear is deservedly celebrated amongst the dramas of Shakespeare"[28] to the brutal bluntness of D. H. Lawrence's: "James Joyce bores me stiff—too terribly would-be and done-on-purpose, utterly without spontaneity or real life. Gertrude Stein amuses me for a while, but soon palls."[29] While some of the judgments in literary criticism will focus on what an author is judged to be like by the general population of readers on whose behalf he presumes to speak as a critic, others are concerned only with the effect the author produces on the mind and feelings of that particular critic, much in the manner of Kant's account of the "singular representation of intuition referable to the feeling of pleasure, and, as such, only a private judgement."[30]

Yet other judgments are not so much "liking/disliking" but "rating" statements. They are concerned with the "placing" of authors on a scale of excellence based on a total achievement: "there is no English poet under forty," writes Pound of Lawrence, "who can get within shot of him."[31] A more ambitious and complicated rating statement is that of Matthew Arnold on the superiority of Wordsworth's poetry to all except Shakespeare and Milton:

> Yet I firmly believe that the poetical performance of Wordsworth is, after that of Shakespeare and Milton, of which all the world now recognises the worth, undoubtedly the most considerable in our language from the Elizabethan age to the present time . . . taking the roll of our chief poetical names, besides Shakespeare and Milton, from the age of Elizabeth downwards, and going through it,—Spenser, Dryden, Pope, Gray, Goldsmith,

Cowper, Burns, Coleridge, Scott, Campbell, Moore, Byron, Shelley, Keats (I mention those only who are dead),—I think it certain that Wordsworth's name deserves to stand, and will finally stand, above them all. Several of the poets named have gifts and excellences which Wordsworth has not. But taking the performances of each as a whole, I say that Wordsworth seems to me to have left a body of poetical work superior in power, in interest, in the qualities which give enduring freshness, to that which any of the others has left.[32]

Here the critic is blending a sequence of "global" judgments (in Olsen's terms) into one supraglobal assessment of the total of poetry. At a lower level, judgments set out to record perceived distinctions of value between the work of authors, and do not *rate* the authors but *weigh* their vices and virtues. Judgment is in this sense a matter of holding opposites in the scales: Shakespeare is "the poet of nature" (writes Samuel Johnson), but with his excellences there are also faults, and "faults sufficient to obscure and overwhelm any other merit."[33]

Varieties of Judgment

But regardless of the scope or extension of what is *being* judged, literary judgments can be broken down into at least three varieties that I shall now examine. These differences appear to suggest the importance to meaning in criticism of the linguistic and aesthetic *forms* in which judgments occur.

Qualified Superlatives

First, many literary judgments rest on the critic's finding unique, outstanding, or exceptional qualities in literary works. A perception of the outstanding or exceptional performance seems to underlie the concept of the "great author" (or "great work") much resisted by contemporary materialist and poststructuralist criticism; while from another perspective, as John M. Ellis has complained, summary assessments of the greatness of authors have tended to assume an unwarranted distinction in discussions of critical value and to dominate the commonly received idea of evaluative criticism.[34] But rarely does a critic pass a judgment of the simple form "Shakespeare is the greatest writer in English" or x or y are the "greatest poems" without some limiting reservation. Never are these the greatest poets or greatest poems in *all* imaginable respects—or on grounds of pure unparticularized greatness. As Pope once wrote in judging the poetry of Homer, "No Author or Man ever excell'd all the World in more than one Faculty,"[35] and the attribution of greatness or uniqueness to an author or work usually involves some reservation that channels the exceptional praise. This then qualifies the superlative. Thus, Dryden annunciates Shakespeare's greatness by referring to the largeness and comprehensiveness of his "soul."[36] For Johnson, *King Lear* is deservedly celebrated among the dramas of Shakespeare, but with reference to the fact that in this, beyond any other play, Shakespeare keeps the attention "so strongly fixed," and so on. (*Hamlet,* by comparison, is praised for "variety.")[37] Likewise, when Johnson writes of Cowley's *Miscellanies* in the *Lives of the Poets* that "Such an assemblage of diversified excellence no other poet has hitherto afforded," the uniqueness that sets Cowley above other poets records a distinctive quality.[38] Arnold does the same when he writes that "Milton, of all our English race, is by his diction and rhythm the one artist of the highest rank in the great style whom we have."[39] Being of the highest rank in "the great style" is here further delimited by an intimation of the exact devices of style (i.e., diction and rhythm) that guarantee Milton's success.

When passing an exceptionally favorable judgment, the critic does not always have to say *why* a particular author is great. Thus, when T. S. Eliot is writing of Milton's "greatness," he asserts only that "what he could do well he did better than any one else has ever done," and we have to read Eliot's essay through to discover what Milton did best. But except when criticism is establishing the status of newly appearing literary work, much of the effort of judgment seems to consist in justifying a preexisting valuation: "While it must be admitted that Milton is a very great poet indeed, it is something of a puzzle to decide in what his greatness consists"[40]—a judgment that recalls Eliot's observation of Keats that he "seems . . . [to him] a great poet. . . . But I am not so much concerned with the degree of his greatness as with its kind."[41] When F. R. Leavis embarks on his essay on Wordsworth, a similar consideration prevails: "Wordsworth's greatness and its nature seem to be, in a general way, pretty justly recognized in current acceptance, the established habit of many years. Clear criterial recognition, however, explicit in critical statement, is another matter."[42] Judgment here is not a reranking act. It is better defined as a re-description of why a particular rank is accepted.

Complex Comparatives

According to T. S. Eliot, "People tend to believe that there is just some one essence of poetry, for which we can find the formula, and that poets can be ranged according to their possession of a greater or less quantity of this essence."[43] In practice, however, many judgments are relative judgments of a fairly complex kind. If criticism, according to Beardsley, is a "principled activity," it is nevertheless rooted in the terms of its particular occasion and its criterial matrix. Comparisons are required. The comparison between Author A and Author B sometimes takes place on identical grounds (e.g., degrees of "greatness"), but the terms of comparison may themselves be susceptible to shift, to undulate and to change. The very conception of greatness may alter. Moreover, many "rating" statements found in the general literature of criticism are ratings relative to some other performance whose value—as the critic explains—requires its own unique justification. Thus Ezra Pound can write that "Crabbe will perhaps keep better than Browning, he will have a savour of freshness; of course he is *not* 'the greater poet' of the two, but then he gives such sound satisfaction in his best moments."[44]

Without grappling directly with the question of who is the "greater" writer, W. W. Robson catches the subtle mix of affinities and distinctions between C. S. Lewis and G. K. Chesterton in a judgment thus:

> They were both Christian apologists who reached large audiences, and they shared a point of view, at the same time hierarchical and democratic.... As a critic, Chesterton was much more original than Lewis, but Lewis with his greater knowledge and scholarship was more responsible; Chesterton was a journalist, not a scholar.... Chesterton is too highly coloured, Lewis too richly flavoured.... Lewis was totally free from what is bad in Chesterton. ... On the other hand, Lewis did not have Chesterton's artistic gift.[45]

The poise of such judgments is that of a delicate system in complex balance. If the writers go too far in *some* direction (being too highly colored, being too richly flavored), they do not transgress in the *same* direction; nor are their points of reference simply opposed (color on the one hand; flavor on the other). The same is true when Johnson is comparing Dryden and Pope: "There is more dignity in the knowledge of Dryden, and more certainty in that of Pope." Again, what looks initially like a judgmental contrast between a positive and a negative, evolves into a statement in which different positive attributes are compared:

> If the flights of Dryden ... are higher, Pope continues longer on the wing. If of Dryden's fire the blaze is brighter, of Pope's the heat is more regular and constant. Dryden often surpasses expectation, and Pope never falls below it. Dryden is read with frequent astonishment, and Pope with perpetual delight.[46]

Johnson later went on to profess a special fondness for the memory of Dryden; but in his comparison between Dryden and Pope, as in Robson's attempt to match the work of Chesterton as a whole to the work of Lewis as a whole, there is a sequence of contrasts. Each implies gradations of success—height of flight, length on the wing, brightness of blaze, regularity of heat, and so forth. The formula for these contrasts is not binary merely (Dryden flies high; Pope flies low). Nor is it simply the distinction that exists between altitude and duration (Dryden flies high; Pope flies long). The statement proposes a series of constants, such as flight, and different variables are functions of these—on the one hand, the height reached by Dryden and, on the other, Pope's length "on the wing"; or where the constant "fire" produces the brightness of Dryden alongside Pope's more regular heat. Johnson is establishing further evaluative sub-scales based on different properties of height and of fire.

Dual-Valuation Criteria

Thirdly and finally, we see that one and the same criterion of critical judgment can tend in both positive and negative directions at once. Thus Robson can write of Milton that "A certain *uncritical* element in . . . [his] genius is at once his strength and his weakness,"[47] and of Lewis, again, that his "boyish romanticism is responsible for some of . . . [his] worst sillinesses; but it is also responsible for what was best and purest in his response to literature."[48] Such statements allow critics to relate the strengths and weaknesses of writers to the same impulse, temperament, or cause. In the process of weighing, the judgment turns on its own axis: "It is not a wilful paradox to assert that the greatness of each of these writers," proclaims T. S. Eliot of Goethe, La Rochefoucauld, La Bruyère, and Vauvenargues, "is indissolubly attached to his practice of the error, of his own specific variation of the error. . . . They would not have been as great as they were but for the limitations which prevented them from being greater than they were."[49] In Johnson, likewise, a single source, that of "great labour, directed by great abilities," is diffused alike through the praise and the blame. This is the center of gravity on which his judgment of metaphysical poetry is poised: "Yet great labour directed by great abilities is never wholly lost: if they frequently threw away their wit upon false conceits, they likewise sometimes struck out unexpected truth: if their conceits were far-fetched, they were often worth the carriage."[50] Dual-valuation criteria of this kind enable critics to articulate their mixed feelings—the coexistence of good and bad.

The Limits and Uncertainty of Judgment

None of these cases, however, helps us towards a satisfyingly *contained* conception of judgment. But if the present analysis complicates the problem of judgment vis-à-vis criticism, it also resists the attack on both of these concepts as an elitist and concerted authoritarian cause. Williams has condemned the crudity of ex cathedra statements disintegrated from the complexities of the literary response, and judgments in criticism often suggest propositions impregnable to doubt—the "mystical intuitions" of A. J. Ayer—despite the reasons once given by Montaigne about the weaknesses of the imperfect human faculty that gives rise to them:

> 'Tis not only Feavers, Debauches, and great Accidents that overthrow our Judgements, the least things in the World will do it. We are not to doubt, though we are not sensible of it, but that if a continued Feaver can overwhelm the Soul, a *Tertian* will in some proportionate measure alter it. If an *Apoplexy* can stupifie, and totally extinguish the sight of our Understanding, we are not to doubt but that a great Cold will dazzle it. . . . there is hardly one single hour in a Man's whole Life, wherein our Judgement is in its due place and right condition. . . . [51]

—or (as also pertinent to the meaning of the term in Pope's *Essay*), the definition of "judgment" formed by John Locke:

> The faculty, which God has given man to supply the want of certain knowledge, is judgment, whereby the mind takes any proposition to be true or false, without perceiving a demonstrative evidence in the proofs.[52]

The interest of Leavis's comments is in this context his enthusiasm for the *limits* of judgment. For Leavis, judgments are statements open to be controverted. Thus the types of statement analyzed and distinguished here are not the same as the "eternal verities" decried by Terry Eagleton in *Literary Theory*, or the "idealist criticism" dismissed unhistorically by Dollimore and Sinfield in defense of "new historicist" thought;[53] they are attempted answers to the kinds of questions that Leavis imagines are typically posed by criticism: "Where does this come? How does it stand in relation to . . . ?" Judgments of this kind do not preempt alternative propositions; in deconstructive language, the judicial "verdict" is undecidable, a reassertion of difference. In this aspect, literary judgments share in the problems now more commonly examined in terms of interpretation.

From this discussion of judgment we can, therefore, derive a conception that goes *some* way at least to shape a definition of criticism, a determinacy within the undecidable universe of conflicting notions that criticism is bound to create. Much purely aesthetic analysis of judgment has dwelt on the truth, or objectivity, or correctness of judgments, or sometimes upon their acceptability to others. This is the defining criterion favored by Alan Tormey: "[T]he *case* for a critical judgment," he writes, "rests on the extent of its acceptance among independent judgers[,] not on something like 'degree of confirmation.'"[54] The problem in the situation of criticism is that a critic whose judgments proved completely acceptable to the community of "independent judgers" would be completely and instantly neutralized as a critic. A critical judgment may be interesting on account of the perception that it intends to convey some once-and-for-all truth; but its authority stands by dialectical necessity in a critical relationship to, and at a distance from, the "acceptable"—the difference denoted by Wittgenstein between a "*comfortable* certainty" and "a certainty that is still struggling."[55] Judgments are accepted as "possible truths" in being admitted to controversies where the possibility of truth is important, and criticism is not interested in debating deliberate lies. Theory, judgment, evaluation, interpretation—all have their part to play in defining criticism; but they do not finally define this central term, because none of these concepts is adequate to replace "criticism" in the range and relations of its literary work. And since the constituents of criticism also function as species of genera widely outside the social practice of criticism, criticism itself is the abiding concept to which we pragmatically have to return. But the time has come to look more directly at criticism within its historical mode and to consider the temporal dimension of defining. This will prepare the ground for the merits of the poetical definition of criticism by Alexander Pope.

Part III:
The Idea of History and the Idea of Criticism

8
Truth, History, and Literary Criticism

Such once were *Criticks*; such the Happy *Few*
—Alexander Pope, *An Essay on Criticism*

The history of literary criticism, in fact, is the history of all and only what has been written about literature, subject only to such principles of exclusion and emphasis as historians share.
—F. E. Sparshott, "The Problem of the Problem of Criticism"

As a symbolic structure, the historical narrative does not *reproduce* the events it describes; it tells us in what direction to think about the events and charges our thought about the events with different emotional valencies. The historical narrative does not *image* the things it indicates; it *calls to mind* images of the things it indicates, in the same way that a metaphor does.... Properly understood, histories ought never to be read as unambiguous signs of the events they report, but rather as symbolic structures, extended metaphors, that "liken" the events reported in them to some form with which we have already become familiar in our literary culture.
—Hayden White, *Tropics of Discourse*

HISTORY AS DEFINITION

ALL WRITING ABOUT CRITICISM IS "HISTORICAL" IN SOME WAY: INSOFAR AS SOMETHING exists as criticism, it exists in the past—from Aristotle's *Poetics* down to last week's Sunday newspaper reviews. Moreover, many general studies of literary criticism adopt a roughly chronological arrangement for organizational or explanatory purposes even when "history" does not appear in their title. There is a sense in which to analyze criticism at all is to rewrite its history, and history has a purchase on literary criticism in any number of ways. Examples might include the act of self-historicization that F. R. Leavis, writing in the twentieth-century, turned into a critical art form in its own right, and where the consciousness of his personal role in criticism's recent history dissolves into an alternately bitter or nostalgic remembrance of things past.[1] The same can be said (on another level entirely) of Clive James's decision to republish with an "auto-critique"[2] a collection of his own early literary reviews, while at a different extreme history may also include what Chris Baldick has called "the social mission" of literary criticism, criticism seen against a "historical" background of social and political change, and where it is placed in a context of events that are judged to belong to "history."[3] When the historian or critic interweaves history and criticism, and places them in narrative order, we learn how criticism is part of the cultural flow that rolls down the ages.

In another regard, "the history of criticism" is simply the name we give to a type of book, a generic subdivision of the literary field. In the terms applied by C. S. Lewis to literature,[4] this is *Poiema* and it is *Logos*, an objêt d'art of ambitious textual dimensions, a patchwork of narration, discussion, analysis, summary, and judgment. Some histories of criticism resemble guidebooks or sketches. They give a history in outline, a navigational chart on a global scale, minus the detail of villages and minor roads; others more closely resemble a huge encyclopedia or atlas, a comprehensive house of records where all knowledge is stored. To ask what they mean, what is their *Logos*, is to ask how they are used. Histories of criticism contain a great deal of what we did not know that is rationally interesting. They tell us what works exist, in what order they appeared, how many of them there are, what needs they met in their time, and what their contemporaries thought of them. They connect and contrast critics and critical texts. But if we as often consult them as read them through, histories of criticism nevertheless also express "what criticism is"—the nature of its "being"—condensed from the vast span of years to the reading experience of a few hours or days. We see that in the enormous scope of critical affairs what the individual critic can do is tiny. In a time of frantic innovation we see from the larger scale how little new exists under the sun. Histories of criticism convey an actual sense and an ideal sense: criticism "now" in this very hour and this very minute, and criticism "then" as it was alongside what is presently called by that name.

So much for the use and merits of the form: to turn now to its critical problems.

The History of Criticism and the History of "X"

The first is the material, the criticism that this is a history of. To set bounds to the task, the critical historian somehow needs to limit the thing it is his or her business to treat, and on some principle. But what principle counts?

Different principles have been tried. Writing at the turn of the last century, George Saintsbury thought of criticism as

> pretty much the same thing as the reasoned exercise of Literary Taste—the attempt, by examination of literature, to find out what it is that makes literature pleasant, and therefore good—the discovery, classification, and as far as possible tracing to their sources, of the qualities of poetry and prose, of style and metre, the classification of literary kinds, the examination and "proving," as arms are proved, of literary means and weapons, not neglecting the observation of literary fashions and the like.[5]

This emphasis on the logical subject of a critical history as "the reasoned exercise of Literary Taste" is, of course, another definition of criticism open to dispute (as "taste" and "reason" have themselves come under attack), and later critical historians have adopted a different stress. In *A History of Modern Criticism, 1750–1950*, René Wellek, whose multivolume narrative extends the spatial field beyond Saintsbury's "Europe" to Russia and America, criticism is broadened out from Saintsbury's "examination of literature" to "*any* discourse on literature" (my emphasis). Even then it remains, according to Wellek, "clearly circumscribed by its theme, as many other sciences are, and the multitude of problems and approaches is precisely the topic of the books."[6] For Wimsatt and Brooks, in the meantime, the history in question is "an argumentative history of literary argument in the West,"[7] where the arguments inside criticism unite chronological and logical modes of organization according to constrictions that Wellek does not impose. Yet other historians (like George Watson) can be found writing a history of "the art of analysing literary English works" and focusing on "revolutionary figures" or "major English critics."[8] In more recent years Baldick has rejected the idea of a history that is "a succession of studies in the thought of individual critics" in favor of "an introduction to the changing 'agenda' . . . of critical discussion." This "continually unfolding series of dialogues" maps "the successive debates, movements, and schools within the critical arena."[9] Such are some of the varied ways of defining criticism implicit and explicit within the literature of critical history.

Two approaches to the material or "objects" of critical history have generally found favor and are worthy of note. They seem, however, to do more to suggest something of the peculiar generic and situational problems faced by the history of criticism than the clarity or security of its historical method.

The first is to appeal to the history of ideas. This is the approach taken by René Wellek:

> It should be frankly recognized that the history of criticism is a topic which has its own inherent interest, even without relation to the history of

the practice of writing: it is simply a branch of the history of ideas which is in only loose relationship with the actual literature produced at the time. No doubt one can show the influence of the theory on the practice and, to a minor degree, of the practice on the theory, but this is a new and difficult question which should not be confused with the internal history of criticism.... The historian of criticism need only ask what Wordsworth meant by his doctrine, whether what he said makes sense, and what were the context, the background, and the influence on other critics of his theory.... [10]

We may agree that the history in question must be the history of criticism and not something else, and the method adopted by Wellek is designed to satisfy this criterion. But where Wellek's primary aim is to distinguish the history of criticism from the history of literature, the objection must be that it is reductive ("simply a branch," "need only ask"); and that if the distinction required is achieved, it is achieved at too high a cost to criticism's definition.[11] Moreover, if we think of the history of criticism as a history of ideas, then we do not need a separate history of criticism, since all that can be said about it—in its historical aspect—is contained in the history of ideas, the sequence of neoclassical, romantic, modernist, postmodernist, and culturally relative "events" (or other comparable categories or gestalts defined according to such "Kuhnian" paradigms)[12] arranged in chronological order. But although many historians have proceeded as if this were indeed the case, it is not plausible to suggest that the only feature of historical interest in a literary critic is his "doctrine," and in no other context would this definition hold water. (We have seen that emotions, responses, liking/disliking expressions, ratings, failed or successful acts of persuasion, and rhetorical play, along with detailed practical analyses, all have their place.) Many have tried to treat major literary critics in this limited way; but a history of criticism constructed along such lines is bound to read like a monument to dead ideology.

An alternative to Wellek's approach is to regard not the ideas but the texts themselves as the "objects" of historical attention, as "events" in their own right. This is suggested by the sense in which the texts must be "objectively" (i.e., dispassionately) studied by the historian, by the work as a critical scholar that belongs to the historian's role. According to this convention, commendably enough, the historian of criticism reads the text of Plato and not a second- or third-hand survey of Plato's work drawn from the digests made by earlier historians. Saintsbury, whose three-volume history of criticism appeared around the turn of the last century, based his historical study on "the earliest texts to the present day," and he made a point of mentioning "Texts" as "the chief object."[13] In more recent years, Baldick has constructed a history of what he calls a kind of "*writing* in English," a history of "a special genre of literature—criticism."[14]

The problem here is created by a merging of the mediate and immediate relations of the critical texts, a confusion between living remains and what it is they have left behind. The documents of history normally have a mediate function. They are the evidence we use—with some proposition or hypothesis in mind—about what really happened in the past. (We do not want a decorative myth or fanciful legend in place of the history.) In the history of criticism, by contrast, the texts mediate opinions, attitudes, values, and ideas about literature (that is, about other texts, themselves the "objects" of critical analysis). But we are not interested in a history of literature, or the history of what literature itself is about; we are interested in a history of criticism. How, then, in the name of history, can the texts mediate themselves? How can they "be" criticism and be "about" it? In a limited way, of course, some of what we call "criticism" *is* the object of the critic's attention. Attacks on other critics' work or definitions of the critical function and the critical ideal belong both to the body of criticism and to the texts that historians use—mediately. They are sign and signified at once. And it is true that the historian of criticism may sometimes have some "objects" other than texts to deal with. She may discuss the personal history of a critic, where and when she lived, was educated, died, and so on. But a history of criticism which elevated the biographical aspects of a critic's achievement above all else would seem strangely restricted, and the task of the critical historian is not normally interpreted in this way. (Suetonius's *The Lives of the Grammarians*, "perhaps the earliest work directly devoted to what might be called the history of criticism,"[15] may be one exception to this rule.)

The first objection that can be lodged against this theory of the textual object in the history of criticism therefore rests on the historical convention that a text is a source "of" or authority "for" events, and is not the same as the event itself. An act of reference is implied.[16] Two other possible objections are these:

1. the original difficulty of deciding what counts as a critical text and what does not;
2. the fact that the objects of history must have finished happening—they must be past.

In the first case, the question arises: do we include such items as Pope's notes to his translation of Homer, the essays of Montaigne, Hopkins's letters, or works like Coetzee's *Foe*?—not to mention all the other overlapping works that are also history, or science, or some other thing? We have seen that the number of ambiguous cases of "literary criticism" seems at least as large as the number of uncontentiously "critical" texts. It is therefore not surprising that when Baldick, for example, looks at the texts, he sees only "a bastard discourse" that recognizes the "impossibility of settling any definition of "criticism" in pure form."[17] If the objects of critical history are texts, we are left wondering what kind of texts a history of criticism is a history of.

In the second instance, we see that even the oldest texts of criticism are present to our eyes, destruction by fire, flood, exposure to sunlight or atmospheric pollution permitting. Therefore, unless the historian is working from obscure manuscript sources to which she has privileged access, and which she does not quote, we do not generally need the historian's pair of eyes in order to see what they say. We are able to provide our own eyewitness accounts, and through these the reader seems able to verify or falsify the history firsthand. But because they are present to us, and part of the cognizable world of criticism, the question arises as to whether the texts as texts can be truly the *objects* of historical thought. Because what needs to be done can be done adequately by the literary critic (or the critic of criticism) the historian, qua historian, would seem to have no distinctive use for the texts, and not surprisingly, the task of composing histories of criticism is not considered the business of historians in most university Departments of History. Nothing would define her work as work within the historical mode. In this view, the very reasons that Wellek gives to distinguish and identify the matter of critical history may also be seen as reasons to exclude it from the class of objects of historical study: "Obviously, the history of criticism differs profoundly from political, social, or economic history in one salient respect: the texts on which the history of criticism is based are immediately accessible, and they can be read, commented upon, interpreted, argued about, and criticized in turn, as if they had been written yesterday, even though they may have been written (like the *Poetics* of Aristotle) 2300 or so years ago."[18]

Another perplexity is where to start and where to end the history. Individual narratives display differences in the manner or tone of their telling: the endless patience and conscientious scholarship of a Wellek over decades of research, the personality and quirkiness of a Saintsbury, his relentless opinions and the dubious charm of his "period" judgments; but these narratives are not ones that anyone could summarize or condense (like a five-minute *Hamlet* or student's potted *Great Expectations*). There may be characters, but there is no action and no plot. There can therefore be little or none of the nonintellectual suspense that is sometimes felt when reading other kinds of historical narratives where there is some emotional engagement (redescriptions of scenes from the Napoleonic Wars or the Russian front). Their mode is didactic or polemical, not dramatic. They are workaday. Some historians have ruled out the treatment of "present history": "This book is a history, not a manifesto," writes George Watson, "and the historian who discourses about the present inevitably describes less accurately than he should wish."[19] Others (Saintsbury, for example) have tried to be all-encompassing, or (like Wellek, or Eagleton,[20] or Baldick) their beginnings and ends have determined how we interpret the moral of criticism, the significance of the whole occurrence whose exposition is the sum of the local episodes. Suppose that Wellek had started his history at 1650 and not 1750. What would he have failed to suggest about criticism that he succeeds in expressing? What would Wimsatt and Brooks, in their *Short History*, have lost if their chapters on classical criticism had never been written? What did Baldick gain by starting at 1890 and not 1790? Answers to these questions would reveal what the historian is trying to say.

But whatever the limits of the history in chronological terms, the inescapable difficulty of this structure is the problem of the historical event. There is a sense in which events are reported and a sense in which they are constructed or made. What would have happened (and happened in any case) even if the historian had failed to record it is difficult to disentangle from what the historian has inserted to support the narrative, or has noticed, judged, appreciated, valued, and so on, according to patterns visible only with the benefit of hindsight, or because he or she has some personal attitude or doctrine to assert that requires the selection of some occurrences and the rejection of others. Clearly, the events of history as a whole are called events because the historian has chosen to put them together in a certain way, as in the Battle of Hastings, the Storming of the Bastille, or the Conquest of Everest. A criterion of significance and relevance is implied. This is the argument used by the philosophy of history against the concept of the imaginary "Ideal Chronicler." "According to this argument," writes Gordon Graham in *The Shape of the Past*, "events are not singly countable in the way that the concept of an ideal chronicle requires—is a battle one event or innumerably many?—and the identification of events requires active interpretation which the passivity of the imaginary device does not possess."[21]

Even when the battles are fought using pens rather than swords, there seems no paradigmatic size for the units of significance constituted or reported in the shape of events by the history of criticism. This can be the heroic achievement of a single critic: "The extent of James's revolution in the criticism of the novel," wrote George Watson, "is difficult to overstate. Before he wrote, none of the ordinary assumptions of twentieth-century novel-criticism were current."[22] In a similar vein Matthew Arnold bears a special relation to "The 'great and famous power' of historical criticism, against which no other Victorian critic before the nineties raised his voice."[23] But the "event" can also be a school of criticism in which many different individual voices are heard: Deconstruction is in this sense an event. On another level the event can be a single critical statement that stands on its own. When Samuel Johnson attacked the dramatic unities of time and place in his *Preface to Shakespeare* of 1765 we say that an era crumbled and a new one began. For Terry Eagleton, writing a "history" of literary theory that begins with the story of "the rise of English," the events of the narrative are extended through the two parallel dimensions of history and criticism:

> *The Pleasure of the Text* was published five years after a social eruption which rocked France's political fathers to their roots. In 1968 the student movement had swept across Europe, striking against the authoritarianism of the educational institutions and in France briefly threatening the capitalist state itself. For a dramatic moment, that state teetered on the brink of ruin: its police and army fought in the streets with students who were struggling to forge solidarity with the working class. Unable to provide a coherent political leadership, plunged into a confused melée of socialism, anarchism and infantile behind-baring, the student movement was rolled back and dissipated; betrayed by their supine Stalinist leaders, the working-class movement was unable to assume power. Charles de Gaulle returned from a hasty exile, and the French state regrouped its forces in the name of patriotism, law and order.
>
> Post-structuralism was a product of that blend of euphoria and disillusionment, liberation and dissipation, carnival and catastrophe, which was 1968.[24]

It is in the logical connection between the events that the difficulties I have reviewed in this chapter are linked to the general problems notorious within the discussion of narrative structure. Of these, the most significant source of the moral or meaning of a history of criticism is causation—the sense, present in Eagleton's passage from *Literary Theory*, in which the one is "a product of" the other. The passage implies that were it not that such or such a thing had happened in the past, the present would not be what it is. This sense of the past as a cause of the present, its *conditio sine qua non*, may sometimes take a premonitory, deterministic, form. For example in "The Heritage of Classical Criticism" related in volume 1 of the recently published *Cambridge History*, we learn that "[t]he Classical critics . . . created the basic critical vocabulary and terminology which has been used ever since, and they anticipated many of the critical issues and stances of modern times."[25] Sometimes the present is where long-dormant tendencies finally assert their nature. Stephen Bann writes of the history of semiotics in volume 8 of the *Cambridge History* that "the possibility of a science of the sign . . . has only come to fulfillment in the twentieth century, and particularly in the post-war period."[26] In Wimsatt and Brooks's *Short History*, the past is continually imposing itself on the present: "If we look around the critical scene and especially the American critical scene during the first decades of our own century, we see distinct aftermaths of all the 19th-century events which we have just been tracing."[27]

But the core of the problem is now this: if the present is the end to which the past is the means, what existed in the past could not have been criticism but something that has now ceased to exist. It has played its part in constructing criticism and has since faded away. Criticism cannot be the means to its own end. Therefore, whatever this something is that becomes an object of historical thought by ceasing to be, the history of it cannot be the history of criticism.[28]

Here we have a crucial difficulty for the history of criticism. It is that the historian has to compose a history of change, when to do so the concept must be suprahistorical: a constant. For there to be a history of x, x must have existed as x for a period of time. But there is nothing to suggest that the concept to which the term "criticism" now applies has remained the same over the time covered by even the shortest of histories, or that it existed at all for most of this period. Indeed, it is the point of the history to show that it has not.[29] Thus, with the single exception of the fact that we use the same word "criticism" to describe the range of historical cases, the critical work of the ancient Greek and Roman writers is arguably *nothing like* what goes by the name of "criticism" in an Eliot, a Leavis, or a Derrida, and this appreciation of change contributes to the moral of the history. The difficulty of holding on to the concept "criticism" is well illustrated by the fact that historians of "criticism today" are engaged in showing how criticism is in process of being transformed into something else that is not criticism: a general science of signs, Theory, postmodernism, cultural studies, and so forth. As Raymond Williams points out in *Keywords* (under "criticism"), this is not just a question of terms: "The point would . . . be, not to find some other term to replace it, while continuing the same kind of activity, but to get rid of the [critical] habit. . . ."[30] And despite the nominal commitment to "criticism" advertised by its title, the penultimate volume of *The Cambridge History of Literary Criticism* is devoted to the history of *theories: From Formalism to Poststructuralism*. Such theories now "stand for" criticism. They are what criticism "is."

The other side of this coin is seen when we look back to the past to take stock of criticism in its partially realized state, as a fragment of the whole it was later to become. This is not criticism but the thing that criticism has evolved from, the relic of an archaic something we have now left behind. The dead critics are in this historical conception irretrievably alien—historical phenomena in the pejorative sense: "What do we read it for?" we have seen that Leavis asks of the criticism of Samuel Johnson. "Not for enlightenment about the authors with whom it deals (though it may impart some), and not for direct instruction in critical thinking."[31] Like the story of literature told by literary history, the story of criticism seems sometimes to resemble the plan of a great novel whose moral (like *Middlemarch*) unfolds by tracing the progress of the heroine's soul from illusion to reality. Criticism is imagined in these terms as a latter-day *construction* of history, ideologically contrived on politically untenable grounds and ripe for demythologization. As the tracing of its rise and importance shows, its *only* authority to exist is historical.

Literary and Fictional Form in the History of Criticism

In its role as *Poiema*, the history of criticism falls therefore between several stools—criticism itself, history itself, prose narrative or fable, exhibitionist political writing, the personal memoir, and the social, moral, or philosophical treatise. It is all of these things, and yet not precisely any of them at any time; and like all representational forms, it is poised somewhere between opposite extremes on a continuous scale. Where it shares certain devices of fiction (such as story), it lacks others. One difference would be the fact that its characters (the critics themselves) have to be real people.[32] And if its events are difficult to fix or define, they are clearly not the same in kind as a history of the Second World War, the French Revolution, or colonial expansionism. The history of criticism shares with history and fiction an approach to the theme of time, including time's ironies: we see how quickly new ideas become orthodoxies; or how some writers stand time's test, while others are celebrated in one period and then collapse into insignificance at another. But its determinism is as often optimistic as pessimistic or tragic. If we consider the history of criticism as the history of a single concept, we find that its essence only reveals itself gradually to us as its variant forms make their appearance through historical change. This means that while histories of criticism may not show us criticism "as we know it," they may extend our awareness of its essential character to work that we would (in current terms) not recognize as criticism.

As concerns the radical division of present and past, histories seem in one respect to have us appreciate different ages as self-enclosed, or externally related: we are at the end of a scale or a series of point-instant "events" separated by spaces on an imaginary line. The alternative to this organization is a history that is not a series but a world (to recall the distinction adopted by R. G. Collingwood). The events are not point-instants but parts of a process in which a cause does not precede its effect by any discernible temporal lapse.³³ The principle that Collingwood announces—with reference to history—is that the present encloses the past. Past and the present are indivisibly necessary to the comprehension of any concept of which we are conscious:

> The way in which . . . [experience] is organized is time, and this in fact is just what time is: it is a manifold of parts which, unlike those of space, interpenetrate one another, the present including the past. This temporal organization is peculiar to consciousness, and is the foundation of freedom: for, because the present contains the past in itself the present is not determined by the past as something external to it, a cause of which it is the effect: the present is a free and living activity which embraces and sustains its own past by its own act.³⁴

If we now extend this theory of temporal organization to criticism, histories of criticism will seem to conform to what Louis O. Mink has called (with reference to both fiction and history) a "mode of comprehension."³⁵ Just as the Collingwoodian or "idealist" theory is a history where the past does not exist, but may be thought, so the historian of criticism in theory has free-range to enter into the critical problems of the past as problems in the here and now of criticism: "To discover what this [past] thought was, the historian must think it again for himself."³⁶ But how, then, is the historian of criticism any different from the critic whose history he writes? Both want to know certain things. Does Wordsworth, or does Wordsworth not, use the Johnsonian phrases "general nature" and the "language of men" to designate his ambitions as an original poet? Does Aristotle, or does he not, emphasize the unities of time and place in the drama? The answers to these questions are both ascertainable facts in the history of criticism and the kind of evidence a critic (qua critic) may marshal for critical purposes. The difference is that an interpretation of textual material that is based on the facts is the end of the critic's thought, but for the historian it is a means to the end of writing the true history of the dead and gone real situation that was the critic's.

But a question does remain about the "truth" of this history. Where the historical narrative runs into autobiography the question is transformed into the problem of reportage. Leavis (in 1963) describes the appearance of his wife's *Fiction and the Reading Public* (thirty years earlier in 1932) as "a contemporary event" that "worked in the intellectual climate as a pervasive and potent influence."³⁷ But the fact that Leavis was there in 1932 (or that he is talking about his wife) is not the factor that makes the statement historically true. In the same way the reality principle on which histories of criticism operate seems close to "verisimilitude," a lifelikeness whose test of truth is that histories of criticism are required to be *psychologically* plausible. This in its turn, however, does not make the events of criticism *entirely* the artifacts of its narrative plan, and Judy Simons (for one) exaggerates when she argues that history is "*merely* another fiction, a narrative interpretation of events from a particular viewpoint" (my emphasis).[38] The historian of criticism can construct myths of its history disguised as facts: fiction is often made out of history, as C. S. Forester's "Hornblower" novels or the plots of ancient classical and Renaissance epics would suggest. (And the sense in which critics may fantasize about their personal historical relations is brought out well by Richard Rorty in his essay on Derrida.)[39] But a fantasist is not what we take the historian to be. To recall W. W. Robson's reflections on the distinctions between history and fiction: there may be a presumption of fact in historical writing that the novelist is free to revolt against; but to go to an extreme and to bring the history of criticism *entirely* under the aspect of a "discursive practice" is to confuse the issue, since this cannot eliminate culpable negligence or intentional deceit. "Skeptical" theories that insist that criticism is a historically constructed myth must from this perspective revise their skepticist claims. With this in mind, and with a sense of the contradictions that allow a historical text of criticism to survive into the present, we are now ready to consider more closely that part of the critical past whose evidential basis is Pope's *Essay*. What kind of definition of criticism is Pope's?

9

Pope's *Essay* and the Poetic "Idea of Criticism"

Understanding is a part of knowing *how*. The knowledge that is required for understanding intelligent performances of a specific kind is some degree of competence in performances of that kind. The competent critic of prose-style, experimental technique, or embroidery, must at least know how to write, experiment or sew.... [T]he one necessary condition is that he has some mastery of the art or procedure, examples of which he is to appraise....
—Gilbert Ryle, *The Concept of Mind*

All human beings carry about a set of words which they employ to justify their actions, their beliefs, and their lives. These are the words in which we formulate praise of our friends and contempt for our enemies, our long-term projects, our deepest self-doubts and our highest hopes. They are the words in which we tell, sometimes prospectively and sometimes retrospectively, the story of our lives. I shall call these words a person's "final vocabulary."

It is "final" in the sense that if doubt is cast on the worth of these words, their user has no noncircular argumentative recourse. Those words are as far as he can go with language; beyond them there is only helpless passivity or a resort to force.
—Richard Rorty, *Contingency, Irony, and Solidarity*

[I]f you don't believe in literary criticism, then your belief that literature itself matters will have the support of an honoured convention, but must be suspect of resting very much on that.... To make my point effectively it is necessary to have recourse to the concrete: you cannot cogently present the idea of criticism as a matter of generalities.
—F. R. Leavis, "The Responsible Critic, or The Function of Criticism at Any Time"

Four Platitudes and Pope's *Essay*

Pope's *Essay on Criticism* of 1711 is at once an essay in verse, a work of literature, and a "statement" defining criticism.[1] It is a critical document by a creative writer that creatively unites the critical and the creative within the bounds of a single work. I do not think it is generally read in these terms; or rather, I do not think the implications of these exceptionally obvious facts about the *Essay*'s aesthetic status are interpreted with sufficient historical breadth to suggest what the poem may have to say to critics now. But there are exceptions to this rule. In his essay "An Introduction to Literary Criticism by Way of Sidney's *Apologie for Poetrie*" of 1983, H. A. Mason was not concerned with normative statements about criticism which seem (in Ellis's terms) to compete with each other, but with thoughts we have always had,[2] and in this he raised the problem that we are seeking to explore in this study.

The first thing to be aware of," writes Mason, "is that when we read a work that itself purports to be a piece of criticism we ourselves are performing a piece of criticism in reading it."[3] Moreover, he argues, the act of judgment that we associate with an act of criticism is not confined to the sorts of judgments we make in literary contexts: "[W]e are performing criticism all day long" (79). We make choices about all kinds of things in everyday life—what hat to wear, for example. Such choices are continuous with critical choices, and the making of them can improve with practice. The same general laws apply:

> Literary criticism is almost entirely a matter of *finesse* and subtle discriminations. Yet anyone who has made blunders in choosing hats knows that almost everybody can improve, that tact in dressing can be acquired, that in short we can learn by experience. (80)

Mason's point is that some delving into the self is required, some investigation into the consonance between our privately maintained conception of criticism and that of other people. He poses a series of questions on the implications of our holding an entirely personal view of this matter:

> So before we can hope to do anything with Sidney we must do something with ourselves. We must ask ourselves what criticism is. First, each of us must say: what does criticism mean to me? And then we must discover if our idea of criticism is a peculiar whim, if it is something that we could not expect anybody else to agree with. Would any one of you be satisfied with an idea of criticism that could not be shared? That could not bear examination by a close friend? (80–81)

What Mason has to say can be isolated in what he called "four platitudes." Together these constitute "a law of criticism," which is "that all its problems run into each other. . . . The art of criticism is to establish precision in vagueness" (82), and Mason at this point linked his conception of how criticism *may be* defined to how it *was once* defined, by Pope, in the early years of the eighteenth century. What can be achieved by definers of criticism comes very close to translation into today's situation of the meaning of what he calls Pope's "masterly essay" (83), a work he sees as bearing comparison with Erasmus's *The Praise of Folly*. The problem, according to Mason, is that definitions are "what we aspire towards," but definitions are also "what we most often have to break away from if we are to be true to the facts as we find and feel them": "The difficulty in defining criticism is on all fours with that felt in trying to define poetry" (82). The first platitude in Mason's list is therefore that criticism is rare and that it is "even rarer than great poetry":

> The fat volumes of the history of literary criticism contain the names and summaries of the works of critics who may have seemed to be alive in their day. But it is certain that they are not all alive now, they do not speak to us, they do not find us. (82)

The explanation that Mason gives for the rarity value of literary criticism compared with poetry is a moral one—it requires "a conquest over pride, vanity and fear" (83). To modern ears, this movement onto ethical ground may be reminiscent of Arnold, but it conjures up for Mason one of the primary lessons that Pope has to teach the modern age about the relationship between the critical valuer and the thing that is valued:

> That an essay on criticism must in part become a treatise on the seven deadly sins was shewn to be a necessity by Pope in his masterly essay on the subject, first published in 1711. May I here and now put into prose what he so admirably presented in verse? In an act of criticism there are of necessity at least two constituent parts: the critic and the work of art. Let us call them the valuer and the valued. Criticism lies in discovering the right relation between them. Do I have to insist that when, for instance, we open the Sunday papers, that when we open the *New Statesman* or when we open the *Spectator*, we rarely find there the right relation between the valuer and the valued? That the emphasis there is all on the valuer at the expense of the valued? That at bottom the valuer prefers himself to the valued? And what is this but pride and vanity? (83)

Mason contends that by the same token we hate good criticism as we hate good art: the good critic "implicitly rebukes us" (83).

The second platitude about criticism that Mason proposes is that "criticism is essentially occasional" (84). Here Mason is referring to Pope's power as a poet and as a creator to enact the critical concept he describes or asserts. Mason uses this aspect of Pope's achievement to tilt at the systematized theory of criticism as distinct from the practice of a critic engaged with particular works and particular authors: "For there is something unnatural in just talking about criticism instead of doing some and I would state it as a law of critical writing that the only talk about criticism that is worth anything is that which in some way exhibits the qualities it is trying to define" (84). Good criticism does not just happen, says Mason. The critic cannot choose to write. He or she cannot just "do" authors, as a student might be encouraged to select a hitherto unresearched poet or novelist as the subject for a Ph.D. There must be a challenge to respond to, a new (or old but newly comprehended) work of some kind that inspires and draws forth the critical account from a deep level of the self. Unless the work of art is itself worthy, no worthwhile criticism can result. Weak art cannot produce great criticism. To this Mason adds the injunction that criticism has to be not only occasional but also "short." Its natural form is the essay. Nothing can be proved or demonstrated in a work of criticism:

> I think criticism must be short because of the limitations of criticism itself. For the critic can only point to this and that in the great work of art and say to the reader: don't you see? And if we don't see, we don't. The critic can't make us see. That is why on the whole we don't see. That is why I doubt my qualifications to talk about criticism. For you must be a critic to be a judge of criticism. I don't think it was affected modesty in Pope that made him describe his remarks on criticism as short flights. (85–86)

It follows from the connections observable between his meditations on the *Essay on Criticism* of Pope (a poem published when the poet was around twenty years old) and Mason's own role in his lectures as a teacher of undergraduate students that his third platitude should be that "criticism is characteristically the work of the young":

> We all, I think, perform one critical act the moment we first take stock of the world we find ourselves born into and decide to take up some attitude to that world. . . . True criticism is . . . a life-choice taken at the deepest level. It is a choice that in our consciousness seems to make itself rather than be made by us. . . . As with poetry we may apply Samuel Johnson's phrase: great criticism is that which is both natural and new. (86)

And in his fourth and final platitude, Mason introduces the need for control over critical "tone"—the demand for "urbanity." The essence of this tone, writes Mason, "is at bottom reverence for the persons whose opinions we wish to change or redirect" by the criticism:

> By casting an air of urbanity over all we fiercely assert, we implicitly draw into the critical remark that necessary humility which says: we can all err, we all have erred. The critic does not rejoice to add one jot to the necessary pain of parting with the habits that sloth, pride, vanity and fear have manacled on to us. (93)

Seeing and Supposing Criticism

My suggestion throughout this discussion has been that the past of criticism is not in the main fruitfully conceived in historically serial or consecutive terms. I have claimed that the model of history used in representations of criticism is often too narrowly based upon the history of ideas, upon a teleology, and upon a positivistic theory of critical events, and that in differentiating or connecting cultural artifacts such as criticism on temporal grounds, the difficulties of defining the "event"—and thus the contents of the concept "criticism," of which tone and aesthetic effect are part of the meaning—become acute. The history of criticism, I have suggested, is a complex mixture, on at least two discursive levels, of imagination, interpretation, evaluation, and narration. But when we turn to past works of criticism that are also poems, we see how the problem cannot be contained within the limits of historiographical theory, or of aesthetics. It is, as Mason seems to suggest, a practical critical one. The solution of the problem dictates consideration of how old works of criticism are perceived outside aesthetic theory and the historical mode.[4]

Because its status as an "art object" is in tension with its status as a historical "event," Pope's *Essay on Criticism* raises in seminal and historical form the contradictions that arise in the representation of literary criticism. There is an aesthetic issue: the *Essay* is a poem and a work of art; and there is an historical problem: the poem belongs to the past. The aesthetic issue concerns the *Essay*'s metadiscursive qualities. The subject of the poem (or rather its "object," what it is "about") is "criticism." But how does it manage to be "about" criticism? "About" in what sense? The problem can be considered in representational terms, and with respect to criteria of precision and vagueness as applied to the link between poem and object. Such a problem can be seen as an aspect of "point of view," where the object is "seen" through or in the words of the poem. Finally, it can be addressed in relation to what we still *suppose* that criticism is.[5]

To take the question from the aspect of reference failure first. If Pope's

Essay = *x* and criticism = *y,* then if *x* corresponds to *y* in all its aspects, attributes, essentials, and so on, the poem defines criticism. But what if there are things about criticism that we judge the poem fails to embrace—the full variety of literary criticism since the time of Pope for example? The correspondence is then approximate or vague. This does not require that the thing the poem is trying to represent need be vague: it is a judgment of vagueness and imprecision in the representation. And yet the concept may indeed be vague, and the representation an accurate or precise representation of vagueness.[6] To say it is "vague" is not to say it is "confused" (as Ellis does), since to say it is "confused" implies the possibility that it could be clearer if possessed by clearer minds. But to say it is "vague" does not have to imply this. It may *clearly* overlap with other concepts. The amount of clarity it can have is then precisely caught in the poem, as in other poems that seek to isolate abstract concepts—Marvell's "Definition of Love," for example, or Rochester's "Upon Nothing," or Cowley's "Ode on Wit," and the *Essay* is in this respect more like these poems than the various "Arts of Poetry" with which it is routinely compared.[7]

The capacity of poetry to fix abstractions is not confined to entire individual poems. It includes the devices of personification, symbolism, and the whole apparatus used by poets to capture the invisible presence that must logically exist for the world to be as it is. Something hitherto very diffuse is contained and shaped so that its image lives on in that form. This does not have to be a less accurate depiction of something than would occur in historical narrative, or in the definitions of empirical science. Indeed, it is open to question whether any form *can* transcribe or represent any thing with total and complete precision, just as any distance may be measured very accurately, but never exactly. The question would be whether the precision available to poetical representation is less than that achievable in prose, or geometrical, mathematical, or musical notation. We cannot safely assume that poetry is the less determinate medium or that, if its objects are typically vague or large or hard to define (love, wit, nothingness, criticism, etc.), the evocation is less precise. The fuzzy edges of criticism will not be precisely caught by fuzzy thought. Pope portrays the overlap between criticism and creative art in terms of the differential effects produced by the want of the same essential constituent:

> 'Tis hard to say, if greater Want of Skill
> Appear in *Writing* or in *Judging* ill;
> But, of the two, less dang'rous is th'Offence,
> To tire our *Patience*, than mis-lead our *Sense*:
> Some few in *that*, but Numbers err in *this*,
> Ten Censure wrong for one who Writes amiss;

> A *Fool* might once *himself* alone expose,
> Now *One* in *Verse* makes many more in *Prose*.
>
> (lines 1–8)

But can this distinction be seen? The second respect in which the *Essay on Criticism* can be considered to stand in relation to its object "criticism" is in the form of a "view" taken from the "point of view" that is supposed to be occupied by the poet and that we are invited to share as readers of the poem. Now one can suggest—when loosely speaking—that the poem conveys Pope's "view" of criticism, and by this we mean only that the poem contains his opinions, thoughts, and ideas about it. As for the constituents of criticism, we can say that Pope "sees" them in the poem in the two senses of the word. Visual metaphors abound to indicate both comprehension and cognition:

> Yet if we look more closely,

says Pope, we shall find that

> Most have the *Seeds* of Judgment in their Mind.
>
> (lines 19–20)

Again:

> But as the slightest Sketch, if justly trac'd,
> Is by ill *Colouring* but the more disgrac'd,
> So by *false Learning* is *good Sense* defac'd. . . .
>
> (lines 23–25)

And in the process of becoming critics (as in the process of striving as artists), we learn that

> Th'*increasing* Prospect *tires* our wandering Eyes,
> Hills peep o'er Hills, and *Alps* on *Alps* arise!
>
> (lines 231–32)

The "view of criticism" corresponds with the view the critic takes of art. Some things can only be seen when the "point of view" is correctly adjusted, when its object is brought into focus:

> Some Figures *monstrous* and *mis-shap'd* appear,
> Consider'd *singly*, or beheld too *near*,
> Which, but *proportion'd* to their *Light,* or *Place*,
> Due Distance *reconciles* to Form and Grace.
>
> (lines 171–74)

Others are invisible, as in the description of "the'informing Soul" (line 76) that is "*It self unseen* but in th'*Effects*, remains" (line 79).[8]

But the object/viewer paradigm is of limited value in grasping the poem's relation to its stated object, since the object (according to the poem's other threads) remains internal to the viewer.[9] For Pope the critic must "make each Day a *Critick* on the last"(line 570) and enact his precepts as Longinus had enacted his, who is "*himself* that great *Sublime* he draws" (line 680). This task of realization is at the center of his poem, and it will therefore be useful, at this point, to recall the division between the different types of concepts that Collingwood had drawn from Kant in his own extended treatment of an interwoven "idea of history." The first of these, as we saw in chapter 2, is "empirical." The second is "transcendental." In his description of "The Transcendental Ideas" in section 2 of his "First Book of the Transcendental Dialectic" of *The Critique of Pure Reason*, Kant brings to a focus his detailed discussion of the distinction between these two types,[10] and we have seen that the concepts that he entitled "empirical" *require* an explicit definition. But if we try to define "criticism" as an empirical concept we run into the same difficulty encountered in trying to define "literature" in terms of the "literary": we become trapped in the dead end of debates about intrinsic properties, attributes about which we can never completely agree because of criticism's own endlessly dialectical nature. We have seen that a possible escape is the conclusion reached by some of literature's recent would-be definers such as Ellis: that literature is a social construct whose meaning rests (nonreferentially) on the circumstances in which we use the word. I have suggested that this does not dispense with the need for a criterion of use, a test to determine whether it is indeed as literature or as criticism that any text or utterance is used.

It is this circularity (possessing the concept being necessary even to think about it) which Collingwood saw as the distinguishing feature of Kant's transcendental ideas. Kant had referred to transcendental concepts as a priori, and as Collingwood was later to deduce, it is impossible to stand wholly outside such concepts in order to define them (as definers of literature have discovered when casting their eyes over literary works and wondering which are the essentially literary ones, which are peripheral). Thus trying to define a transcendental concept is rather like trying to see the spot concealed by our own feet. Failure to recognize this condition of defining criticism is the source of most of the difficulty connecting the poetical "art" value of the *Essay* with the modern "problem of criticism." Perhaps the most common mistake is to externalize the poem itself as a series of refutable propositions, summaries, or excerptible synopses of neoclassical literary and critical ideas (in the plural), of which in an obvious respect it is an amalgam, just as it is a source of some of the best-known aphorisms in English

("*Fools* rush in . . . " [line 625], etc.). Modern definitional glosses have then been sought for these ideas (the key terms "Nature," "Sense," "Wit," and "Judgment," for example)—but usually with limited explanatory success beyond the formulaic.[11]

And this difficulty, I should like to argue, is because we have lost the sense of the *Essay* as a poem, as a simultaneously creative and constative work having "art status" and therefore standing in relation to "criticism" in the same complex way that criticism is related to art—as object to itself. Such an argument calls into question the representational or transcriptional model of defining criticism with its attendant problems of correspondence failure and correspondence success, and the sense in which the object of the poem can be "seen" mediately through or in the images and words. To resolve this difficulty, we must now examine the distinction between definition by proposition and definition by supposition.

The material of Pope's *Essay on Criticism* can be rendered, and is often explained—both historically and critically—as a sequence of prose replications of its successive and separate propositions (much as it is possible to separate out the philosophy of the *Essay on Man* that Pope worked up in verse from his conversations with Bolingbroke and to denude this of the poetry). Some of the most famous propositions in the *Essay on Criticism* include:

> In *Poets* as true *Genius* is but rare,
> True *Taste* as seldom is the *Critick's* Share. . . .
>
> (lines 11–12)

> A *little Learning* is a dang'rous Thing. . . .
>
> (line 215)

> *True Wit* is *Nature* to Advantage drest. . . .
>
> (line 297)

And so forth. But the *Essay* will not succeed in defining criticism as a train of "versified" thoughts.[12] (Critics of Pope have often been inclined to regard his polished versification as a fairly *external* act, a "sugared coating" as it were, of commonplace things that remain commonplace). Pope uses poetic imagery in order to sweeten or decorate his preexistent ideas, but brings the verse and the thinking, the ideas and the poetry, together as part of the same essential.[13] There are the famous lines on the unity of thought and expression, Wit and Nature, form and matter, which stand at the center of the poem:

> *True Wit* is *Nature* to Advantage drest,
> What oft was *Thought*, but ne'er so well *Exprest*,

> *Something*, whose Truth convinc'd at Sight we find,
> That gives us back the Image of our Mind:
>
> (lines 297–300)

And there is then the development of this "thought" by means of an image. Two heterogeneous ideas are yoked in a manner reminiscent of a metaphysical poet:

> As Shades more sweetly recommend the Light,
> So modest Plainness sets off sprightly Wit:
> For *Works* may have more *Wit* than does 'em good,
> As *Bodies* perish though Excess of *Blood*.
>
> (lines 301–4)

But it is one thing to say that the *Essay on Criticism uses* imagery, another to say where all the imagery points. Pope's *Essay* reads today as a versified credo *of* and *for* its time. Partly, this is due to artistic obstacles relating to literary fashion and generic prestige. No one writes essays on criticism in verse anymore,[14] and even poems in heroic couplets are rare. The fact that all the proposing seems at least as important as the suggesting, evoking, symbolizing, and so on, has given the *Essay* an apparently rationalist foundation. We are now comparatively unused to the sense in which modest plainness sets off sprightly wit. It is therefore necessary to do more than to point to the local imagery of the *Essay on Criticism* in order to reclaim the sense in which the form is working to define a concept of "criticism" able to penetrate our own thwarted struggles to say what criticism is.

A solution can, I suggest, be found in the poem's disunified "unity." What Pope successively intuits—the ideas, the tags, the commonplace wisdoms, clichés, and propositions that he gathers up from everywhere around him, from authors great and small—are reproduced in terms of a conception that is not itself an explicit proposition about criticism. At the same time, the propositions appearing within the poem are "about" many things and are understood in succession as items in any linear text. We can reread the poem (in which case the fit of the parts may be more clearly apparent the second time round, and we may carry more with us as we read). And as a work of written literature rather than visual art, a time series must be assumed. So we learn, at line 68, of the order of events. The question is where to begin, what to attend to first.

> First follow NATURE, and your Judgment frame
> By her just Standard, which is still the same:
> *Unerring Nature,* still divinely bright. . . .
>
> (lines 68–70)

Twenty lines later the emphasis has changed from the freedom and liberty of Nature to that which restrains it:

> Those RULES of old *discover'd*, not *devis'd*,
> Are *Nature* still, but *Nature* Methodiz'd. . . .
>
> (lines 88–89)

In the same way, *because* the individual couplets that contain them are so extremely memorable, we do not forget the lines on Nature when we are reading about Rules. Pope builds up a total. The total of 1 + 1 is 2. But if by the time I encounter the second digit in this act of arithmetical addition I have forgotten the first, then the total of 1 + 1 is always elusive. The method of the *Essay on Criticism* is not formally logical (as the *Essay on Man* attempted to be) but accretive, harmonic, or hymnal. It brings together qualities of balance, intricacy, ardor, and sadness available in other arts.[15] There is the "balance" of the heroic couplets themselves, the "intricacy" of the relations between the critical terms, the "ardor" of the evocation of "Nature," the "Sublime," and "True Wit," the "sadness" of the various kinds of human failure to live up to the ideal. The *Essay* is in this respect not a work of reason, but of apprehension, or, to adopt Kant's term, "apperception." Most readers will be aware of the poem's loose-coupled form, its seeming absence of conscious or conspicuous structure. If there is, inevitably, an order of events in the poem, there is no overall order, no managed interlocking of parts.[16]

It is the fluidity of relations between the parts that replaces order.[17] Thus when we are reading about the freedoms of Nature, we are at the same time seeing how Nature is captured and her light is imparted. Nature is there as a standard against which we may frame our Judgment. Through these relationships, Pope apprehends the parts of the unity that make up the whole. Thus, the passage on Nature continues with references to the sense in which the freedoms of Nature are subject to a guiding hand, to restraint. Nature is the presence, or constant, that establishes the key relationships between the elements of the situation of criticism, its source, end, and test:

> *Unerring Nature*, still divinely bright,
> One *clear, unchang'd*, and *Universal* Light,
> Life, Force, and Beauty, must to all impart,
> At once the *Source*, and *End*, and *Test* of *Art*.
> *Art* from that Fund each *just Supply* provides,
> Works *without Show*, and *without Pomp* presides:
> In some fair Body thus th'informing Soul
> With Spirit feeds, with Vigour fills the whole,
> Each Motion guides, and ev'ry Nerve sustains;

> *It self unseen*, but in th' *Effects*, remains.
> Some, to whom Heav'n in Wit has been profuse,
> Want as much more, to turn it to its use;
> For *Wit* and *Judgment* often are at strife,
> Tho' meant each other's Aid, like *Man* and *Wife*.
> 'Tis more to *guide* than *spur* the Muse's Steed;
> Restrain his Fury, than provoke his Speed;
> The winged Courser, like a gen'rous Horse,
> Shows most true Mettle when you *check* his Course.
>
> (lines 70–87)

Likewise when we come to "Those RULES," we find that they are not, after all, a wholly separate or wholly new theme, but "Are *Nature* still . . . " (line 89).

First, then, the poem is committed to "criticism" as a complete idea—as a synthesis, "the joint Force and full *Result* of all" (line 246). The representation of this "allness" is the product of a unitary consciousness: the definition has a definer—Alexander Pope. Then, the *Essay* achieves completeness for itself and its subject by working within the terms of its own partiality and limits as art. It is not an exhaustive account saying all that could be said about criticism. But this sense of completeness is not that of a theoretical treatise: it is an appearance *created by thought*, "transcendental" in the respect that its existence as a unity is not separable from the work the mind has to do in thinking about criticism. This does not exclude reference within the poem to characters and events that really did exist or occur: John Dennis, Dryden, William Walsh, and so on, or things like "language," "rhyme," "judgment," or Dryden's *Fables* that exist today. But how this "appearance" is related to the object of the poem may be gathered from the following analysis of Kant:

> Appearances are the sole objects which can be given to us immediately, and that in them which relates immediately to the object is called intuition. But these appearances are not things in themselves; they are only representations, which in turn have their object—an object which cannot itself be intuited by us, and which may, therefore, be named the non-empirical, that is, the transcendental object $= x$.[18]

The transcendental, according to this account, is the kind of concept, based on an object, in this case criticism, which experience denies to intuition. You cannot look around you and see criticism. You only see different conceptions of criticism, codes of belief, principles, theories, practices, approaches, a chaos of conflicting and overlapping opinions, and so on. Consequently, the only way of expressing and comprehending this concept precisely is via Art. Art (in this case a poem) is thus the chosen medium (the "appearance") for our experience of criticism (the "object"). The power of Pope's rhetorical technique in defining criticism entails the capacity to produce an experience of criticism as a whole (that we could not otherwise experience—by merely looking around us). And because the thing that criticism is is created as art, it can be experienced; yet since the experience (the poem itself) is only an imitation (a representation of the invisible "object" criticism as a whole) it permits a distanced, and therefore more holistic and inclusive, apprehension.[19] This is the sense that Collingwood, writing on definitions in his *Essay on Philosophical Method*, was to give to complete "expositions" of philosophical concepts:

> In the case of such a concept no line could be drawn between definition and theorems; the entire exposition would be a statement at once of its essence, and of its properties regarded as the elements constituting that essence. This would be a definition, for it would state the essence; the concept would remain undefined only in the sense that there would be no one phrase or sentence which could be taken out of its context and called the definition.[20]

Pope never actually *says* what "criticism is" in his *Essay*, but *reveals* his object—criticism-as-a-whole—for our contemplation. The object is discovered, not devised. It gives us back the image of our mind and causes us to reflect on what before we always already knew. Thus the *Essay on Criticism* is tenable as a definition in a further sense that is in tune with Collingwood's thought (and anticipates deconstructive modes of "repetition"): it is entirely confined to that which everyone already knows. A new thought about criticism, never before thought, is just that —a new thought: it is not a definition. Pope's *Essay* is part of the reflective rather than the progressive tradition. In the foreword to his *Philosophical Remarks* Wittgenstein distinguished the spirit of his own writings from that of "the vast stream of European and American civilization in which all of us stand," and he added:

> *That* spirit expresses itself in an onwards movement, in building ever larger and more complicated structures; the other in striving after clarity and perspicuity in no matter what structure. The first tries to grasp the world by way of its periphery—in its variety; the second at its centre—in its essence. And so the first adds one construction to another, moving on and up, as it were, from one stage to the next, while the other remains where it is and what it tries to grasp is always the same.[21]

But if Pope, like Wittgenstein, tries to secure in the *Essay* what "is always the same," it is not that Pope's *Essay* provides us with a definitive critical philosophy or theory of criticism that makes it worth applying to the present of criticism. My suggestion is that the poem qua poem instantiates one *kind* of definition (the "poetic") that is neither wholly objective nor wholly subjective. Compared with statements of the form "criticism is . . . ," the *Essay* points to the value of a different and superior kind of precision. This is the limit of my claim. It is a lesser claim than that of Samuel Johnson in his "Life of Pope" of 1781 where he placed Alexander Pope among "the first criticks and the first poets" purely on the grounds of his *Essay*.[22] It is a higher claim for the poem than that made by the major critics of the twentieth century. The *Essay* has received less attention than Pope's more widely acknowledged satirical writing, his poetical-philosophical endeavors in the *Essay on Man,* or even his Homer. But our current difficulty with "criticism" is one exceptionally pressing reason to keep open the conceptual and aesthetic links with Pope.

The Priority of Ideality

A distinction has been drawn in this study between a preferred perspective and two opposing forms of the effort to define criticism, the one being an overreaction to the shortcomings of the other. The first is that criticism is definable by intrinsic properties, by its attributes, and as a genre. The second is that the concept of criticism is socially constructed. I have argued that the first of these two alternatives seems to give too much weight to cognizable features of criticism empirically circumscribed, while the second seems to leave the capacity for independent thought, the personal creative effort required to define, too far out of the equation. My suggestion is that personal experience is essential to grasp the idea of criticism; but that the vital experience required is the communal and social experience of reflecting upon criticism from *within* its boundaries.[23] That I *ought* to commend the idea of criticism on these grounds may seem another matter. Perhaps I will seem to invoke a romantic transcendence or "eternal verity," prior or superior to things in this world, a God in Nature or ghost in the machine—something more vague, plastic, and flexible than "theory" or part of the "spectral woof of impalpable abstractions" rightly satirized by F. H. Bradley.[24] I will add that I commend the idea that Pope evokes only as a postulate or presupposition that secures coherence for critical activity by permitting a clearly conceived state of disorder. It is the standard by which, having tried to practice critical thought, we know we have succeeded or failed. That is my reason for returning to the language of Pope. Without the idea we have no knowledge of his work that exceeds the verbal.

What, then, does this experience I *say* I am valuing tend to produce—

if not a theory of criticism, a philosophy of criticism, or a definition of criticism? I have not found these terms satisfactory, nor ultimately consonant with the problem as I would perceive it. They seem to me to be too worked out, too finalist in their implications, too prone to oversophistication, too intellectualized in the wrong sense, too likely to lead to a rigid system, too subject to the necessity for proof to constitute presuppositions (in Collingwood's sense), too dependent on proof to explain how criticism is known in the way that we know it. My emphasis has been that in talking of criticism, in a poststructuralist landscape, the most important things will generally be found to be those whose significance is felt more through realization than proof. We need to state them because we need to know that we know them. And we need to know that we know them because criticism is so large and various, and so important to so many people; so that in reconstructing the idea of criticism, which is also the future of criticism, and the essence of what we take for granted about it, there is an element of relearning one's ABC. To return to the defining relations between criticism and theory will provide one example. I will end this chapter with a brief illustrative attempt to clarify this aspect of the current scene by stating the obvious.

First, the object of literary criticism is literature. Second, the theory of literature is part of the theory in criticism and is continuous with criticism. Third, the theory of literature may—when, as sometimes happens, literature is more loosely defined—also be the theory of the criticism of literature. Fourth, the theory of literature may be the generic name for *theories* (in the plural) of the features and aspects of literature (style, narrative, character, prose, poetry, and so forth), and also (nowadays) theories of many extraliterary things that have generated theories of their own that are not theories of literature—life, morals, power, sexuality, politics, and society. It may be a theory of the history of literature, as any literature becomes a document in the history of literature once it is written, and any criticism a document in the history of criticism once it is written. A theory of criticism or a theory of literature is thus a theory of history seen from another point of view. There is a philosophy of history, and there is a philosophy of the history of criticism and a philosophy of the history of literature. And there is a philosophy of the history of the theory of criticism and a philosophy of the history of the theory of literature. And so on. To talk about criticism is to decide which of these things one is wanting to talk about—for they are not the same, and it should not be beneath our dignity to confess this. A final point in this series: the object of the theory of criticism is criticism, and this theory is contained in its object and its object in it.

To replace "theory" we want a word that allows for greater circulation of air, that captures its relative vagueness with relative precision because of the kind of precision it seeks. The *idea* of criticism gestures toward the history of criticism and the history of philosophy in their own right; but it seems to me a better word—assuming we can jump the hurdle of idealist versus realist philosophy and put this aspect of the history of the word behind us. But the key relations are not verbal, nor are they specific to philosophy, with its focus on thought and ideas: they are ethical, situational, and communal. They reflect the relations between those who write books, those who read them, and those who want to know what it is that they have to say. On this plane, the tragic, comic, and ironic inconsequentiality of the critical process has been movingly stated by Samuel Johnson. In criticism's infinite regress can be found a kind of change and a kind of stasis. Johnson's phrase for this model of the history of criticism is "motion without progress." I will end with his remarks: "It is no pleasure to me," he writes in his *Preface to Shakespeare* of 1765,

> in revising my volumes, to observe how much paper is wasted in confutation. Whoever considers the revolutions of learning, and the various questions of greater or less importance, upon which wit and reason have exercised their powers, must lament the unsuccessfulness of enquiry, and the slow advances of truth, when he reflects, that great part of the labour of every writer is only the destruction of those that went before him. The first care of the builder of a new system, is to demolish the fabricks which are standing. The chief desire of him that comments an authour, is to shew how much other commentators have corrupted and obscured him. The opinions prevalent in one age, as truths above the reach of controversy, are confuted and rejected in another, and rise again to reception in remoter times. Thus the human mind is kept in motion without progress. Thus sometimes truth and errour, and sometimes contrarieties of errour, take each others place by reciprocal invasion. The tide of seeming knowledge which is poured over one generation, retires and leaves another naked and barren; the sudden meteors of intelligence which for a while appear to shoot their beams into the regions of obscurity, on a sudden withdraw their lustre, and leave mortals again to grope their way.
>
> These elevations and depressions of renown, and the contradictions to which all improvers of knowledge must for ever be exposed, since they are not escaped by the highest and brightest of mankind, may surely be endured with patience by criticks and annotators, who can rank themselves but as the satellites of their authours. How canst thou beg for life, says Homer's hero to his captive, when thou knowest that thou art now to suffer only what must another day be suffered by Achilles.[25]

10

Conclusion:
Pastness, Presence, and Pope's *Essay*

The general nature of tradition is such that only the part of the past that is not past offers the possibility of historical knowledge. The classical, however, as Hegel says, is "that which is self-significant (selbst bedeutende) and hence also self-interpretive (selber Deutende)." But that ultimately means that the classical preserves itself precisely *because* it is significant in itself and interprets itself; i.e., it speaks in such a way that it is not a statement about what is past—documentary evidence that still needs to be interpreted—rather, it says something to the present as if it were said specifically to it. What we call "classical" does not first require the overcoming of historical distance, for in its own constant mediation it overcomes this distance by itself. The classical, then, is certainly "timeless," but this timelessness is a mode of historical being. . . . But understanding it will always involve *more* than merely historically reconstructing the past "world" to which the work belongs. Our understanding will always retain the consciousness that we too belong to that world, and correlatively, that the work too belongs to our world.

This is just what the word "classical" means: that the duration of a work's power to speak directly is fundamentally unlimited. However much the concept of the classical expresses distance and unattainability and is part of cultural consciousness, the phrase "classical culture" still implies something of the continuing validity of the classical. Cultural consciousness manifests an ultimate community and sharing with the world from which a classical work speaks.
—Hans-Georg Gadamer, *Truth and Method*

And Things *unknown* propos'd as Things *forgot*
—Alexander Pope, *An Essay on Criticism*

DEFINITION AND TEMPORALITY

I SHARE WITH EZRA POUND THE VIEW THAT "IT DOESN'T . . . SO MUCH MATTER where you begin the examination of a subject, so long as you keep on until you get round again to your starting point": "As it were, you start on a sphere, or a cube; [and] you must keep on until you have seen it from all sides."[1] Clearly, we have not by any means examined the problem of criticism from all its sides in this study; but we have examined it from a number of them, and enough, I hope by now, to think that the subject will stand of its own accord, like a stool or a table—to continue Pound's comparison—with at least three legs and possibly more. In this book I have suggested why, in the task of defining, an idealist conception of criticism must be preferred both to social-constructivist and empirical-cognitive definitional modes. To conclude this book with reference to the idea of criticism might be thought to revive the old controversy once prominent in the history of philosophy, and in drawing attention to the *Essay on Criticism* of Pope I will moreover seem to be raking over the ashes of yet another corpse. In the wreckage of the poststructuralist landscape or the glamour of the postmodern, the idea of criticism will therefore appear as a bourgeois delusion, and whatever I say a doomed attempt to hark back, "after theory," to a cause long lost, or some prelapsarian innocent state. Given what I have said in their praise, it will seem a nostalgic attachment to the writings of Johnson and Pope. But for the reasons Gadamer suggests with respect to the "classic" texts in *Truth and Method*, those who seek contact with the critics of past times must shed nostalgia if they are to reinvigorate the historical mode. That Pope's *Essay* has a role in one serially historical sense is true: for several decades after the poem appeared, the rhythm and movement of its lines, its rhymes, and its images were the subject of wide imitation and persistent allusion. Many of its phrases have passed into the language even when their source in the poem is forgotten; but I would argue that this is also a reason for giving the poem a role in the resolution of a modern theoretical problem. As its predecessor English critical essays in verse signally could not, we see how the poem is on several fronts opening communications with the future.

To recapitulate: the problem arises of how to write or teach criticism when we do not know—or know but are not able to say (when nothing goes without saying)—what criticism is. But while we do not have to explain how we breathe or eat in order to perform those two indispensable functions of human life, performing criticism seems to require some consciousness of essence, some exposure of its deep heart and center in contrast to its penumbral or peripheral regions. Among the defining tasks of criticism, then, is the task of accounting for itself. "Criticism," writes Johnson in his satirical portrait of Dick Minim "is a study by which men grow important and formidable at very small expence"[2]—and I have claimed that there are many such propositional statements in the "literature" of criticism, not all as genially ironic as Johnson's. I have touched on all of the following ways of defining criticism at some point:

1. the historical: the story told from a point of view in the present of what criticism has been thought in the past "to be," using critical histories;
2. the persuasive: a normative account of what it *ought* to be in the future;
3. the functional: a description of what it characteristically does, or according to its "point";
4. the institutional or environmental: an agreed practice to whose rules and conventions practitioners subscribe, as this is defined by the elements of its situation: author, work, critic, the world, and so on;
5. the etymological or lexicographical, as in a dictionary or "verbal" definition;
6. definition by aggregation of the variant "species" of the "genus": taste, judgment, theory, valuation, scholarship, journalism, interpretation, appreciation, depreciation, and so forth, or by drawing a line between criticism and any one of these items;
7. the ostensive: citing standard examples or instances of the concept, or as a collection of theories or approaches.

What Collingwood has claimed about "civilization" in this connection can be affirmed of "literary criticism": it is "a thing about which a good deal has been said by many persons over a space of many years. It is not a new subject of discourse. Something has already for a long time been called by that name. The word is established."[3] But although the word "criticism" is "established," its use—and the concept to which it refers—has been open to fundamental challenge in recent years. As Richard Shusterman has written:

> The problems of defining poetry (or more generally literature) and criticism did not depart with Eliot. They are still with us and increasingly more troubling. Scepticism about finding a common and peculiar object or essence for precisely defining literature and criticism and clearly demarcating them from each other and from other textual practices has led some deconstructionist and Marxist critics to a more radical scepticism which challenges the integrity and proper existence of these disciplines.[4]

To advance the things that criticism is concerned to define, including criticism, has usually therefore expressed itself in a will to jettison the word and replace it with others: "Theory" with a capital "T," "deconstruction," "reading," "rereading," "misreading," or the study of cultural practice. In this, critics seem sometimes to have deserted the *idea* of criticism for the trivially pluralist universe of its novel terminologies.⁵ But I have claimed that this does not prove that criticism can be dismissed as a bourgeois hallucination or mystical presence, or that if we turn to the dictionary definition of criticism and find it unhelpful (as we certainly will), it will do to define criticism vaguely, or not at all, as F. R. Leavis claims when he says that you cannot "cogently present the idea of criticism as a matter of generalities."⁶ And since the idea of criticism is itself a critical idea, forged by the hands of critics and none other than critics, it can be defended against criticism that seeks to abolish the word. Anyone trying to disintegrate criticism must expect and get a critical response—or succeed by default.

The present (as it always is, and as it always was when the past was the present) is a time of crisis in criticism. Modern critics have exceptional difficulty in accepting each other's conclusions, and in understanding each other's arguments. But my argument is open to one objection to which I am entirely sympathetic. The problem is that while the idea of criticism is part of criticism, one can't undertake criticism without getting rid of all fixed ideas. I do not think the whole objection need be brushed aside by this paradox; for we are not actually concerned with encapsulations of criticism that define absolutely—like those in geometry that define a triangle as a figure having three sides. The idea of criticism is the residue left when all possible propositions as to criticism's nature have been refuted. The definition exists to make our hold on what we are doing as critics qualitatively stronger, and I have argued that the idea has to be there in the mind in the first place, and that no definition can assure a total realization of criticism in dictionary terms. Nor will the study of criticism produce discoveries in the sense that they are made in medicine, or in surveying the heavens, and no one who knows the field could suppose that criticism's business is to publish "results" for others to build on. As Wendell V. Harris has written: "Criticism is not cumulative: it cannot be so long as there is no possibility of testing literary theories, incorporating those verified into a relatively consistent structure, and dismissing the others."⁷

In the same way, I have also observed, the problem of critics who fail to understand each other can not be solved by regulating their exchanges according to the terms of a creed, as members of one religion share a codified system of public beliefs. It is sometimes suggested that the expression of critical opinions is controlled rather by conventions of conduct ("working" and not "ruling" definitions), and this is surely correct—but again, only up to a point. For complicity with these conventions is only provisional, their precise identity only emerging after a sufficient experience of the practice of criticism. The exchanges between critics take place according to social as well as logical rules (of the kind that philosophy discovers or analyzes). The peculiarity of the present phase of criticism (in contrast with the age of

Addison, Johnson, or Pope) concerns the decorum of the *communis criticorum:* that critics should not *need* terms especially comprehensible to those with whom they disagree.

But such peculiarities enhance—they do not remove—the need to revisit the idea of criticism according to Pope. Vagueness in the local arguments made by critics is not the same as vagueness in criticism's conceptual identity. For the idea of criticism to be *sufficiently* clear, we have to shut our eyes to sides of what we are seeing: we distinguish between different ways of thinking about the same works of criticism whose textual and discursive attributes are not distinct.[8] At one moment these may be instances of the concept "literature," at the next of "criticism," without our need to identify the empirical features of "works." Thus works can be instances of the idea of "criticism" in one sense even if their textual attributes clearly suggest a deviation from the normal use of the term.

The fallacy is not that there are such things as "standard cases," or that there is no possibility of normal use;[9] it is that there is any clearly *observable* line between the ambiguous cases and the standard ones that would enable us to say what single logical feature makes the usage normal. But what are the standard cases of literary criticism—an essay by T. S. Eliot on Dryden or *Hamlet* perhaps? a whole book on the art of fiction by David Lodge? Aristotle's *Treatise on Poetry* in English translation? Joseph Addison's *Spectator* papers on Milton's *Paradise Lost*? The answer is there are no standard cases within this list other than where we suppose them. Correspondingly, the standard cases of criticism only seem standard cases until we analyze them. The concept presents us with a field that shades incrementally from one thing to another in the same way that the red of the rainbow gradually turns into purple. Granted, some works of criticism seem to be written deliberately to confuse the issue of what is a literary and what a critical work; but to think of Johnson's criticism, or Coleridge's, or Arnold's, or T. S. Eliot's may also be to appreciate the sense in which paradigmatic works of criticism have under some aspect to become literature if they are to establish themselves as works belonging to the history of criticism and to contribute to the definition of criticism by that means. The truth is that the instances of criticism are never completely identified as works. An idea of criticism ensures that units of significance aside from the unity of the work are normally described as criticism—a judgment, an interpretation, an evaluation, a suggestion or countersuggestion, a theory developed over several publications. Contributions to the theory may be separated by time, as a composite of the work of different theorists, so that the distance between criticism and the critical work is comparable to the distance between the idea of fiction and a work like *Jude the Obscure* when we call this a "novel." Conventions are available to help us give names to the form; but these are not a reliable guide to the concept. Examples of criticism in the merely generic sense can exist from which criticism in essence is absent.

Where criticism is written by creative artists two views have arisen. One is that criticism composed by creators of art implies a special authority we may with great difficulty disregard: the understanding that, in Gilbert Ryle's phrase, is "a part of knowing *how.*" The other is that the criticism of creators wants sufficient disinterest to have critical value. There are many examples to support both views. Some of the most distinguished critics in English literature were creators of exceptional merit: Ben Jonson, Dryden, Johnson, Wordsworth, Coleridge, Keats (who wrote criticism in his *Letters*), Byron and Gerard Manley Hopkins (in theirs), George Eliot and Henry James (in their essays and reviews), and so on. More recent examples might include the writings of Lionel Trilling say, or Ted Hughes—the latter's many reviews, his *Poetry in the Making*, his preface to Emily Dickinson's poems, his selections from Shakespeare, and his *Shakespeare and the Goddess of Complete Being.* Such instances take us, once again, "outside the academic fold" of literary criticism. Although it can be said of Dryden's criticism (as Johnson said of it) that "His observations were framed rather for those that were learning to write, than for those that read only to talk,"[10] it remains a pertinent question whether Dryden's "Prefaces" were really more than *self-*justifications designed to pave the way for his poems. The same question could be put to Wordsworth's preface to his *Lyrical Ballads*. And again, why in their critical essays are George Eliot and Henry James so preoccupied with the art of the *novel?* There seems always to be some seepage from a writer's strictly creative ambitions to his or her work as a critic. And when this is evident it seems to subtract from the criticism. Modern academic criticism provides by contrast for a distance between the critic and the object of the criticism.

Such oppositions are, however, complicated in a number of ways. The problem is contained in the terms we use when we wonder to what extent a text may be considered as "art" and to what extent it is part of "science"; or when we examine the nature of the creative faculty, and decide to include amongst its elements the subfaculties of "judgment," "evaluation," "self-analysis," "self-criticism," and so forth. The qualities characteristic of criticism in its distinction from creation arise as attributes of creation. Moreover, the proposition that criticism and creation share their essential attributes is open to be refuted by other criticism, just as the doctrine of "art for art's sake" has its parallel in the practice of criticism for criticism's sake. From Shakespeare and Tolstoy the modern critic turns to Eagleton and Lacan. For reasons of this kind, and just at the point where avant-garde literary art has embraced the province of criticism, critics complain of much modern criticism that it tends to marginalize literature. One of the failures of attempts to talk in general terms about the field of critical studies has been the ruling out of all the very many ways in which criticism operates as art, *is* art in any definition of the term that recognizes the critical functioning of literary texts.

Criticism and literary art enjoy thereby a fundamental generic instability. Sometimes criticism is embedded *within* a literary work, as in the comic discourses on drama in *Hamlet* or in Stoppard. Criticism *in* literature is not always *of* literature, whether in the debate on African art between Gerald and Birkin in D. H. Lawrence's *Women in Love*,[11] or in the wider sense that a novel (say) analyzes the phenomenon of cultural identity (like *Midnight's Children*). The object of critical attention may be real, like India in the 1940s, or indeterminantly fictional, like the object of Keats's meditation on a Grecian urn. Two literary art forms come very close to criticism but are hard to define as such: the verse translation and the satire or parody. As for the latter, Pope's *Rape of the Lock* is a joke at the expense of Homer; Howard Jacobson's *Peeping Tom* ridicules Thomas Hardy; Milan Kundera's *Book of Laughter and Forgetting* describes the antics of a club of great writers in Prague whose members—Boccaccio, Goethe, Verlaine, and Petrarch—spend their time squabbling over girlfriends and wives and so deflating their namesakes on the great stage of European literature. And then, of course, there is the substantial body of writing by poets on poets, and *in* poetry: Ben Jonson on Shakespeare, Cowley on Crashaw, Rochester on Waller, Dryden on Oldham, and so forth. These are the kinds of problems and complications that attempts to define criticism must try to address.

I have discussed a range of statements of the form "criticism is . . ." in this book. These are propositions, but we have seen that although they differ widely in content, for which they are the declarative vehicles, they are not actually exclusive of other suggestions we might make about criticism, and it would not be interesting or fruitful to take issue with them. No one could usefully deny that criticism is a "discourse," or a "system," or a "study." Terms such as these define while not conflicting with the common usage of the word. The most important characteristic of such statements is that they establish a set of "defining relations," and one consequence of hearing criticism called an "art," a "philosophy," or "a form of theology" is that we reflect on the meaning of these terms in their relation to criticism. But this meaning is unstable. Thus criticism may be an "art," but for one critic it is "the art of knowing the hidden roads that go from poem to poem," while for another it is "the art of putting questions." For one it is "the exercise of . . . . [a] quality"; for another "an exercise in persuasion."[12] Saying what criticism "is" is going to suggest all sorts of relationships between criticism and the other concepts: to say that criticism "is discrimination" is one thing; to say that criticism "is the endeavour to discriminate" places the emphasis quite elsewhere. It includes within "criticism" the whole range of unsuccessful attempts to tell things apart.

Criticism would be poorer without such statements. It is not that any one of the statements is *in itself* more justified or more true than anything actually formulated by Pope. Only if *all* the paradigm figures, propositions, questions, and issues raised by Pope in his *Essay* could be proved to be *not* paradigm figures, propositions, questions, or issues to be raised in connection with the modern analysis of the concept "criticism" would it be appropriate to link temporal criteria of differentiation with aesthetic or intellectual ones in any hard-and-fast way. According to Rorty, "literary criticism," has been "stretched" over recent years:

> It is a familiar fact that the term "literary criticism" has been stretched further and further in the course of our century. It originally meant comparison and evaluation of plays, poems, and novels—with perhaps an occasional glance at the visual arts. Then it got extended to cover past criticism (for example, Dryden's, Shelley's, Arnold's, and Eliot's prose, as well as their verse). Then, quite quickly, it got extended to the books which had supplied past critics with their critical vocabulary and were supplying present critics with theirs. . . .
>
> Once the range of literary criticism is stretched that far there is, of course, less and less point in calling it *literary* criticism. But for accidental historical reasons, having to do with the way in which intellectuals got jobs in universities by pretending to pursue academic specialties, the name has stuck. So instead of changing the term "literary criticism" to something like "culture criticism," we have instead stretched the word "literature" to cover whatever the literary critics criticize.[13]

But this underplays the aesthetic dimension of statements on the nature of criticism. Whenever critics suggest that criticism has been "redefined," what they really mean is that another set of propositions about criticism has entered the fray, and a different set of defining relations. We have seen that the new propositions will not be *totally* random statements. Criticism is not "defined" by statements using the verb "to be" in the sense that any one statement allows nothing more to be said; but the existence of such statements at every turn within the literature of criticism is one of the ways that the concept, as far as it is knowable, becomes expressible. Trying to say what criticism "is" would not be so often attempted were it consistently thought it could not be attempted with success, and within what F. R. Leavis called a "logical ethos," the statements have a tactical status and evocative function. They reflect the "inevitable opportunism" that Leavis detected in a "living principle" whose constituents "can't be, in the ordinary sense of the word, defined."[14] All the statements on what criticism "is" turn out to be partial synonyms, temporary or incomplete substitutions; they are working definitions whose use when we draw them together is to render each other intelligible. An idea of criticism is logically presupposed by the partiality we detect in these independent verbal representations.

Conclusions

To return to the concerns expressed at the start of this book.

Criticism and Historicity

In the beginning, I examined an inference that "old" (i.e., pre-twentieth-century) literary criticism was too routinely regarded in a condition of distanced historicity, in obsolete, relevance-restricted terms that failed to engage with modern theoretical analysis. Too often, the historical representation of past criticism has consisted of an external sequence of theoretical norms organized according to overarching paradigms of cultural classification. This externalization of the history of criticism, I have argued, has had consequences for the understanding of criticism, because it has transformed the critical present into another stage in the history of ideas defined seriatim *by* its ideas; the intellectual description of criticism present and criticism past is framed within philosophies of history where the present tends to be cast as an *advance upon* the past. This inclination to elevate the present over the past is not, of course, without precedent historically. Pope, like Paul de Man[15] and others, makes clear how far our own attempts to organize the past of criticism are preconceived within the seventeenth-century Ancients and Moderns debate. Such temporal polarity has been an issue in the seventeenth, eighteenth, nineteenth, and twentieth centuries alike; but it was in the following poetic terms that Pope particularized the defining origins of criticism in the *Essay:*

> But where's the Man, who Counsel *can* bestow,
> Still *pleas'd* to *teach*, and yet not *proud* to *know*?
> Unbiass'd, or by *Favour* or by *Spite;*
> Not *dully prepossest,* nor *blindly right;*
> Tho' Learn'd, well-bred; and tho' well-bred, sincere;
> Modestly bold, and Humanly severe?
> Who to a *Friend* his Faults can freely show,
> And gladly praise the Merit of a *Foe?*
> Blest with *Taste* exact, yet unconfin'd;
> A *Knowledge* both of *Books* and *Humankind;*
> *Gen'rous Converse;* a *Soul* exempt from *Pride;*

> And *Love to Praise*, with *Reason* on his Side?
> Such once were *Criticks*, such the Happy *Few*,
> *Athens* and *Rome* in better Ages knew.
> The mighty *Stagyrite* first left the Shore,
> Spread all his Sails, and durst the Deeps explore. . . . .
> Horace still charms with graceful Negligence,
> And without Method *talks* us into Sense,
> Will like a *Friend* familiarly convey
> The *truest Notions* in the *easiest way*. . . . .
> In grave *Quintilian*'s copious Work we find
> The justest *Rules*, and clearest *Method* join'd. . . . .
> Thee, bold *Longinus!* all the Nine inspire,
> And bless *their Critick* with a *Poet's Fire*.
> An ardent *Judge*, who Zealous in his Trust,
> With *Warmth* gives Sentence, yet is always *Just;*
> Whose *own Example* strengthens all his Laws,
> And *Is himself* that great *Sublime* he draws.
> (lines 631–46, 653–56, 669–70, 675–80)

When Pope writes in his *Essay on Criticism* that "Such once were *Criticks*, such the Happy *Few*, / *Athens* and *Rome* in better Ages knew" (lines 643–44), he is charting poetically (rhapsodically, not rationalistically) the decline and fall of literary criticism from Greek and Roman times to *his* present day; but the process he outlines is complicated by every variety of fluctuation, interruption, and reversal. His lines construct a setting for his own contribution to the process, and Pope's survey of his historical antecedents provides an *occasion* for interventions both as poet and as critic. The passage is a preamble to the *Essay*'s simultaneously detached yet intensely personal close and to the self-portrait of the poet, who is "Averse alike to *Flatter*, or *Offend*" (line 703). The relation here between the history of criticism, collapsed from its mythically perfect state, and the act of personal assertion captures the essence of the relationship between history and definition as modes of self-realization. That there is, or has been, a decline and fall provides the impetus for Pope's intervention; at the same time, one cannot fail to associate the latest in the line of critics with the great dead lamented by Pope. In this, Pope both basks in the reflected glory of his ancestor critics while enacting the process of criticism's conscious dependence on history to exist at all. Here the past is not *simply* a "burden," a dead weight to be thrown off and disowned. The passage brings Pope into voluntary partnership with the expired critics and poets recalled and historically reordered through his lines, but it also involves a competitive element expressed in common with the lines translated by Pope from Chaucer in *The Temple of Fame*, and recalled by Johnson in his *Preface to Shakespeare* of 1765:

> Criticks I saw, that other's names efface,
> And fix their own, with labour, in the place;
> Their own, like others, soon their place resigned,
> Or disappear'd, and left the first behind.[16]

That Pope was responding here to what de Man has called the "spontaneity of being modern"[17] derives from his consciousness of a process that is at once larger than any single lifetime but does not efface the individual writer and critic. The same creative interplay of present and past, of individual and universal, pervades Pope's poetry, from his poetical versions of the *Iliad* and the *Odyssey* of Homer, through the consciously adopted Horatian persona of his satirical writing and the harsher ridicule of the *Dunciad*, to the carefully crafted "Epitaphs" scrutinized at different times by both Johnson and Wordsworth.

It is in the history of criticism according to Pope, then, that we find the most imposing challenge to the logical priority of the present over the chronological priority of the past. We are made alive to the way that the Ancient and the Modern are *already* locked in mutual criticism, as—classically—they are in the juxtapositions organized by the symbolic form of the *Essay*. Here the present of criticism is played off against the Longinian, Aristotelian, and Horatian past. But Pope, too—as his poem's treatment of "Wit" throughout will suggest—has also "reconstructed criticism," and the past of criticism that his poem creates is not an unyielding edifice that we cannot take something from. As Ricoeur observes, some of what we call the past is connected to its past context in a less interesting way than it serves as a mirror image for us. The plight of modern conceptualizations of the past of eighteenth-century criticism is appropriately described in Ricoeur's account of the "enigma of temporal distance," which is

> an over-determined enigma owing to the axiological shift that has made us strangers to the customs of past times, to the point that the otherness of the past in relation to the present is more important than the survival of the past in the present. When curiosity gains the upper hand over sympathy, the stranger becomes alien. The difference that separates gets substituted for the difference that binds together.[18]

By the kind of writing it is, the past of criticism transcends its occasion and moves out of the contexts of the culturally specific paradigm and into the arena of literary value. It reaches beyond the dominance of the categories of "old" and "new," "neoclassical" and "poststructuralist," to the issues and problems characteristic of the self-created critical community constituted by the evolving practice of criticism. Collingwood called this historical process of self-definition "consciousness."[19] T. S. Eliot wrote in his *Four*

Quartets that "To be conscious is not to be in time."[20] In the seventeenth and eighteenth centuries the value I have in mind was describable in terms of "Eternal" or "general nature." Its presence is a central criterion in Pope's description of criticism, and his exhortation to

> Regard not then if Wit be *Old* or *New*,
> But blame the *False,* and value still the *True*.
>   (lines 406–7)

This seems so easy to say that the statement's collapse into cliché was virtually assured. But the statement could not have become a cliché (like much else in the *Essay*) had its inspirational force not been felt, not by one generation—the generation alive at the poem's appearance in 1711—but by many thereafter. The fact is, it has always been so convenient to use the immediate contextual field of the *Essay* to depreciate Pope that his poem's transtemporality (and its place within this other field) has become obscured to the point where historical work on Pope or the *Essay* seems to have little hope of recovering its answering significance for us. Contextual research on the *Essay*—as conducted by such historical and cultural experts as David Womersley or Christa Knellwolf—sets the poem against the foil of its historical universe; but it also runs the risk of digging us deeper into the pastness of the poem, and reinstating its divide from the present.[21] My argument in this book has been that an opening up of the channels of communication will come by returning to the present problems of criticism and by reintroducing the poem into a broadened canon of thinking and feeling about criticism that goes beyond Theory in the au courant sense. Recognition of the cultural resistance to this procedure is the initial step.

Criticism and the "New"

The relevance of this discussion to the second preliminary concern of this study should now be clear—this is the illusion, stated in characteristic form by Richard Rorty, that the idea of criticism has been abolished or substantially redefined in recent years. We have seen that the illusion this statement promotes is encouraged by a cultural need to sever the ties with criticism's past. But Pope's definition in his *Essay on Criticism* shows that the experience of resistance to the intellectual fashions of one's time is not substantially novel, and Pope was among the writers of the past who as poet, satirist and translator was signally able to express this. But the irony of the condition, as we have just observed, is precisely that it deprives us of access to such "traditional" modes of liberation as Pope's. Unresisted and unchecked by criticism in the past, a temporal apartheid arises within the present from which there is no escape.

Several studies of late have begun to historicize and explain what John M. Ellis in his recent book has called the "race-gender-class" thesis in modern criticism—the definition of academic modes of literary criticism in terms of one grand and paradoxical combination of antiexclusionism and anti-Enlightenment.[22] Others, approaching the problem from a point of view grounded in philosophical aesthetics, have drawn attention to the autonomous institution of literary practice independent of the priorities of social studies, political thought, or psychosexual inquiry. These latter analysts—such as Stein Olsen—have made efficacious and important interventions. Unless literary criticism can defend its object of interest on its own terms, then it is a phenomenon without a history, and it must have been the history of some other thing from the eighteenth century we were interested in. But a turn in the direction of Pope's *Essay on Criticism* suggests that the community of criticism may have inherited the value-system of the poem so fundamentally that its cultural politics are no longer *consciously* part of its knowledge. To take the poem seriously as a definition of criticism is to see that the "classical" values foregrounded in the poem—disinterest, creativity, balance, sanity, a sharp comic sense, skepticism about all temporally defined values, an opposition to the sectarian formulas productive of false debate—are still values. They do not always seem to be values. The present scene (like Pope's) is riven with sectarian critical politics, historicism, misunderstanding—all the confusions we *see*. But values can be maintained as values without having to be realized in the manners and procedures of a critical culture. Values would be meaningless without some tension between them and the cognizable realities of a time. Their own value is to preserve the possibility of change for the better. Pope was under no illusions about the value systems successfully realized in the critical universe of his day. He would not otherwise have been so formidable a satirist of them.

The Language of Criticism

This brings me to the third of the concerns articulated at the start of this book—the question of language. I have dwelt at length in this book on aspects of vocabulary and grammar by means of which criticism is ordinarily circumscribed. Much seems to hang on the possibility of meaning being shared. I have suggested, from the outset, that the meaning of "criticism" is shared in one sense (we know what it means) and not in another: the world has different conceptions of criticism, different theories as to its function, purpose, essence, or value. Its relationship to "theory" "judgment," "interpretation," and so forth have all proved ways in which it has been possible to put some other meaning in the place of criticism. But I have argued that neither "criticism" (the word) nor "criticism" (the idea) is easily disposed of, and that this coincidence of conceptual and terminological durability is part of the understanding we have taken from Pope. *That* we know this may be a consequence of also comprehending how little new can be said, and of a Bloomian misprizing of the past in the face of this fact. The industrialization of critical production within the academy is kept in motion by *original* work. And so there arises the pressure of expediency to limit the claims to special attention made by the old critics and (in Pope's case) the old definers of criticism. One might conveniently point to the 1960s (say) as a radical schism, a challenge even to the existence of criticism and literature made when we substitute other words for "criticism," or when we address the subject of "literature" in terms of its pervasive "textuality." But literature is still written. Critics of literature still offer views on its quality. Readers of literature, while forming independent opinions, are undivertibly interested in the views on the quality of literature offered by critics. Contrary to the dominant linguistic strain in recent cultural relativism, changing the vocabulary of the paradigm does not *in itself* alter its structure, and we have seen that the word "criticism" has not, after all, been abandoned. Abolitionists share with their imagined opponents in critical suppositions—questioning, skepticism, interrogation, and so forth—and operate in the modes of confutation and resistance that confirm the idea of criticism. There is irony in the fact that it is precisely these critics who insist that assumptions be stated and that tacit values be made plain. If the assumptions of abolitionist criticism were stated more clearly, then the extent of their working within the critical paradigm would be exposed.

Criticism and Community

This leads to the fourth and final difficulty broached at the beginning of this book: the identity and strength of the critical community. This difficulty is inescapably a social question in some sense, and the site where social and aesthetic considerations inextricably combine. The fact that they do is one of the reasons why it seems not satisfactory to adopt a *purely* aesthetic view of the problems raised by criticism. There is a danger, one not totally avoided by aesthetic theorists working with and through philosophical concepts, of a different kind of hermeticism from the one taken issue with so far. In a certain aspect, "radical conspiracy theorists" are right to suspect the ideologically and socially neutral "aesthetic point of view." Now, the aesthetic qualities of Pope's *Essay on Criticism* are part of its transcendence as a definition of criticism. But the poem also contains an account of social relations that suggests a social relation with the critical present. The passage in question, quoted above, is justly famous, but its fame needs to carry more weight in discussions of the extended critical society of present and past. Mason has referred to the ideal of "urbanity" he saw exposed by Pope's poem, but in the current climate such appeals are likely to cut little ice. They are too resonant of a connoisseuring, donnish detachment; they nourish prejudices about Pope as a model of an eighteenth-century "polite" culture founded on class privilege and social exploitation. But this particular passage from the poem is concerned with the question of how we treat friends and how we treat foes and the relationship that the critic has to these two tribal groups. It sheds a further light on the attitude that the critic is bound to take up when confronted with works from the present and works from the past. The critic is one who

> . . . to a *Friend* his Faults can freely show,
> And gladly praise the Merit of a *Foe*.
>
> (lines 637–38)[23]

Such a critic is

> Blest with a *Taste* exact, yet unconfin'd;
> A *Knowledge* both of *Books* and *Humankind*
>
> (lines 639–40)

The linkage here between books and humankind is one of the most important sociocritical morals that can be taken away from Pope's poem. The poem transcends its context of origin at such a point. It thereby enacts its historical role.

Summary of Conclusions

One could object that the *Essay on Criticism* is of dubious value in the study of the definition of criticism, because the poem is in obvious ways unique. As a one-time event, an argument can be made that the *Essay* is an instance of nothing except itself. And if the poem fails to typify a category or class of statements, this would seem to forbid our drawing general morals about how to define criticism from its use as a case study here. But this uniqueness is (ipso facto) its historical value, and to the extent that the poem is trying with a degree of undervalued poetic success to solve a problem whose solution remains elusive to this day, it is part of the past that is not yet over, "that is not even past." Pope's *Essay* is not an abstract formula for criticism such as philosophy, critical theory, or aesthetics might try to supply, and like many works of literature it focuses a human situation, here combining religion, literature, criticism, social morality, and the self-conscious ambition of Pope.[24] At the same time, the function of Pope's poem has been to show how the definition of criticism tends towards its ideal when its statement converges with art. That the definition of criticism *can be* art I have attempted to establish, and it will be evident from my treatment of the *Essay* that as a work of art I believe it to be good. But while it can be appreciated aesthetically, it is not itself part of aesthetics. Pope turns "criticism" into one of the defining events of human life.

Several consequences flow from the findings made in this study and can be summed up as follows.

1. In this account (contra the modernist, abolitionist or versions of the poststructuralist view), *the definition of criticism is only intelligible in holistic terms which include its past as part of its present, as this is disclosed through a sufficiently profound and developed philosophy of history and model of time.*

2. *Criticism is not identified by its classifiable works or their textual, discursive, or formal features, and its history cannot be satisfactorily contrived by these means.* It follows that any value ascribed to one or another school or "theory" in modern criticism cannot be located in the form of its approach, its specific terminology, analytical or theoretical practices, or Rortian "final language." The importance of the text, the theory, or the school is evident only by seeing a particular instance under the aspect of the idea of criticism, as taking up a critical stance within a situation, network, and background involving an author, a work, a reader, and a world. The example is determined as criticism *occasionally*, as far as it conforms to conditions of satisfaction identified at the level of supposition rather than proposition. The example thus serves the useful purpose of criticism, which is sustained by antecedent conventions and not, I have argued, according to aprioristic social or political categories that annex criticism to fields having useful purposes of their own.

3. To support this claim, the present account has also developed a description of what I have called an "idealist" definition of criticism. I have argued that in comparing types of definition, *the precise formulation of criticism is language- and literature-dependent, and thus open to critical inspection on literary terms.* Because definitions are not exempt from judgments according to textual rules or aesthetic criteria, some may be preferred to others on these grounds. The art of Pope shows that there are *degrees of success* in the definition of criticism.

4. Furthermore, each of these conclusions moves value away from the world of all-or-nothing logic characteristic of recent statements of the form "criticism is . . . ," from a "revolutionary" criticism, or traditional accounts by such critics as Arnold, Eliot, or Eagleton of its "function," and relocates it in modes of apperception which relegitimate the *Essay on Criticism* of

Pope (to take only the most obvious but strangely neglected example). The fact that they do, I argue, involves no special claim for the values of eighteenth-century criticism per se, over and against the values to be found in the present, the nineteenth century or the twentieth century. There is no "historical" value in that sense, but a way of understanding what our hold on the concept of criticism would be like if the *Essay* had not existed, or existed and all the copies had been lost and all recollection of the poem effaced. It is a way of imagining what our culture would be like without anyone ever having had an idea of criticism—not to mention the passion and insight to write a poem about it.

AFTERWORD

The Logic of Cultural Studies

> Theory's gumbo-effect is why Cultural Studies, the studying of anything and everything "cultural," can claim coherence. Anything at all, in short, which can be thought of as if made textually, imagined as imagined, as narrated, as constructed language-like, and thus "readable," is now being "read."
> —Valentine Cunningham, *Reading after Theory*

That cultural studies has sought to redefine criticism there seems no reason to doubt. "Far from constituting a new 'Copernican revolution' or paradigm-change as is sometimes claimed," writes Patrick Parrinder, "the theory 'boom'"

> appears to be a symptom of deeper, underlying changes in literature and its academic study. Literature, in the sense of the masterpieces of the canon or the "great tradition," has come to seem too narrow an object to be viewed in isolation from other social forms. The movement for the unification of the social sciences under the rubric of semiotics and discourse theory, the study of "signifying systems" or of "discursive practices" necessarily includes the study of literature in its aims. Literary criticism has been struggling to become cultural just as cultural theory was struggling to become, if not more literary, at least more alive to the categories of language and narrative.[1]

The intersection of criticism with cultural studies takes many forms. Within the terms of a broad definition, it could, for example, be located in the vast universalizing critiques of Western art to be found in, say, Camille Paglia's *Sexual Personae* or even Harold Bloom's *The Western Canon*—works that aspire to discuss art and literature totalistically, in terms of whole civilizations at many significant levels. Alternatively, the phrase "cultural studies" may be reasonably thought to refer to the general human and cultural engagement we find in writers like Arnold, Eliot, Trilling, Williams, or Leavis, whose standing as critics of literature is enhanced by their being able to extend their interests beyond the range of literary works and purely literary values to questions of civilization, community, and society. And then again, and more canonically, perhaps, the practice of cultural studies may be taken to allude to the kind of writing originating in the discussion of politics, economics, or society that literary criticism has taken over and transgressively applied as part of criticism: work such as Walter Benjamin's, Theodor Adorno's, or Louis Althusser's. In these and other ways, a fundamental challenge to criticism's definition and distinctness has come from the direction of cultural studies.

The right of cultural studies to exist—whether as an adjunct to criticism or as its controlling context—has been commonly asserted on the basis of a certain inexorable logic: this is the "common sense" adopted by anyone seeking to extrapolate from a position of proven soundness to ensure that a given or accepted principle is uniformly applied. Cultural studies emerged in the forms relevant to the present inquiry when existing tools of literary criticism, still considered to have use in their time, were taken up and applied to artifacts not traditionally considered literature. Its advent was prompted by an increasingly acute awareness of the relationship between the divisions of contemporary society—education and opportunity, on the one hand, and the meaning and scope of culture, on the other. Hitherto, the word had seemed to rule out all but the tastes and practices of an elite, "cultured" class. Now, with the advent of cultural studies, the culture of the whole of society, in all its forms, could be treated with an equity of care for the value invested in any part of the culture by its particular users. The appearance of cultural studies came with the credentials of an egalitarian crusade. Its motive was essentially corrective; its ethic was the moral generosity of a libertarian social vision.

So the logic of cultural studies was devised to serve the highly commendable function of bridging a gap between two different worlds. On one side of the case there was the literary imagination, made more esoteric by the progress of twentieth-century literary modernism. On the other there was the popular domain open to all capable of experience. Within the politics of academic life, this widening of the bounds had a tactical value for cultural studies. By claiming the whole of experience for its distinctive field, cultural studies became universalist—all that can be summed up in the idea of a social study, a combined or general humanity—and it was for this reason able to promote itself above literary criticism and to assume a more comprehensive authority. In a far more obvious sense, its "logic" was that consequent on the discovery that the object of criticism's traditional attention—literature itself—is a category that has unreliable, indefinable limits and no monopoly stake in the capital of human interest. Cultural studies could appropriate literary criticism by exploiting the fact that the limits of literature cannot be precisely drawn. If they exist, their existence cannot be seen. They are not empirically available.

Viewed from the wider perspective of history, the interest of cultural studies in the relations between literary studies and cultural forms is one expression of relations between literature and life, or the conjunction of "Books and Humankind," that critics from the time of Pope and Johnson have valued. The study of popular culture could decisively assert such links. Critics promoting cultural theory (Williams and Eagleton, for example) have at some stage in their earlier careers come under the influence of this doctrine, one that is traceable to Arnold and, latterly, to Leavis. This is the focus of the work of Richard Hoggart, the founding father of cultural studies in Britain. Hoggart's achievement—in what can be viewed as cultural studies in its prestructuralist phase—was to place the phenomenon of the literary work within an array of diverse cultural and anthropological phenomena drawn from the daily experience of ordinary human lives in their linguistic and ritualistic particulars. The array in question does not challenge the existence of literature. Rather, cultural studies serves here to supply the works of literature with a vast and various context. It seeks merely to resist the idea that cultural experience need be remote, and that access to it need be confined to the privileged few. But the tools of analysis were originally, and essentially, literary ones.

The subject was soon to take on a wholly different emphasis that seems to subvert or even reverse this original and irresistible logic. As the principles and approaches of cultural studies came to be associated with the influence, exerted from outside Britain, of the writings of structuralist criticism (and the constituents of that criticism: Marxism, linguistics, and Freudianism), the leading assumptions were epitomized by, and for the purposes of discussion may be isolated in, the writings of the French critic Roland Barthes. Now, the emphasis came to fall not on the text in its social context, but on the text itself, and on its status as a "signifying practice" in its own right. In an essay entitled "The Two Criticisms" (1963), Barthes expressed his irritation with the tendency of what he describes as "academic" (as opposed to "interpretative") criticism. Literary texts were too often used as a means to explore matters that fall outside literature—the personality and life of the author, for example. This is what Barthes went on to call "the *elsewhere* of literature": "The critic must admit that it is his very object, in its most general form, literature, which resists or evades him, not the biographical 'secret' of his author."[2]

Literature *should* be read to learn more about literature, but according to Barthes it generally is not. The specifically literary text was no longer to be regarded as the key to a chronologically coincident social moment (like

Hoggart's working-class Britain in the 1950s, say). Instead, it was now to be seen in a form dissolved into all other signifying phenomena and as socially produced; as something constructed by ideology, specifically bourgeois ideology. Literature was no longer a window opening onto society but a dysfunctional, because politically incorrect, consequence of society's forces. What began as a logical widening of critical attention from "canonical" literature to (say) film, or popular fiction (detective stories, romances, newspapers, advertisements, etc.) had evolved into a critical philosophy denying the separate identity of literature, canonical or otherwise, and asserting the universal artifact of the Text. Moreover, as "bourgeois liberal humanism" became the standard butt of Theory, its implication was now a pronounced antihumanism.

But the value of this recent development will depend on the security of an analogy that must, like any other, hold at a number of points. In *Reading the Popular* (1989), the cultural critic John Fiske, for example, is concerned with the sense in which the phenomena and practices of popular culture provide a "signifying system." Following Barthes, Fiske draws on a combination of Marxism and Saussurean linguistics to establish the structures of textual signification appropriate to each subject that he treats. In so doing he goes beyond the narrowly semiotic account of a text's internal relations to suggest the sense in which the text inscribes the structures of the wider (consumer) culture. The critic is now no longer concerned (as Barthes in his treatments of Balzac or Racine) with "texts" in the literary sense, but with the beach, video pleasures, shopping, quizzes, the Sears Tower in Chicago. Fiske follows the Barthes of *Mythologies* and *The Pleasure of the Text* to reveal a popular culture located in, and empowered by, Pleasure. Such pleasure subverts capitalist domination. This it does by appropriating capitalism's typical forms for popular use.

The vastly entertaining qualities of this critical practice are not open to doubt. Madonna's appropriation of capitalist-patriarchal images of woman (underwear, leather, etc.) is seen to subvert and mock such images to produce an enjoyable shock. Madonna controls patriarchy by embracing its forms as her own. The dimensions of our everyday (real) experience within capitalist culture are valued and validated by this stroke. The method encourages thought about ordinary but really significant things that are the experience of the West, and of mass participation in popular culture, and it suggests the complex way in which such images work. It is a complexity that seeks comparison with that conventionally imputed to canonical literature. The effect is to turn these "ordinary" phenomena into things that are far from ordinary and to draw out the special significance that they inherently have.

The same had been true of the work of Roland Barthes. Here again, we are to suppose an analogy between the production of material commodities and the production of literature-as-commodity. This analogy steers the description of criticism toward the materialist as distinct from the idealist paradigm explored in this study. Thus in his essay on "The New Citroen" (1957), for example, Barthes could write of the Citroen D.S. 19 [3] that "cars today are almost the exact equivalent of the great Gothic cathedrals: I mean the supreme creation of an era, conceived with passion by unknown artists, and consumed in image if not in usage by a whole population which appropriates them as a purely magical object."[4] The cultural artifact of the car lends itself to Barthes's conception of cultural production exceptionally well. It is, quite literally, socially constructed in the sense that it has no single author. Its creation is intersubjective. Its system of production—the assembly line in the case of those vehicles manufactured in bulk for the mass—is one of the great stories of Western capitalist efficiency. The student of culture, confronted by the end product of this process, subverts the oppressive intentions of the manufacturing economy by appropriating the product for pleasure, savoring the shapes and curves. These enable the car to share the formal properties of other objects, religious and fantastic:

> It is well known that smoothness is always an attribute of perfection because its opposite reveals a technical human operation of assembling: Christ's robe was seamless, just as the airships of science-fiction are made of unbroken metal. The *D.S. 19* has no pretensions about being as smooth as cake-icing. . . .[5]

But Barthes's method, like Fiske's, raises the problems that are characteristic of the logic of cultural studies. Is everything a text or are only certain things? If everything is a text (in which case the greater proportion of texts is still waiting to be analyzed), then the attention given by the cultural analyst to some texts rather than others means that a judgment has had to be made. And if it is argued that nothing can assert a stronger claim to critical attention than anything else, then why (in Fiske's case, for example) pick on the beach, or Madonna, or the Sears Tower, or rather why pick on them *first?* If, on the other hand, only *some* things are texts, then who determines their textual nature: who decides the principles and how they should be applied? There is clearly a danger that the canonical hierarchy will be replaced by the substitute hierarchy of texts privileged simply by the fact that they are open to analysis leading to certain conclusions about capitalism's pervasive presence and its vulnerability to subversion. The logic of this "pantextualist" theory depends on our accepting the Althusserian-Marxist proposition that literature is in effect a commodity (like any other).

Now, *in a sense* it is. From the emergence in the eighteenth century of a culture of print, the world of books has been notoriously the domain of consumer capitalism (and latterly its "dot.com" varieties). Literature will reflect its society, and will be shaped by the ideology, technocracy, and political assumptions out of which society is made. Poems and novels are—again, *in a sense*—texts. But it would surely constitute a mistake to translate this witty reading of contemporary culture into a method having *no* essential distinction from the method of literary criticism—as if the elements of its whole situation, as we have described them above, were the same in *every* respect. If nothing else, it would be to miss the deliberate comedy and playfulness of the conjunction. For works of literature, except in the sense that texts are constructed from paper and ink, are not made out of things in the same way that cars are made out of metal. As Freadman and Miller have pointed out, "ideology and text are not determinate objects in the way that most ordinary instances of raw materials and products (say, steel and a car) are,"[6] and a similar problem occurs with the idea that readers "consume" textual commodities. How, for example, in the role of consumer, does one enforce one's consumer rights? If I buy an electric toaster that does not work, the device goes back to the shop and money is refunded. But can I do that with *Paradise Lost*? No. *Paradise Lost* is a commodity in a fundamentally different sense from an electric toaster and in a sense that cultural studies—in seeking a logical consistency and an explanatory code for all commodities—must opt to underplay. Its commodity status is only metaphorically and not literally described by the Althusserian-Marxist model.[7] In order to get literary texts to correspond to commodities, or literary works to correspond to texts, other elements in the situational equation have to be frozen. Examination shows they are fluid. They differ according to the interactions of expectation and intent that apply to their different situations.

This distinction leads to a much more specialized role for cultural studies than criticism "proper" perhaps ever had. In practice, of course, the identity of the material of cultural studies is as much governed by implicit understandings, by hierarchical habits, by suppositions as the definition of literature or criticism is, and these objects are controlled by conventions of choice that are similarly undefinitive. As a study of "popular" culture, cultural studies is therefore most often confined unaccountably to particular modes of the popular—television and advertisements rather than gardening, goldfish breeding, or pigeon fancying, so that popular artifacts and practices are selected to be "read," but not judged, according to tacit criteria of selection. In this, cultural studies seems at odds with its founding aims and with the power of the metaphors of "opening up" and "breaking down" that logically justify its important claims. As others have observed,[8] cultural studies in practice seems strangely shy of the mass of cultural objects that make up the world around us, including the spirit of popular judgmentalism that guides the principles of consumer choice, and is evidenced in phone-in voting to shows on radio or TV. In this, the appropriation of literary criticism by cultural studies seems less like a revolution, and more like the last act in a drama of corporate appropriation.

Notes

INTRODUCTION

1. "It is an odd feature of the extensive discussions in contemporary literary theory," notes John Searle, "that the authors sometimes make very general remarks about the nature of language, without making use of principles and distinctions that are commonly accepted in logic, linguistics, and the philosophy of language." "Literary Theory and Its Discontents," in *Beyond Poststructuralism*, ed. Wendell V. Harris (University Park: Pennsylvania State University Press, 1996), 102.

2. H. Aram Veeser presumes that this movement "challenges the norm of disembodied objectivity to which humanists have increasingly aspired"—and thus constructs a straw man out of the critical past. See the introduction to *The New Historicism*, ed. H. Aram Veeser (New York and London: Routledge, 1989), ix.

3. I take the expression from John M. Ellis, *Literature Lost: Social Agendas and the Corruption of the Humanities* (New Haven and London: Yale University Press, 1997). This work has provoked both commendation and strong hostility. For the latter see the review by Joseph Carroll, *TLS*, 12 June 1998, 27, who claims that Ellis "fails to realize that in their combined effect the three chief elements of current criticism—deconstruction, Marxism and Freudianism—constitute a comprehensive explanatory system." Something of the heat generated by Ellis's book can be felt from the stinging rebuttal to Carroll's review by Robert Wilcocks, who writes that "The 'un-naïve' reader will have realised [in reading Carroll] that this review is an ingenious attempt to sabotage clear thinking in the humanities." He says, "How anyone in the 1990s can write that 'Freudianism provides an explanatory apparatus for individual identity and sexual and family relations' is beyond me" (*TLS*, 31 July 1998, 15).

More recently, Ellis's volume has been conscripted in support of arguments used by Martin C. Battestin to launch his attack on New Historicist criticism in "Historical Criticism and the Question of Contemporaneity." See *AJ* 12 (2001): 361–79. But see also the reply by Jill Campbell in the same volume, "In Defense of Literature: A Response to Martin C. Battestin" (381–98), on behalf of modern critical movements. The present flowering of Theory is for Campbell a testimony to literature's own inexhaustible value; it is more a response to the richness of the literary than the expression of the theorists' will to dominate and exclude.

4. Such a history might begin with Ben Jonson's remark continued in the epigraph to this book: "To judge of poets is only the faculty of poets; and not of all poets, but the best." See *Timber or Discoveries: Made Upon Men and Matter* (1641; reprint, London: Dent, 1951), 123. René Wellek has surveyed the European history of the term "criticism" as it

replaced "poetics" and "rhetoric" and from its origins in the Greek *krités* or "judge," and he implies a role for Pope's conception within the modern extension of the term. He points out that *kritikós,* meaning "a judge of literature," "occurs as early as the end of the fourth century B.C.," but that "the expansion of the term [criticism] to include both the whole system of literary theory and what we would today call practical criticism and day-to-day reviewing happened only in the seventeenth century." See *Concepts of Criticism* (New Haven and London: Yale University Press, 1963), 22, 24.

5. Quotations from the *Essay* are taken from *Pastoral Poetry and "An Essay on Criticism,"* ed. E. Audra and Aubrey Williams, vol. 1 of *The Twickenham Edition of the Poems of Alexander Pope* (London: Methuen, 1961). Line numbers are given in the text.

6. Paul Hernadi, ed., *What Is Criticism?* (Bloomington: Indiana University Press, 1981); F. E. Sparshott, *The Concept of Criticism* (Oxford: Oxford University Press, 1967).

7. M. C. Beardsley, *Aesthetics: Problems in the Philosophy of Criticism* (New York: Harcourt, Brace, and World, 1958).

8. Stein Haugom Olsen, *The Structure of Literary Understanding* (Cambridge: Cambridge University Press, 1978) and *The End of Literary Theory* (Cambridge: Cambridge University Press, 1987); John M. Ellis, *Against Deconstruction* (Princeton: Princeton University Press, 1989) and *Literature Lost;* Richard Freadman and Seumas Miller, *Re-Thinking Theory: A Critique of Contemporary Literary Theory and an Alternative Account* (Cambridge: Cambridge University Press, 1992); Peter Lamarque and Stein Haugon Olsen, *Truth, Fiction, and Literature: A Philosophical Perspective* (Oxford: Oxford University Press, 1994); John Harwood, *Eliot to Derrida: The Poverty of Interpretation* (London: Macmillan, 1995); Wendell V. Harris, *Literary Meaning: Reclaiming the Study of Literature* (London: Macmillan, 1996); Peter Lamarque, *Fictional Points of View* (Ithaca and London: Cornell University Press, 1996); Valentine Cunningham, *Reading after Theory* (Oxford: Blackwell, 2002); Frederick Crews, "In the Big House of Theory," *NYRB,* 29 May 1986, 36–40; W. W. Robson, *"The Definition of Literature" and Other Essays* (Cambridge: Cambridge University Press, 1982).

9. They can be supplemented by essays taking a more or less satirical approach to the topic of Theory. For a very pungent example, see Cedric Watts, "Bottom's Children: The Fallacies of Structuralist, Post-structuralist, and Deconstructionist Literary Theory," in *Reconstructing Literature,* ed. Laurence Lerner (Oxford: Blackwell, 1983), 20–35; also Raymond Tallis, "The Survival of Theory," in *Theorrhoea and After* (New York: St. Martin's Press, 1999), 29–72.

10. Cunningham, *Reading after Theory,* esp. 13–37.

11. I refer in particular to Hans Robert Jauss, "Literary History as a Challenge to Literary Theory," *NLH* 2 (1970–71): 7–37; Hans-Georg Gadamer, *Truth and Method,* trans. Joel Weinsheimer and Donald G. Marshall, revised 2d ed. (London: Sheed and Ward, 1989); Paul Ricoeur, *Time and Narrative,* trans. Kathleen Blamey and David Pellauer, 3 vols. (Chicago and London: University of Chicago Press, 1984–88). For Jauss, neither Marxist aesthetics nor the historical methods of philological scholarship "recognizes the true role of the reader to whom the literary work is primarily addressed, a role as unalterable for aesthetic as for historical appreciation" (7–8). But the aesthetic and literary nature of the *critical* text permits the same principle to be applied to critical history. Both Jauss and Gadamer are indebted to the development of "the logic of question and answer" as set forth by Collingwood in *An Autobiography* (Oxford: Oxford University Press, 1939).

12. See, for example, the essay by Dominick LaCapra entitled "Writing the History of Criticism Now?" in *History and Criticism* (Ithaca and London: Cornell University Press, 1985), 95–114. LaCapra appeals to Jacques Derrida as a historical model for understanding the critical past, where "the principal condition of history would be the movement of repeti-

tion with difference" (105), but he does not recall—as he might easily have done—the Collingwoodian and Gadamerian concepts of "reenactment," which equally support his point.

13. Crews notes as a unifying principle that "while the gurus of theoreticism differ sharply among themselves, in another sense they are much alike: all of them neglect or openly dismiss the principle of intersubjective skepticism, the core of any empirical commitment." Crews, "In the Big House of Theory," 39.

14. One of the most forceful analyses is John M. Ellis's *Against Deconstruction*. The present book follows through on some of the consequences of this analysis for criticism generally and for eighteenth-century critical history in particular, and works from the premise that the deconstruction of deconstruction has in practice *happened*.

15. The effect of this "culturalization" has been increasingly to interpret the study of literature as a means to ends beyond literature itself—"life" in one specifically cultural, periodized, and thus ultimately historicist sense. On the evidence of the broadened "postdisciplinary" Anglophone literature of criticism of recent years, the philosophical affinities of criticism with continental philosophy have often occluded or ignored the role of British philosophical traditions, even where they bear most closely on literary and critical problems in English literature and themselves overlap with continental thought. For a compensatory account of Collingwood's pertinence to mainstream British literary criticism in the twentieth century, see my "'The True Creative Mind': R. G. Collingwood's Critical Humanism," *BJA* 41, no. 3 (July 2001): 293–311.

16. Frank Kermode, "Art among the Ruins," *NYRB*, 5 July 2001, 59–63.

17. Robin Headlam Wells, Glenn Burgess, and Rowland Wymer have noted that in the first half of the twentieth century "historicist thinking, in literature as well as history departments, was a good deal more subtle than New Historicists and Cultural Materialists have been generally willing to acknowledge." See the preface to *Neo-Historicism: Studies in Renaissance Literature, History, and Politics 5* (Cambridge: D. S. Brewer, 2000): xi.

18. F. R. Leavis, "Johnson as Critic," *Scrutiny* 12, no. 3 (1944): 187.

19. See, for example, G. F. Parker's chapter entitled "Taking Johnson Seriously" in his *Johnson's Shakespeare* (Oxford: Clarendon Press, 1989), 1–14.

20. Raman Selden and Stan Smith, "General Editors' Preface," in *Feminist Literary Criticism*, ed. Mary Eagleton (London and New York: Longman, 1991), iv.

21. For a fuller discussion of this trend, see my essays on the criticism of Terry Eagleton and of Catherine Belsey, which are chapters 1 and 2 of *Modern Critics in Practice: Critical Portraits of British Literary Critics* (New York: St. Martin's Press, 1990). For a discussion of Belsey's relation to Leavis, see Gary Day, "Leavis and Post-Structuralism," in *F. R. Leavis: Essays and Documents,* ed. Ian MacKillop and Richard Storer (Sheffield, U.K.: Sheffield Academic Press, 1995), 174–89.

22. For an elaboration of this problem see Raymond Tallis's "Preface to the Second Edition, Theorrhoea 1988–1995: The Band Plays On," in *Not Saussure: A Critique of Post-Saussurean Literary Theory* (London: Macmillan, 1995), x–xxiii.

23. On recent disputes over the politics of truth, see Gerald Graff: "This debate has not progressed in twenty-five years; today the opposing sides continue to talk past each other without hearing what's being said." "Preface to the 1995 Edition," in *Literature against Itself: Literary Ideas in Modern Society* (Chicago: Elephant Paperbacks, 1995), xv.

24. As prominent and influential examples of poststructuralist "Renaissance Studies" see, for example, Catherine Belsey, *The Subject of Tragedy: Identity and Difference in Renaissance Drama* (London and New York: Methuen, 1985); Jonathan Dollimore and Alan Sinfield, eds., *Political Shakespeare: New Essays in Cultural Materialism* (Manchester: Manchester University Press, 1985); and Howard Felperin, *Beyond Deconstruction: The Uses and Abuses of Literary Theory* (Oxford: Clarendon Press, 1985) (on Shakespeare's

Sonnets). Foucaultian explorations of power and sexuality combine with scholarly refurbishment of the "Early Modern Period" in Stephen Greenblatt's *Renaissance Self-Fashioning: From More to Shakespeare* (Chicago and London: University of Chicago Press, 1980).

25. Evidence of the *desirability* of this fragmentation within critical subcommunities is suggested by Stanley Fish's reply to M. H. Abrams's attack on deconstructionists' private strategies of interpretation: "What Abrams and those who agree with him do not realize is that communication occurs only *within* such a system (or context, or situation, or interpretive community) and that understanding achieved by two or more persons is specific to that system and determinate only within its confines." See *Is There a Text in This Class?: The Authority of Interpretive Communities* (Cambridge: Harvard University Press, 1980), 304. One might respond that as far as some schools of criticism are unable to speak to other critics in other schools, or to readers and writers more generally, they have relinquished their raison d'être as explicators and communicators of literature and criticism.

26. See John Gross, afterword (1991) to *The Rise and Fall of the Man of Letters: Aspects of English Literary Life since 1800* (1969; reprint, Harmondsworth, England: Penguin Books, 1991), 321–35; and Bernard Bergonzi, *Exploding English* (Oxford: Oxford University Press, 1990). The phrase "movement slogans" is Frederick Crews's.

27. Robson, *"Definition of Literature" and Other Essays*, viii.

28. Ellis, *Against Deconstruction*, 158.

29. Wendell V. Harris, in the introduction to *Beyond Poststructuralism*, suggests that "what is needed is not another pretentious all-embracing theory, not another attempt at making it all new, but a cleansing of the stables together with a return to thinking about what makes literature valuable, what makes it worthy of a place in the curriculum" (xii).

Chapter 1. Defining Literature/Defining Criticism

1. Conversely, as Jonathan Culler has recently noted, "Investigations of the nature of literature seem to have functioned above all as moves in arguments about critical method." See "The Literary in Theory," in *What's Left of Theory? New Work on the Politics of Literary Theory*, ed. Judith Butler, John Guillory, and Kendall Thomas (New York: Routledge, 2000), 276.

2. Christopher Butler, "What Is a Literary Work?" *NLH* 5 (1973): 17, notes that "Any critic or critical theorist . . . must be in a position to accept or reject some description of his subject matter. But the difficulty for most critics . . . lies in giving some general specification which will be critically useful." He concludes that a literary work is institutionally constituted by the circumstances governing its production "and guaranteeing its relationship to human purposes" (29).

3. An exhaustive treatment of vague terms—to which I shall return in discussing Pope's account of "criticism" in his *Essay*—can be found in Timothy Williamson, *Vagueness* (London and New York: Routledge, 1994). See esp. chapter 2, "The Ideal of Precision," 36–69.

4. The distinction between "propositions" and "absolute presuppositions," the latter being logically prior to the former and the metaphysical basis for questions of this kind, was definitively explored by Collingwood in *An Essay on Metaphysics* (Oxford: Clarendon Press, 1940). See esp. chapter 4, "On Presupposing," and chapter 5, "The Science of Absolute Presuppositions." The implications for the theory of history of this Collingwoodian distinction have been amplified in Rex Martin's extensive introduction to his revised edition of *An Essay on Metaphysics* (Oxford: Clarendon Press, 1998), xv–ci. Martin's edition represents an important reentry point for Collingwoodian concepts into current theory of criticism and the philosophy of its historical mode.

5. To this list one might add (from the continental tradition) the chapter entitled "The Notion of Literature" in Tzvetan Todorov's *Genres in Discourse*, trans. Catherine Porter (Cambridge: Cambridge University Press, 1990), 1–12. Todorov critiques definitions of literature under the headings of the "functional" and the "structural," and successively as "imitation," "fiction," the "beautiful," and so on, in order to deny the "structural notion of 'literature'" (11) in favor of "the theory of discourse and . . . the analysis of its genres" (12). There are many other important contributions to the theme of defining literature. See, for example, the indispensable collection of essays edited by Paul Hernadi that appeared under the title *What Is Literature?* (Bloomington: Indiana University Press, 1978). In common with popular discussions of "literature" by Hillis Miller and Peter Widdowson, all such treatments engage with a subdivision of the problem posed by Tolstoy in *What Is Art?* (1898) and by numerous professional aestheticians. For a recent account of various attempts to address the problem of art (including surveys of "Antiessential," "Functional," "Procedural," "Institutional," "Historical," and "Intentional" definitions), see Stephen Davies, *Definitions of Art* (Ithaca and London: Cornell University Press, 1991).

6. René Wellek and Austin Warren, *Theory of Literature* (1949; reprint, Harmondsworth, England: Penguin Books, 1993), 22.

7. John M. Ellis, *The Theory of Literary Criticism: A Logical Analysis* (Berkeley: University of California Press, 1974), 24n.

8. An unusually thorough exploration of this question has since appeared in Lamarque and Olsen's *Truth, Fiction, and Literature*. See also Lamarque, *Fictional Points of View*.

9. Robson, *"Definition of Literature" and Other Essays*, 3.

10. Terry Eagleton, *Literary Theory: An Introduction* (Oxford: Blackwell, 1983), 3, 4.

11. In *Literature Lost*, Ellis claims that Eagleton fails to understand the logic of definition. One might alternatively suggest that Eagleton comprehends only a simplistic logic—one prey to the fallacy of the excluded middle.

12. Eagleton's notion of canon formation has affinities with that of Barbara Herrnstein Smith, "Contingencies of Value," in *Canons,* ed. Robert von Hallberg (Chicago and London: University of Chicago Press, 1984), 5–39, and is similarly political. Critiques of the political grounds of canonization can be found in Willie van Peer, "Canon Formation: Ideology or Aesthetic Quality?" *BJA* 36, no. 2 (April 1996): 97–108; Harold Bloom, chapter 1 ("An Elegy for the Canon") of *The Western Canon: The Books and School of the Ages* (New York: Harcourt Brace, 1994), 15–41; and Stein Haugom Olsen, "The Canon and Artistic Failure," *BJA* 41, no. 3 (July 2001): 261–78.

13. Imre Salusinszky, *Criticism in Society* (New York and London: Methuen New Accents, 1987), 1.

14. This phrase is used pejoratively by Arnold, and in a different, neutral sense by I. A. Richards.

15. Matthew Arnold, "The Function of Criticism at the Present Time" (1864), reprinted in *The Oxford Authors Matthew Arnold*, ed. Miriam Allott and Robert H. Super (Oxford: Oxford University Press, 1986), 327–28.

16. T. S. Eliot, "The Function of Criticism" (1923), reprinted in *Selected Essays* (London: Faber and Faber, 1932), 24–25.

17. T. S. Eliot, "The Frontiers of Criticism" (1956), reprinted in *On Poetry and Poets* (London: Faber and Faber, 1957), 115.

18. See Yvor Winters, *The Function of Criticism: Problems and Exercises* (1957; reprint, London: Routledge and Kegan Paul, 1962). Winters "defines" the function of criticism implicitly as part of his attempt to perform it.

19. See F. R. Leavis, "The Responsible Critic or the Function of Criticism at Any Time," *Scrutiny* 19 (1953): 162–83; reprinted in *A Selection from "Scrutiny"* (Cambridge: Cambridge University Press, 1968), 2:280–303. According to Ian MacKillop, Leavis planned

an unwritten book on the subject of criticism's function. See *F. R. Leavis: A Life in Criticism* (London: Allen Lane, 1995), 298. The book was to include past work on Johnson, Coleridge, and Arnold, "with chapters added on Eliot and Lawrence. He wanted a concentrated work that would present 'an Idea, and (in my way) not an abstract one.'"

20. Terry Eagleton, *The Function of Criticism: From the Spectator to Post-Structuralism* (London: Verso, 1984), 123–24.

21. I. A. Richards, *The Principles of Literary Criticism* (1924; reprint, London: Routledge, 1989), 1.

22. Northrop Frye, "Polemical Introduction," in *Anatomy of Criticism: Four Essays* (Princeton: Princeton University Press, 1957), 1–6. This essay first appeared as "The Function of Criticism at the Present Time," *University of Toronto Quarterly,* October 1949.

23. Roland Barthes, "What Is Criticism?" (1963), reprinted in *Critical Essays*, trans. Richard Howard (Evanston, Ill.: Northwestern University Press, 1972), 258.

24. Lamarque and Olsen, *Truth, Fiction, and Literature,* 332.

25. Oscar Wilde, "The Critic as Artist" (1891), in *The Complete Works of Oscar Wilde* (Glasgow: Harper Collins, 1994), 1125.

26. Frye, "Polemical Introduction," 8. For John M. Ellis, "The prevailing critical consensus . . . has long insisted on pluralism, on the value of different critical viewpoints, and on criticism's lacking the character of a science" (*Against Deconstruction*, 155).

27. John M. Ellis, "The Logic of the Question 'What Is Criticism?,'" in Hernadi, *What Is Criticism?*, 18–19.

28. R. G. Collingwood, *An Essay on Philosophical Method* (1933; reprint, Bristol: Thoemmes Press, 1995), 92.

Chapter 2. On Definition and Debate

1. In the numbered list that follows, and with the exception of item 7, the italics are mine.

2. Arnold, "The Function of Criticism at the Present Time," 325.

3. Wilde, "The Critic as Artist," 1125.

4. T. S. Eliot, "The Perfect Critic," in *The Sacred Wood: Essays on Poetry and Criticism* (1920; reprint, London: Routledge, 1989), 15.

5. I. A. Richards, preface to *Principles of Literary Criticism* (1924; reprint, London: Routledge, 1989), vii.

6. I. A. Richards, *Practical Criticism: A Study of Literary Judgment* (1929; reprint, London: Routledge, 1991), 11.

7. R. G. Cox, "Auden as Critic and Poet," *Scrutiny* 18, no. 2 (autumn 1951): 159.

8. Cleanth Brooks, "The Formalist Critic," *Kenyon Review* 13 (1951): 71–81, reprinted in *Twentieth-Century Literary Theory: A Reader,* ed. K. M. Newton (London: Macmillan, 1988), 45.

9. Frye, "Polemical Introduction," 12; 16.

10. Wellek, *Concepts of Criticism*, 316–17.

11. E. D. Hirsch Jr., "Intrinsic Criticism," in *Validity in Interpretation* (New Haven: Yale University Press, 1967), 144.

12. Barthes, *Critical Essays*, 260.

13. M. C. Beardsley, *The Possibility of Criticism* (Detroit: Wayne State University Press, 1970), 11.

14. Georges Poulet, "The Self and Other in Critical Consciousness," *Diacritics* 2 (1972): 46–50, reprinted in Newton, *Twentieth-Century Literary Theory*, 82, 84.

15. George Steiner, "F. R. Leavis," in *Twentieth Century Literary Criticism: A Reader,* ed. David Lodge (London and New York: Longman, 1972), 626.
16. Harold Bloom, *The Anxiety of Influence: A Theory of Poetry* (New York: Oxford University Press, 1973), 96.
17. Francis Mulhern, *The Moment of Scrutiny* (London: New Left Books, 1979), 331.
18. John Carey, "Viewpoint from the *TLS*" (1980), reprinted in *Original Copy: Selected Reviews and Journalism, 1969–1986* (London: Faber and Faber, 1987), 29.
19. Clive James, "These Staggering Questions," *London Review of Books* (1980), reprinted in *From the Land of Shadows* (London: Pan Books, 1983), 205.
20. Edward Said, *The World, the Text, and the Critic* (London: Faber and Faber, 1984), 25, 51.
21. H. A. Mason, "An Introduction to Literary Criticism by Way of Sidney's *Apologie for Poetrie*," *CQ* 12, nos. 2 and 3 (1983): 79, 86.
22. H. A. Mason, "The Miraculous Birth or The Founding of Modern European Literary Criticism," *CQ* 11, no. 2 (1982): 297.
23. Chris Baldick, *Criticism and Literary Theory, 1890 to the Present* (New York and London: Longman, 1996), 3.
24. For an analysis of "intraverbal equations" of this type, see William Empson, "A Is B," in *The Structure of Complex Words* (1951; reprint, Harmondsworth, England: Penguin Books, 1995), 350–74.
25. See R. G. Collingwood, *The Principles of Art* (1938; reprint, Oxford: Oxford University Press, 1958), 1: "It is one of those problems where what we want to do is to clarify and systematize ideas we already possess." See also his "Preliminary Discussion: The Idea of a Philosophy of Something, and, in Particular, a Philosophy of History" (1927), reprinted in his *The Idea of History*, ed. Jan van der Dussen (Oxford: Oxford University Press, 1994), 342: "The essence of history . . . is an open secret in the sense that every historical critic believes himself, rightly or wrongly, to possess it, to grasp it as an immanent criterion in his everyday work."
26. Ludwig Wittgenstein, "Lectures on Aesthetics," in *Lectures and Conversations on Aesthetics, Psychology, and Religious Belief*, ed. Cyril Barrett (Oxford: Blackwell, 1966), 1.
27. See C. K. Ogden and I. A Richards, "The Theory of Definition," chapter 6 of *The Meaning of Meaning* (New York: Harcourt Brace, 1956), 123. See also the comment that "no one who does not believe with Nansen's Greenland Eskimos 'that there is a spiritual affinity between two people of the same name', can fail to see the futility of . . . attempts to define by Essence" (109n).
28. Said, *World, the Text, and the Critic*, 26.
29. Cox, "Auden as Critic and Poet," 159.
30. Barthes, *Critical Essays*, 260.
31. T. S. Eliot, "The Age of Dryden," in *The Use of Poetry and the Use of Criticism* (London: Faber and Faber, 1933), 60.
32. Terry Eagleton, *Criticism and Ideology: A Study in Marxist Literary Theory* (London: New Left Books, 1976), 43.
33. Harris, *Literary Meaning*, 209.
34. Collingwood, *Idea of History*, 338.
35. Richards, *Practical Criticism*, 188.
36. Morris Weitz, *"Hamlet" and the Philosophy of Literary Criticism* (London: Faber and Faber, 1965), 318.
37. For a collection of attempts to answer the question see Hernadi, *What Is Criticism?* As observed in the previous chapter, John M. Ellis queries the logic of the question-answer

approach to definition as unclear regarding the kind of answer that would be appropriate and satisfying: explanatory, factual, or normative. (Ellis, "The Logic of the Question 'What Is Criticism?'" 15–29).

38. See Searle, "Literary Theory and Its Discontents," 129.

39. D. H. Lawrence, "John Galsworthy" (1928), reprinted in *Selected Literary Criticism*, ed. Anthony Beal (1956; reprint, London, Heinemann, 1967), 118–19. The case against criticism as science has won powerful proponents in the twentieth century. T. S. Eliot echoes Lawrence in asserting the danger of pursuing criticism as if it were a science, "which it can never be." See Eliot, "The Frontiers of Criticism," 117.

40. In *Working with Structuralism: Essays and Reviews on Nineteenth- and Twentieth-Century Literature* (London: Routledge, 1981), David Lodge takes issue with Lawrence's claim that criticism can never be a science: "I would maintain—and I think most academic literary critics would share this view—that if the critical account is to be, in Lawrence's words, 'reasoned', it must involve the classifying and analysing which he dismissed so contemptuously, and even a certain amount of jargon." This riposte avoids the point that Lawrence is doing some classifying in his own right by saying that criticism "can never be a science" (3).

41. For a discussion of criticism within these two paradigms of knowledge, see *The Arts and Sciences of Criticism*, ed. David Fuller and Patricia Waugh (Oxford: Oxford University Press, 1999): "All of the essays [in this volume] are in some way about what kind of knowledge literature is or claims (implicitly) to be, and how far similar answers to this question predicate comparable conclusions about what criticism should be" (1).

42. John M. Ellis, "The Definition of Literature," chapter 2 of *Theory of Literary Criticism*, 50. A more politically conscious version of this definition of literature, though not specifically criticism, is given by Eagleton, *Literary Theory*, 11. The relationship between these two views has been discussed in chapter 1.

43. See, for example, James's "*Daniel Deronda*: A Conversation" (1876), reprinted in *Henry James: The Critical Muse: Selected Literary Criticism*, ed. Roger Gard (Harmondsworth, England: Penguin, 1987), 104–21. See also Wilde, "The Critic as Artist," 1108–55.

44. See the afterword to this volume.

45. In "The Study of Poetry," originally published as the general introduction to *The English Poets*, ed. T. H. Ward (London, 1880).

46. Collingwood, "Preliminary Discussion," 357.

47. Kant discusses "The Transcendental Ideas" in section 2 of his "First Book of the Transcendental Dialectic." See the *Critique of Pure Reason* (1781), trans. Norman Kemp Smith (1929; reprint, London: Macmillan, 1993), 315–26.

48. See W. W. Robson, "Evaluative Criticism," chapter 3 of *"Definition of Literature" and Other Essays*, 56.

49. Collingwood, *Idea of History*, 347.

Chapter 3. Criticism, Function, Category, Complement

1. Robson, *"Definition of Literature" and Other Essays*, 1.
2. Ellis, "The Logic of the Question 'What is Criticism?'," 23.
3. Collingwood, *Principles of Art*, 7.
4. Foucault has argued that the idea of the "author" is *of itself* an oppressive concept, another form of inhibiting power: "[H]e is a certain functional principle by which, in our culture, one limits, excludes, and chooses; in short, by which one impedes the free circulation, the free manipulation, the free composition, decomposition, and recomposition of fiction." Michel Foucault, "What Is an Author?" in *The Foucault Reader*, ed. Paul Rabinow (Harmondsworth, England: Penguin, 1991), 119.

5. I. A. Richards, "The Definition of a Poem," in *Principles of Literary Criticism* (1989 reprint ed.), 178.
6. F. R. Leavis, "Mutually Necessary," in *The Critic as Anti-Philosopher: Essays and Papers by F. R. Leavis,* ed. G. Singh (London: Chatto and Windus, 1982), 207.
7. For an idea of this malaise as it is deepened by the local systems of examining critical writing in British schools, see Alan Brown, "On the Subject of Practical Criticism," *CQ* 28, no. 4 (1999): 293–327. For the relationship between the pedagogy of Theory and recent systems of bureaucratic control in school and university critical education, see my "'More Creative than Creation': On the Idea of Criticism and the Student Critic," *Arts and Humanities in Higher Education* 1, no. 1 (June 2002): 59–71.
8. Arnold, "The Function of Criticism at the Present Time," 325.
9. Eliot, "The Function of Criticism at the Present Time," 331.
10. Eliot, *Selected Essays*, 24.
11. Ezra Pound, "Date Line" (1934), reprinted in *Literary Essays of Ezra Pound,* ed. T. S. Eliot (London: Faber and Faber, 1954), 75.
12. Ibid.
13. F. R. Leavis, "Literary Criticism and Philosophy," in *The Common Pursuit* (London: Chatto and Windus, 1952), 213.
14. Eagleton, *Function of Criticism*, 123.
15. Eliot, *Selected Essays*, 24.
16. Or *as* a function, in the way that attempts have sometimes been made to define literature. E.g., Antony Easthope, *Literary into Cultural Studies* (London: Routledge, 1991), 53: "Literature exists not as an essence, an entity, a thing, but as a process, a function." See in this connection the discussion of the definability of literature in chapter 1 of the present study.
17. T. S. Eliot, "To Criticize the Critic" (1961), in *"To Criticize the Critic" and Other Writings* (London: Faber and Faber, 1965), 11–13.
18. Pound, "Date Line," 74–75.
19. Frye, *Anatomy of Criticism*, 341.
20. See, for example, Eagleton, *Literary Theory;* Raman Selden, *A Reader's Guide to Contemporary Literary Theory* (Brighton: Harvester Press, 1985); Ann Jefferson and David Robey, eds., *Modern Literary Theory: A Comparative Introduction* (1982; reprint, London: Batsford, 1993).
21. Eliot, "The Perfect Critic," 15.
22. See Frye, "Polemical Introduction," 12, 16.
23. Bloom, *Anxiety of Influence*, 96.
24. James, "These Staggering Questions," 205.
25. Said, *The World, the Text, and the Critic*, 26.
26. Richards, *Principles of Literary Criticism*, 2.
27. Ludwig Wittgenstein, *The Blue and Brown Books* (1958; reprint, Oxford: Blackwell, 1993), 25.
28. Eliot, "The Frontiers of Criticism," 104.
29. Mason, "An Introduction to Literary Criticism," 82.

Chapter 4. "Outside the Academic Fold"

1. Gross, *The Rise and Fall of the Man of Letters*, 329.
2. John Newton, "Literary Criticism, Universities, Murder," *CQ* 5, no. 4 (summer/autumn 1971): 335.
3. Gross, *Rise and Fall of the Man of Letters*, 330.

4. In so saying, I mean to reiterate and juxtapose perceptions of those sympathetic to Theory and of those hostile or resistant to it.
5. Hans Keller, *Criticism* (London: Faber and Faber, 1987), 93.
6. Terry Eagleton, *Marxism and Literary Criticism* (London: Methuen, 1976), 59.
7. Eliot, "To Criticize the Critic," 12.
8. Carey, *Original Copy*.
9. See, for example, John Fiske, *Reading the Popular* (Boston: Unwin Hyman, 1989).
10. John Carey, "Books, Raw and Cooked," in *Original Copy*, 238.
11. Clive James, review of *Critical Understanding: The Powers and Limits of Pluralism*, by Wayne C. Booth, *London Review of Books* (1980), reprinted as "These Staggering Questions," in *From the Land of Shadows*, 203.
12. In the title of this section I allude to Jeremy Treglown and Bridget Bennett, eds., *Grub Street and the Ivory Tower: Literary Journalism and Literary Scholarship from Fielding to the Internet* (Oxford: Clarendon Press, 1998)—a collection of recent essays by Valentine Cunningham, Hermione Lee, Majorie Perloff, Karl Miller, et al. on different aspects of the journalism/academic divide.
13. Antony Easthope, *British Post-Structuralism since 1968* (London: Routledge, 1988), xii; Eagleton, preface to *Literary Theory*; Julia Kristeva, *Desire in Language: A Semiotic Approach to Literature and Art* (Oxford: Blackwell, 1981), vii; Jacques Derrida, *Of Grammatology*, trans. Gayatri Chakravorty Spivak (Baltimore: Johns Hopkins University Press, 1974), 6.
14. Whether theoretical developments are consistent with theorists' sustaining a sufficient political influence and engagement has been taken up in Butler, Guillory, and Thomas, *What's Left of Theory?*
15. Mason, "An Introduction to Literary Criticism," 83.
16. John Carey, *The Intellectuals and the Masses: Pride and Prejudice among the Literary Intelligentsia, 1880–1939* (London: Faber and Faber, 1992), 215.
17. Leonard Woolf, "Hunting the Highbrow" (1927), reprinted in *CQ* 24, no. 1 (1995): 80–87.

CHAPTER 5. CRITICISM, VALUATION, AND USEFUL PURPOSE

1. Sparshott, *Concept of Criticism*, 119–20 rightly distinguishes between "evaluation" as "estimating" and the verb "to value" meaning put a price on something, but admits that "these distinctions . . . are not reflected in actual usage with any precision."
2. I. A. Richards, preface to *Principles of Literary Criticism* (1989 reprint ed.), vii.
3. F. R. Leavis, "Valuation in Criticism," in *"Valuation in Criticism" and Other Essays*, ed. G. Singh (Cambridge: Cambridge University Press, 1986), 276.
4. Samuel Johnson, "Life of Pope" (1781), in *Lives of the English Poets*, ed. George Birkbeck Hill, 3 vols. (Oxford: Clarendon Press, 1905), 3:94.
5. E. D. Hirsch, "Evaluation as Knowledge," in *The Aims of Interpretation* (Chicago: University of Chicago Press, 1976), 108.
6. Terry Eagleton, "Introduction: What Is Literature?," in *Literary Theory*, 13.
7. This possibility is discussed, and dismissed as an argument against nonevaluative criticism, by W. W. Robson, "Evaluative Criticism, and Criticism without Evaluation," in *"Definition of Literature" and Other Essays*, 50: "It would apply, *mutatis mutandis*, to any field of enquiry."
8. Barbara Herrnstein Smith, *Contingencies of Value: Alternative Perspectives for Critical Theory* (Cambridge: Harvard University Press, 1988), 42.

9. Robert Graves, *Goodbye to All That* (1929; reprint, Harmondsworth, England: Penguin Books, 1981), 240.

10. Smith, *Contingencies of Value*, 19, mentions these critics along with T. S. Eliot and Yvor Winters as examples of "the magisterial mode of literary evaluation."

11. D. H. Lawrence, letter to Edward Garnett, 30 October 1912; to A. W. McLeod, 26 April 1913; to Lady Ottoline Morrell, June 1915; reprinted in *Selected Literary Criticism*, 132, 133, 229, respectively.

12. Frye, "Polemical Introduction," writes: "The first step in developing a genuine poetics is to recognize and get rid of meaningless criticism, or talking about literature in a way that cannot help to build up a systematic structure of knowledge. This includes all the sonorous nonsense that we so often find in critical generalities. . . . It includes all lists of the 'best' novels or poems or writers. . . . all casual, sentimental, and prejudiced value-judgments" (18). It is unclear, perhaps, whether Frye is saying here that all value judgments are necessarily casual, sentimental, and prejudiced, or whether he is just wanting to get rid of those that are.

13. I. A. Richards, "The Critics' Concern with Value," in *Principles of Literary Criticism* (1989 reprint ed.), 26. Richards goes on to say that "The expert in matters of taste is in an awkward position when he differs from the majority."

14. See John Carey, "Viewpoint from the *TLS*," 25. There may be parallels between this idealistic disillusionment with the possibility of an entirely objective or universally valid valuation and twentieth-century criticism's "Quest for the One True Meaning." The latter is surveyed by John Harwood in *Eliot to Derrida:*, 140–59. Cf. also John M. Ellis's account of deconstruction's attack on a naive certainty in preference to some more sophisticated or complex position. *Against Deconstruction*, 138.

15. Peter Widdowson, "'Literary Value' and the Reconstruction of Criticism," *Literature and History* 6, no. 1 (1980): 139. Antony Easthope, "The Question of Literary Value," chapter 3 of *Literary into Cultural Studies*, narrows down the matter to the specific question of "whether the modernist reading as performed by literary study is any indication of literary value" (60).

16. Ludwig Wittgenstein, *On Certainty*, trans. Denis Paul and G. E. M. Anscombe (Oxford: Blackwell, 1969), 59e.

17. Geoffrey Strickland is right to insist that "There is a world of difference . . . between the real objection to what we believe to be true and the merely hypothetical objection that a real objection may be found." See *Structuralism or Criticism? Thoughts on How We Read* (Cambridge: Cambridge University Press, 1981), 62.

18. Smith, *Contingencies of Value*, 3.

19. Eagleton, *Literary Theory*, 13.

20. *The Critical Works of Thomas Rymer*, ed. Curt A. Zimansky (New Haven: Yale University Press, 1956), 164.

21. F. R. Leavis, *Revaluation: Tradition and Development in English Poetry* (1936; reprint, London: Peregrine Books, 1967), 171.

22. John Dryden, "Of Dramatic Poesy: An Essay" (1668), reprinted in *"Of Dramatic Poesy" and Other Critical Essays*, ed. George Watson, 2 vols. (London: Everyman, 1971), 1:67.

23. This is a danger in aesthetic analyses that for the sake of analytic convenience reduce critical judgments to formulas consisting of single statements of the kind "This is good."

24. Keller, *Criticism*, 123.

25. Terry Eagleton, "Value in Art: An Exchange," *New Left Review* 142 (November–December 1983): 76.

26. For a fuller discussion of this issue see the afterword to this volume.
27. Smith, *Contingencies of Value*, 19.
28. Carey, *Original Copy*, 29.
29. *The Life of Samuel Johnson, LL.D.*, ed. John Wilson Croker (London, 1831), 3:337.
30. Olsen, *End of Literary Theory*, has argued along similar lines that "There is, on the part of the reader, an initial expectation of value which the reader brings with him to the work" (154).

CHAPTER 6. CRITICISM AND THE MEANINGS OF "THEORY"

1. See Geoffrey Hartman, "The State of the Art of Criticism," in *The Future of Literary Theory*, ed. Ralph Cohen (London and New York: Routledge, 1989), 86–101.
2. One exception to this rule is the *Norton Anthology of Theory and Criticism*, ed. Vincent B. Leitch (New York and London: W. W. Norton, 2001). Despite a heavy emphasis on twentieth-century material, this volume prints several early essays from as far back as Plato and includes Pope's *Essay on Criticism* in full.
3. Tallis, "Preface to the Second Edition," x–xxiii, notes how little has changed, or is likely to change, in the face of decisive demolitions of theorists' fallacies about art, criticism, language, and reality. For Wendell V. Harris, similarly, "It seems to be one of the characteristics of the field of literary criticism that its practitioners hardly ever explicitly retract any of their previously stated positions." *Beyond Poststructuralism*, xii.
4. John Holloway, "Language, Realism, Subjectivity Objectivity," in Lerner, *Reconstructing Literature*, 60.
5. Harwood, *Eliot to Derrida*, 15, quotes Gerald Graff on the guild mentality of modern scholarship in which "any specialist in a writer or period will be a *promoter* of that writer or period." (See *Professing Literature: An Institutional History* [Chicago: University of Chicago Press, 1987], 228.) It is arguable that this mentality has spread from the treatment of writers and periods to Theory.
6. Samuel Johnson, *Idler* 36 (on "The terrifick diction"), in *The Idler and the Adventurer*, ed. W. J. Bate, John M. Bullitt, and L. F. Powell, vol. 2 of *The Yale Edition of the Works of Samuel Johnson*, ed. John H. Middendorf (New Haven and London: Yale University Press, 1963), 113.
7. Recent examples of the last include K. M. Newton, ed., *Theory into Practice: A Reader in Modern Literary Criticism* (London: Macmillan, 1992); Philip Rice and Patricia Waugh, eds., *Modern Literary Theory: A Reader* (London: Edward Arnold, 1992); and Peter Brooker and Peter Widdowson, eds., *A Practical Reader in Contemporary Literary Theory* (New York: Prentice-Hall, 1996).
8. See Jonson, *Timber or Discoveries: Made upon Men and Matter*, 124.
9. Paul de Man, "The Resistance to Theory" (1982), reprinted in *Modern Criticism and Theory: A Reader*, ed. David Lodge (London and New York: Longman, 1988), 355.
10. Wendell V. Harris, "Theory," in *Dictionary of Concepts in Literary Criticism and Theory* (New York and London: Greenwood Press, 1992), 410.
11. Freadman and Miller, *Re-Thinking Theory*, 196.
12. M. H. Abrams, *A Glossary of Literary Terms*, 6th ed. (London and New York: Harcourt Brace, 1993), 259. Harris, *Literary Meaning*, 133, in turn notes that "In the late 1960s, after discovering that it was useful to speak of 'thematizing,' practitioners moved on to 'theorize' certain aspects of literature and its study."
13. Unless we are being sarcastic, and hinting that the theory in question is unproved, we do not say "According to *a* theory, authorial intention has limited value in the interpretation of texts." What we say is: "According to Theory . . . " In this usage, the writer is

not expected to say which particular "countable" theory or theories he or she has in mind, to name them, or to say what they are "of." The meaning is received without further question.

14. W. J. T. Mitchell, introduction to *Against Theory: Literary Studies and the New Pragmatism,* ed. W. J. T. Mitchell (Chicago: University of Chicago Press, 1985), 6–7.

15. Raman Selden, ed., *From Formalism to Poststructuralism,* vol 8 of *The Cambridge History of Literary Criticism* (Cambridge: Cambridge University Press, 1995), 1–2.

16. De Man, "The Resistance to Theory," 359.

17. Jonathan Culler, *On Deconstruction: Theory and Criticism after Structuralism* (1983; reprint, London: Routledge, 1994), 8.

18. Eagleton, *Literary Theory,* 195–97.

19. See Raman Selden, introduction to *From Formalism to Poststructuralism,* 2; Culler, *On Deconstruction,* 8; Eagleton, *Literary Theory,* 197.

20. Lodge, foreword to *Modern Criticism and Theory,* xi.

21. Christopher Ricks, "Literary Principles as against Theory," in *Essays in Appreciation* (Oxford: Oxford University Press, 1996), 332.

22. Newton, *Twentieth-Century Literary Theory,* 11.

23. Brooker and Widdowson, introduction to *A Practical Reader in Contemporary Literary Theory,* 3.

24. Raymond Williams, *Keywords: A Vocabulary of Culture and Society,* rev. ed. (London: Fontana, 1988), 316–18. Williams's definition is in its turn a counter to the definitions of "theory" and "theorist" recorded in Johnson's *Dictionary* (1755):

> THEORY. *n.s.* Speculation; not practice; scheme; plan or system yet subsisting only in the mind.
> THEORIST. *n.s.* [from *theory*] A speculatist; one given to speculation.

25. Brooker and Widdowson, introduction, 2.

26. Jefferson and Robey, *Modern Literary Theory,* 7.

27. Edward Said, "Traveling Theory," in *The World, the Text, and the Critic,* 241.

28. Culler, *On Deconstruction,* 17.

29. Patrick Parrinder, "Having Your Assumptions Questioned," in *The State of Theory,* ed. Richard Bradford (London: Routledge, 1993), 143.

30. Rice and Waugh, *Modern Literary Theory,* 1.

31. Brooker and Widdowson, *Practical Reader in Contemporary Literary Theory,* 7. Cf. Rice and Waugh's statement of the opt-out veto: "All forms of criticism are founded upon a theory, or an admix of theories, whether they consciously acknowledge that or not" (*Modern Literary Theory,* 1).

32. Terry Eagleton, "The Significance of Theory," in *The Significance of Theory* (Oxford: Blackwell, 1990), 24.

33. Selden, introduction, 1.

34. Helen Taylor "Leaving Parties and Legacies: Reflections across the Binary Divide on a Decade of Englishes," in Bradford, *State of Theory,* 58.

35. Parrinder, "Having Your Assumptions Questioned," 143.

36. Said, *The World, the Text, and the Critic,* 242.

37. See Andrew Marvell, "A Dialogue between the Soul and the Body," in *The Oxford Authors Andrew Marvell* (Oxford: Oxford University Press, 1990), 18–19.

38. Crews writes that "the theory will have demonstrated its cogency if it brings out meaning and coherence in a given text or problem. Of course such bogus experiments succeed every time. All they prove is that any thematic stencil will make its own pattern stand out." "In the Big House of Theory," 42.

39. Freadman and Miller, *Re-Thinking Theory*, 196.
40. Felperin, *Beyond Deconstruction*, 148–49.
41. Harwood, *Eliot to Derrida*, 15.
42. Brooker and Widdowson, *Practical Reader in Contemporary Literary Theory*, 3. K. M. Newton words his point with somewhat more care: "Practice is almost never merely the simple application of theory; applying theory to practice inevitably introduces difference which must have a knock-on effect on theory, thus changing the theory and developing it" (introduction to *Theory into Practice*, 3).

Chapter 7. Criticism, Interpretation, and Judgment

1. Raymond Tallis, "Scholarship Terminable and Interminable: Some Thoughts on the Place of Literary Criticism in a Life of Finite Duration," in *Theorrhoea and After*: "Interpretive criticism gives the critic infinite scope to wheel out his own ideas—not separately tested—and those, more or less digested, of others. Freudian critics, Marxist critics, New Historicist critics, and so on, can slip in their prejudices, resentments, along with the latest ideas that capture their magpie attention, and, by finding them in their author/victims, can advance the most complex, abstract and contentious notions, without having to prove them" (95).

2. Geoffrey H. Hartman, *Saving the Text: Literature/Derrida/Philosophy* (Baltimore and London: Johns Hopkins University Press, 1981).

3. James M. Heath and Michael Payne, introduction to *Text, Interpretation, Theory* (Lewisburg, Pa.: Bucknell University Press, 1985), 11.

4. Sparshott, *Concept of Criticism*, 133.

5. P. D. Juhl, *Interpretation: An Essay on the Philosophy of Literary Criticism* (Princeton: Princeton University Press, 1980).

6. Juhl wrote to contrastive effect of "[t]he sort of statements . . . [that] fall under the category of criticism (in a narrower sense) *as opposed to* interpretation" (ibid., 32, my emphasis). Years earlier, G. Wilson Knight had drawn a distinction between "interpretation" and "criticism" in terms significantly different from the objectivity of philosophical treatments of interpretation: "I would emphasise . . . that poetic 'interpretation' . . . is to be firmly distinguished from 'criticism'. The critic is, and should be, cool and urbane, seeing the poetry he discusses not with the eyes of a lover but as an object; whereas interpretation deliberately immerses itself in its theme and speaks less from the seats of judgement than from the creative centre. It deliberately aims to write of genius from the standpoint not of the reader, but of genius itself; to write of it from *within*. So, while the critic stands on his guard against the lure of the unknown and prefers not to adventure too far from home, interpretation, it must be confessed, is happiest among the vast open spaces of what is, nevertheless, a severely disciplined speculation." G. Wilson Knight, "Prefatory Note," in *The Imperial Theme: Further Interpretations of Shakespeare's Tragedies including the Roman Plays,* 3d ed. (London: Methuen, 1951), vi. In *The Wheel of Fire: Interpretations of Shakespearean Tragedy* (London: Methuen, 1930), Knight had written that "Criticism is a judgement of vision; interpretation a reconstruction of vision" (1).

7. Umberto Eco, with Richard Rorty, Jonathan Culler, and Christine Brooke-Rose, *Interpretation and Overinterpretation*, ed. Stefan Collini (Cambridge: Cambridge University Press, 1992).

8. In Lodge, *Twentieth Century Literary Criticism,* 652–60.

9. Hirsch, *Validity in Interpretation*.

10. Quoted from *The Norton Anthology of English Poetry*, 3d ed. (New York and London: W. W. Norton, 1983), 1361.

11. W. W. Robson, "On Liberty of Interpreting," in *"Definition of Literature" and Other Essays,* 24–25, 27. For Wendell V. Harris, "where the hermeticist's difficulties with the meaning of individual words and sentences are almost wholly artificial, the difficulty of grasping the meaning of a text as a whole is undeniable." *Literary Meaning,* 97.

12. Graff, *Professing Literature,* 233.

13. Johnson, *Preface to Shakespeare* (1765), in *Johnson on Shakespeare,* ed. Arthur Sherbo, vols. 7 and 8 of *The Yale Edition of the Works of Samuel Johnson,* ed. John H. Middendorf (New Haven and London: Yale University Press, 1968), 7:109.

14. Eliot, *On Poetry and Poets,* 109.

15. Johnson, *Johnson on Shakespeare,* 704.

16. Annette Barnes, *On Interpretation: A Critical Analysis* (Oxford: Blackwell, 1988), 3.

17. *The Dunciad,* ed. James Sutherland, vol. 5 of *The Twickenham Edition of the Poems of Alexander Pope* (London: Methuen, 1965), 354.

18. In his foreword to M. H. Abrams's *Doing Things with Texts: Essays in Criticism and Critical Theory* (New York and London: W. W. Norton, 1989), Michael Fischer explains what Abrams means by this term: "This model, often associated with the New Criticism, conceives the paradigmatic critical situation to be an isolated person confronting a single, autonomous work of art and detecting features that are already there, without reference to such 'external' relations as the interests of the perceiver or the truth, usefulness, or morality of the work" (ix).

19. Williams, *Keywords,* 86, s.v. "Criticism."

20. Leavis, "Literary Criticism and Philosophy," 212–13.

21. Raymond Williams, *Keywords,* 86.

22. Olsen, *End of Literary Theory,* 139, 141.

23. William Wordsworth, appendix to the *Lyrical Ballads,* in *The Prose Works of William Wordsworth,* ed. W. J. B. Owen and J. W. Smyser, 3 vols. (Oxford: Clarendon Press, 1974), 1:160–61.

24. Eagleton, *Literary Theory,* 17–18.

25. Dryden, "Of Dramatic Poesy," 1:67.

26. Leavis, *Revaluation,* 171.

27. F. R. Leavis, *New Bearings in English Poetry* (London: Chatto and Windus, 1932), 6.

28. Johnson, *Johnson on Shakespeare,* 703.

29. Letter to Harry Crosby, 6 September 1928, reprinted in Lawrence, *Selected Literary Criticism,* 149.

30. Immanuel Kant, *The Critique of Judgement,* trans. James Creed Meredith (Oxford: Clarendon Press, 1952), 207.

31. Ezra Pound, review of *Love Poems and Others,* by D. H. Lawrence (1913), reprinted in *Literary Essays of Ezra Pound,* 387.

32. Matthew Arnold, preface to *The Poems of Wordsworth* (1879), reprinted in *Essays in Criticism: Second Series,* ed. S. R. Littlewood (1938; reprint, London: Macmillan, 1969), 78–79.

33. Johnson, *Johnson on Shakespeare,* 7:71.

34. See "Evaluation," chapter 4 of Ellis, *Theory of Literary Criticism,* 72–103.

35. Alexander Pope, preface to *The Iliad of Homer* (1715), reprinted in *Translations of Homer,* ed. Maynard Mack, vols. 7–10 of *Twickenham Edition of the Poems of Alexander Pope,* ed. John Butt (London: Methuen, 1967), 7:12.

36. Dryden, "Of Dramatic Poesy," 1:67.

37. Johnson, *Johnson on Shakespeare,* 702, 1011.

38. Samuel Johnson, "Life of Cowley" (1779), reprinted in *Lives,* 1:35.

39. Matthew Arnold, "Milton" (1888), in *Essays in Criticism: Second Series,* 38.

40. T. S. Eliot, "Milton I," in *On Poetry and Poets,* 138.

41. T.S. Eliot, "Shelley and Keats," in *The Use of Poetry and the Use of Criticism*, 100.
42. Leavis, *Revaluation*, 130.
43. Eliot, "Shelley and Keats," 98.
44. Ezra Pound, "The Rev. G. Crabbe, LLB." and "The Future" (1917), in *Literary Essays of Ezra Pound*, 278.
45. W. W. Robson, *Critical Essays* (London: Routledge and Kegan Paul, 1966), 61–62.
46. Johnson, "Life of Pope," 3:222–23.
47. Robson, *Critical Essays*, 110.
48. Ibid., 72.
49. Eliot, "Shelley and Keats," 99–100.
50. Johnson, "Life of Cowley," 1:21.
51. Montaigne, *Essays of Michael Seigneur de Montaigne*, trans. Charles Cotton, 2d. ed. (London, 1963), 2:385.
52. Cited by Samuel Johnson in the *Dictionary* (1755), s.v. "Judgment."
53. Attention to the "social process" of criticism, writes Jonathan Dollimore, "has far-reaching consequences": "To begin with it leads us beyond idealist literary criticism—that preoccupied with supposedly universal truths which find their counterpart in 'man's' essential nature; the criticism in which history, if acknowledged at all, is seen as inessential or a constraint transcended in the affirmation of a transhistorical human condition." See "Shakespeare, Cultural Materialism, and the New Historicism," in Dollimore and Sinfield, *Political Shakespeare*, 4. But this is a false opposition. "History" is not, plainly, "inessential" or "transcended" in literary criticism consonant with philosophical idealism—as the writings of Collingwood, author of *The Idea of History*, demonstrate amply.
54. Alan Tormey, "Critical Judgments," *Theoria* 39 (1973): 43.
55. Wittgenstein, *On Certainty*, 46e.

CHAPTER 8. TRUTH, HISTORY, AND LITERARY CRITICISM

1. See F. R. Leavis, "*Scrutiny:* A Retrospect" (1963), reprinted in *"Valuation in Criticism" and Other Essays*, 218–43. In discussing the influence of Shakespeare criticism by reference to exchanges between Fr. A. J. Stephenson "and F. R. Leavis, and between L. C. Knights and the last-named" (231), Leavis lays claim to personal historical significance through the third person singular.
2. Clive James, *The Metropolitan Critic: Non-Fiction, 1968–1973* (London: Macmillan, 1994).
3. See Chris Baldick, *The Social Mission of English Criticism, 1848–1932* (Oxford: Clarendon Press, 1987).
4. See C. S. Lewis, *An Experiment in Criticism* (Cambridge: Cambridge University Press, 1961), 132.
5. George Saintsbury, *Classical and Medieval Criticism*, vol. 1 of *A History of Criticism and Literary Taste in Europe*, 2d ed. (Edinburgh and London: William Blackwood and Sons, 1902), 4. Saintsbury emphatically rejects the need to offer a more developed and systematized definition of his core material in vol. 3, *Modern Criticism,* 2d ed. (1906): "A man may surely write a *History of England* without including in it an abstract treatise on politics, and describe an interesting country without philosophising on the architecture of its buildings, the family story of its tribes, or the chemical constitution of its natural products" (143).
6. René Wellek, "Introduction to Volumes 5 and 6: Method and Scope," in *English Criticism, 1900–1950,* vol. 5 of *A History of Modern Criticism, 1750–1950* (London: Jonathan

Cape, 1986), xvii. In a review of the first two volumes of the history, Wellek was taken to task by Erich Auerbach, *Romanishe Forschungen* 62 (1956): 387–97, on the grounds that literary criticism does not constitute a unified subject. Wellek reasserted his belief in his subject's integrity in the "Preface to Volumes 3 and 4," in *The Age of Transition,* vol. 3 of *A History of Modern Criticism, 1750–1950* (London: Jonathan Cape, 1966), vii; and in idem, "Introduction to Volumes 5 and 6," xvii.

    7. William K. Wimsatt Jr. and Cleanth Brooks, introduction to *Literary Criticism: A Short History* (New York: Alfred A. Knopf, 1957), vii.

    8. George Watson, preface to *The Literary Critics: A Study of English Descriptive Criticism* (London: Chatto and Windus, 1964), n.p.

    9. Chris Baldick, "Author's Preface," in *Criticism and Literary Theory*, xiii–xiv.

    10. René Wellek, introduction to *The Later Eighteenth Century,* vol. 1 of *A History of Modern Criticism* (London: Jonathan Cape, 1955), 7. By the publication of vols. 3 and 4 in 1966, however, Wellek is suggesting a somewhat less clear-cut division between theory and practice: "The literary opinions, rankings, and judgments of a critic are buttressed, confirmed, and developed by his theories, and theories are drawn from and supported, illustrated, made concrete, and plausible by an inspection of works of art" ("Preface to Volumes 3 and 4," v–vi).

    11. Saintsbury, too, had appealed to a belief in the essentially "simple" nature of his history: "I set before myself and my readers at the outset the promise of a simple survey of the actual critical opinions, actually expressed, in 'judging of authors,' by the actual critics of recorded literature." See *Modern Criticism*, 143.

    12. Patrick Parrinder applies the Kuhnian model of historical development in science to the history of literary criticism in *Authors and Authority: English and American Criticism, 1750–1990* (London: Macmillan, 1991), 3–4.

    13. Saintsbury, *Classical and Medieval Criticism*, 5.

    14. Baldick, "Author's Preface," xiv.

    15. George A. Kennedy, preface to *Classical Criticism,* vol. 1 of *The Cambridge History of Literary Criticism* (Cambridge: Cambridge University Press, 1989), ix.

    16. Cf. Michel Foucault, "Archaeology and the History of Ideas," in *The Archaeology of Knowledge*, trans. A. M. Sheridan Smith (1972; reprint, London: Routledge, 1995). Foucault takes issue with the whole emphasis on historical "reference" under the rubric of "archaeology": "Archaeology tries to define not the thoughts, representations, images, themes, preoccupations that are concealed or revealed in discourses; but those discourses themselves, those discourses as practices obeying certain rules. It does not treat discourse as *document*, as a sign of something else...." (138–39).

    17. Baldick, *Criticism and Literary Theory,* 2–3.

    18. Wellek, "Introduction to Volumes 5 and 6," xv.

    19. Watson, *Literary Critics*, 195.

    20. See Eagleton, *Function of Criticism*. Eagleton's history teaches the "moral" that "Modern European criticism was born of a struggle against the absolutist state" (9). Approximately the same period is covered by Parrinder in *Authors and Authority*. But although criticism and history are differently related in Parrinder's history, he employs the same method of moral-by-example: "[I]n considering criticism as it is and has been, readers will consider what it one day should be" (4).

    21. Gordon Graham, *The Shape of the Past* (Oxford: Oxford University Press, 1997), 21.

    22. Watson, *Literary Critics*, 159.

    23. Ibid., 131.

    24. Eagleton, *Literary Theory*, 141–42. Jonathan Culler, "The Call to History," in *Framing the Sign: Criticism and Its Institutions* (Oxford: Blackwell, 1988), claims that Eagleton

"lacks a well-thought-out model of critical history but is content for the most part to accept current notions of major critical schools . . . and see each as a response to the major wars or crises of civilization that occurred prior to their appearance, or at least in the same decade" (62).

25. George A. Kennedy, "Christianity and Criticism," in *Classical Criticism*, 346.
26. Stephen Bann, "Semiotics," in Selden, *From Formalism to Poststructuralism*, 88.
27. Wimsatt and Brooks, *Literary Criticism*, 729–30.
28. I draw here on a Collingwoodian analysis of the logic of cause and effect. See, for example, *Essay on Metaphysics*, esp. part IIIc: Causation, 285–28.
29. The historical problem is in this aspect a version of the "identity question": "Is x y?"
30. Williams, *Keywords* (1988 reprint ed.), 86.
31. Leavis, "Johnson as Critic," 187.
32. An exception to this rule is where the theories (and not the people who think them up) acquire the power of agency: "Deconstruction holds that . . . ," and so on.
33. For an account of the fallacy of the temporal priority of cause to effect see R. G. Collingwood, "Causation in Theoretical Natural Science," chapter 32 of *An Essay on Metaphysics*, 313–27.
34. Collingwood, *Idea of History*, 187.
35. See Louis O. Mink, "History and Fiction as Modes of Comprehension," in *New Directions in Literary History*, ed. Ralph Cohen (London: Routledge and Kegan Paul, 1974): "An historical narrative does not demonstrate the necessity of events but makes them intelligible by unfolding the story which connects their significance" (111).
36. R. G. Collingwood, "History as Re-Enactment of Past Experience," in *Idea of History*, 283. There are close correspondences between Collingwood's thought on history as a concept and T. S. Eliot's conception of the past of criticism: "The important critic is the person who is absorbed in the present problems of art, and who wishes to bring the forces of the past to bear upon the solution of these problems." See T. S. Eliot, "Imperfect Critics," in *Sacred Wood*, 37–38.
37. Leavis, *"Valuation in Criticism,"* 219.
38. See Judy Simons, "Jane Austen: *Persuasion*," in *Literature in Context*, ed. Rick Rylance and Judy Simons (Houndmills, U.K.: Palgrave, 2001), 100.
39. Richard Rorty, "From Ironist Theory to Private Allusions: Derrida," in *Contingency, Irony, and Solidarity* (Cambridge: Cambridge University Press, 1989): "The later Derrida . . . drops theory—the attempt to see his predecessors steadily and whole—in favor of fantasizing about those predecessors, playing with them, giving free rein to the trains of association they produce" (125).

Chapter 9. Pope's *Essay* and the Poetic "Idea of Criticism"

1. Major studies of Pope give relatively scant attention to the *Essay,* and the poem has inspired few theoretical "rereadings." Useful general summaries of the *Essay* can, however, be found in Bertrand A. Goldgar, introduction to *Literary Criticism of Alexander Pope* (Lincoln and London: University of Nebraska Press, 1965), ix–xxxiv; Yasmine Gooneratne, *Alexander Pope* (Cambridge: Cambridge University Press, 1976), 23–31; David Fairer, *The Poetry of Alexander Pope* (Harmondsworth, England: Penguin, 1989), 30–40; Felicity Rosslyn, *Alexander Pope: A Literary Life* (London: Macmillan, 1990), 33–39; and Ian Gordon, *A Preface to Pope*, 2d ed. (London and New York: Longman, 1993), 145–54. The fullest and most informed account remains, however, that of E. Audra in the introduction to vol. 1 of the *Twickenham Edition* of Pope's poems, *Pastoral Poetry and "An Essay on Criti-*

cism," 197–236. For an assessment of the varied reactions to the poem from the eighteenth century to the twentieth century, see James Reeves, *The Reputation and Writings of Alexander Pope* (New York: Barnes and Noble, 1976), 125–37.

2. Mason, "An Introduction to Literary Criticism," 79–173. A further exception is G. Wilson Knight in *Laureate of Peace: On the Genius of Alexander Pope* (London: Routledge and Kegan Paul, 1955), who writes pertinently that the *Essay* is "strikingly relevant today [in 1955]" and that "The contemporary challenge to us is obvious. A creative intelligence opposes the academic and formalized mind" (40, 42).

3. Mason, "An Introduction to Literary Criticism," 79.

4. A more localized and external "historical context" for the *Essay* has been proposed by David Womersley, who appeals to the aftermath of the War of the Spanish Succession and argues that we should consider the *Essay* "in the context of the politicized poetics generated by the debates arising from international conflict during the reign of Queen Anne." See his introduction to *Augustan Critical Writing* (Harmondsworth, England: Penguin, 1997), xxxii. (For an account of Womersley's idea of history as a means to conceive the *Essay* historically, see Tom Mason and Philip Smallwood, "Introducing the Long Eighteenth Century: Literary History and the New Pedagogy," *CQ* 29, no. 3 [2000]: 191–213, esp. 198–202.) Other "historicist" commentaries on the *Essay* have been provided from a cultural materialist perspective by Laura Brown, *Rereading Literature: Alexander Pope* (Oxford: Blackwell, 1985), who thinks that the poem "joins the representation of the structural principles of a capitalist social order with an informing image of imperial expansion" (50); and from a feminist viewpoint by Christa Knellwolf, who sees the Pope of the *Essay* as engaged in gendered self-construction. See *A Contradiction Still: Representations of Women in the Poetry of Alexander Pope* (Manchester: Manchester University Press, 1998), 86–108. For a related view see Penelope Wilson, "Engendering the reader: 'Wit and Poetry and Pope' once more," in *The Enduring Legacy: Alexander Pope: Tercentenary Essays,* ed. G. S. Rousseau and Pat Rogers (Cambridge: Cambridge University Press, 1988), 63–76. Wilson writes of Pope's "instructions to a *reader*" (my emphasis, 66), though Pope's audience in the poem is strictly the reader *as critic*.

5. Collingwood's distinction between propositions and relative suppositions, on the one hand, and absolute presuppositions, on the other, was made in *Essay on Metaphysics:* "Absolute presuppositions are not verifiable. This does not mean that we should like to verify them but are not able to; it means that the idea of verification is an idea which does not apply to them, because . . . to speak of verifying a presupposition involves supposing that it is a relative presupposition . . . the logical efficacy of a supposition does not depend on its being verifiable, because it does not depend on its being true: it only depends on its being supposed" (32).

6. See Williamson, *Vagueness,* esp. chapter 2, "The Ideal of Precision," 36–69.

7. Perhaps in order to draw attention to the Horatian background, the editor of the *Norton Anthology of Theory and Criticism,* Vincent B. Leitch, refers to "Alexander Pope's versified 'art of poetry'" (438); but while it is a work of art, Pope's poem is actually entitled an "essay" (a provisional account or interim report) and is only mistakenly referred to as an "art" (or the last word on the subject). A prose *Art of Criticism,* by "A Gentleman of Quality," had been published in 1705 shortly in advance of the *Essay,* and is an anonymously translated version of Dominique Bouhours's influential *La Manière de bien penser.* But though the translation is an important source of the poem—unrecorded in the *Twickenham Edition*—the shift from "art" to "essay" signals the distinctive meaning of the critical poem that Pope's own contemporaries did not always appreciate. Other "essays" in verse—on other subjects—preceded Pope's over several years: see the Earl of Roscommon's *Essay on Translated Verse* (1674) and John Sheffield, the Earl of Mulgrave's *Essay on Poetry* (1682); also George Granville, Lord Landsdowne's *Essay upon Unnatural Flights in Poetry* (1701).

But when Addison reviewed Pope's poem in the *Spectator*, no. 253 (20 December 1711), he too had blurred the distinction by referring to it as "The Art of Criticism" and was one of the first to write of Pope's adoption of earlier "precepts"—a criticism that is repeated again and again in the eighteenth, nineteenth, and twentieth centuries. But while Addison admires the beauty and polish of the *Essay,* its point seems to elude him. The very style of condescending elegance that Addison displays in the review comes under scrutiny in the *Essay*. See *The Spectator*, ed. Gregory Smith (New York: Everyman, 1970), 2:251–54. For a reflection on Pope's relation to the Horatian background to the poem, see Reuben A. Brower, *Alexander Pope: The Poetry of Allusion* (Oxford: Oxford University Press, 1959), 188–206.

8. The emphasis on visibility and visuality in the poem's handling of its central concept is brought out by Morris Brownell, *Alexander Pope and the Arts of Georgian England* (Oxford: Clarendon Press, 1978), 52: "In the *Essay on Criticism* (1711) Pope compares the limits of human knowledge and critical myopia to prospect and perspective (222–32); conceits in false wit to ornate costume portraiture (240–47); the seeds of judgement to a painter's sketch (19–22), false learning to 'ill-colouring' (23–35), and mutability of language to fading colours (484–93)."

9. To commend, as I do here, the poetic definition of criticism as the preferred reading of Pope's *Essay* opens the poem to an analytical history of "artworks" more characteristic of aesthetic than critical theory. Stephen Davies, summarizing Arthur Danto's theory of art, notes pertinently that "Mere representations *re*-present their subjects, whereas artworks are *about* their subjects; when artworks are understood as such, they are understood not only as indicating what is seen but also as revealing a way of seeing." *Definitions of Art*, 69. Pope's "way of seeing" in the *Essay*, I argue, creates a foundation for what we are now able to suppose about criticism. It is not outmoded because it is taken for granted.

10. Kant, *Critique of Pure Reason*, 315–26.

11. On the various meanings of "Wit" in the poem, see William Empson, "Wit in the *Essay on Criticism*," in *Structure of Complex Words*, 84–100; see also Edward Niles Hooker, "Pope on Wit: The *Essay on Criticism*," in *Essential Articles for the Study of Alexander Pope*, ed. Maynard Mack (London: Frank Cass, 1964), 175–97.

12. Cf. Terry Eagleton's highly relevant distinction between "philosophy" and "literature" in *Criticism and Ideology:* "Philosophy . . . deals with the lived not as 'spontaneous' response and perception but in terms of the general categories underlying it—categories which may or may not be ideological. . . . In this sense it differs from literature, whose aim is to give us the lived as it were spontaneously; but literature nonetheless resembles it in so far as this 'spontaneity' is in fact phenomenal. Literature, too . . . reveals more or less indirectly the categories of the lived; it is merely that it typically produces those categories so as to conceal them, dissolving them in the 'concrete'. (Pope's *Essay on Man* presents certain categorial propositions, but in so far as the rhetorical strategy of its form is to induce an *experience* of them, it is a literary rather than philosophical text.)" (76).

13. Gordon, *Preface to Pope*, usefully notes that "it is not until one tries to extract a prose meaning from the lines that one realizes how poetically charged they are" (86).

14. Nor were they exactly common *before* Pope, as Maynard Mack points out: "The content of this poem would be quite new to its readers so far as treatment in verse was concerned, there being extant several reputable versified 'Arts' of poetry, including Horace's, but nothing quite like a critical 'Art.'" See *Alexander Pope: A Life* (London: Yale University Press, 1985), 178.

15. I take this collection of terms, as equally pertinent to the interest of the *Essay*, from Roger Scruton's summary of the aesthetic interests of a Brahms melody. See *The Aesthetics of Music* (Oxford: Oxford University Press, 1997), 372.

16. The rights and wrongs of the poem's internal organization were a central issue of commentary from the 1950s. Donald Greene once noted that "there is no real logical order

in the poem at all, beyond that of simple enumeration." See "'Logical Structure' in Eighteenth-Century Poetry," *PQ* 31 (1952): 330. In a footnote to his later essay, "An Anatomy of Pope-bashing" (*Enduring Legacy*, 241–81), Greene recalls that he had earlier argued that Pope's *Essay* is "illogical," "unaware that De Quincey had earlier reached the same conclusion": "[H]owever, I did not regard this as a fault. Like good poetry of other centuries, that of Pope does not make its effect by trying to imitate a scholarly treatise: the *Essay*'s structure is dramatic, not logical" (272n). For an attempt to find organization in the argument of the poem according to rhetorical concepts ("exordium" [lines 1–8], "narratio" [lines 9–45] and "expressio" [lines 46–67], etc.), see John Aden, "'*First* Follow Nature': Strategy and Stratification in *An Essay on Criticism*," *JEGP* 55 (1956): 604–17. Although Aden believes that "To Pope's eighteenth-century readers the poem as a whole exhibited . . . a certain Horatian indifference to method," he argues that "far from being unorganized, the whole first part of the poem is very carefully ordered. . . ." (605). Geoffrey Tillotson, similarly, contends that in all of Pope's "essay" poems "there is often a remarkable organization that fuses together . . . the paragraph-sections of the matter in ways other than the strictly logical or narrative." See *Pope and Human Nature* (Oxford: Clarendon Press, 1958), 199.

17. Patricia Meyer Spacks writes persuasively that "Pope wished to enlarge the function of imagery, to supply a logic of metaphor, thus achieving an organic unity which would demonstrate wit's power to organize as well as to decorate didacticism." See "Imagery and Method in *An Essay on Criticism*," in *Pope: Recent Essays by Several Hands*, ed. Maynard Mack and James A. Winn (Brighton: Harvester Press, 1980), 108. The essay was originally published in *PMLA* 85 (1970): 97–106, and it is reprinted as "Wit Governing Wit: *An Essay on Criticism*," chapter 2 of Spacks, *An Argument of Images: The Poetry of Alexander Pope* (Cambridge: Harvard University Press, 1971), 17–40.

18. Kant, *Critique of Pure Reason*, 137.

19. In shaping this formulation with respect to Pope's *Essay* I am indebted to thoughts encountered in Freadman and Miller's analysis of the workings of the postmodern novel. See *Re-Thinking Theory*.

20. Collingwood, *Essay on Philosophical Method*, 95.

21. Dated November 1930. See *Philosophical Remarks*, ed. Rush Rhees, trans. Raymond Hargreaves and Roger White (1975; reprint, Oxford: Blackwell, 1990).

22. Johnson, "Life of Pope," 3:228. Johnson praised the poem as exhibiting "every mode of excellence that can embellish or dignify didactick composition, selection of matter, novelty of arrangement, justness of precept, splendour of illustration, and propriety of digression" (3:228–29); and earlier in the "Life of Pope" he had described it as a work "which displays such extent of comprehension, such nicety of distinction, such acquaintance with mankind, and such knowledge both of ancient and modern learning as are not often attained by the maturest age and longest experience" (3:94–95).

23. Cf. Stein Haugom Olsen, responding to the concept of "community" by reference to the social realities of race, gender, and class: "It is a *general* point about social practices and institutions that they are defined by concepts and rules that must be internalized by those who enter into the practice. To continue over time social practices or institutions must have *some* members at any one time. However, such social practices/institutions are not defined through their membership. They constitute their own membership: the *only* requirement on this membership is that it has to some extent internalized the concepts and conventions of the practice/institution and applied them. Social practices of this kind cannot therefore be identified through *other* criteria defining a community (e.g. criteria of social identity)." Olsen, "The Canon and Artistic Failure," 275.

24. F. H. Bradley, *The Principles of Logic* (Oxford: Oxford University Press, 1928), 591.

25. Johnson, *Johnson on Shakespeare*, 7:99.

Chapter 10. Conclusion

1. Ezra Pound, *ABC of Reading* (1934; reprint, London: Faber and Faber, 1991), 29.
2. Samuel Johnson, *The Idler* 60, in *The Idler and Adventurer*, 184.
3. R. G. Collingwood, *The New Leviathan*, ed. David Boucher, rev. ed. (Oxford: Oxford University Press, 1992), 280.
4. Richard Shusterman, "Essence, History, and Narrative: T. S. Eliot on the Definition of Poetry and Criticism," *Monist* 71, no. 2 (April 1988): 183.
5. In his introduction to *Keywords*, Raymond Williams could, for example, write of "an idea of criticism which, from Arnold through Leavis, had *culture* as one of its central terms" (12). For Williams, Leavis's "idea" has become one of many.
6. F. R. Leavis, "The Responsible Critic, or the Function of Criticism at Any Time," *Scrutiny* 19, no. 3 (1953): 181.
7. Harris, *Literary Meaning*, 209.
8. The idea of criticism belongs in this respect with the "non-exhibited" definitions of art discussed by Stephen Davies in his *Definitions of Art*.
9. Searle, "Literary Theory and Its Discontents," observes that "It is not necessarily an objection to a conceptual analysis, or to a distinction, that there are no rigorous or precise boundaries to the concept analyzed or the distinction being drawn." He goes on to suggest that while "[t]his is something of a cliché in analytic philosophy," it is not equally a commonplace of literary theory, where all-or-nothing logic more often prevails (102).
10. Samuel Johnson, "Life of Addison," in *Lives*, 2:146.
11. D. H. Lawrence, *Women in Love*, ed. David Farmer, Lindeth Vasey, and John Worthen (Harmondsworth, England: Penguin, 2000), 78–79.
12. Bloom, *Anxiety of Influence*, 96; Mason, "An Introduction to Literary Criticism," 79; Arnold, "The Function of Criticism at the Present Time," 325; Carey, *Original Copy*, 29.
13. Richard Rorty, "Private Irony and Liberal Hope," in *Contingency, Irony, and Solidarity*, 81–82.
14. F. R. Leavis, "Thought, Language and Objectivity," in *The Living Principle* (London: Chatto and Windus, 1975), 51.
15. See Paul de Man, "Literary History and Literary Modernity," chapter 8 of *Blindness and Insight: Essays in the Rhetoric of Contemporary Criticism*, 2d ed. (London: Routledge, 1983). De Man notes that the debate between the Ancients and the Moderns "forced the participants to make comparative critical evaluations of ancient versus contemporary writing" (153), and goes on to explain how "modernity, which is fundamentally a falling away from literature and a rejection of history, also acts as the principle that gives literature duration and historical existence" (162).
16. Johnson, *Johnson on Shakespeare*, 7:109.
17. De Man, *Blindness and Insight*, 142.
18. Ricoeur, *Time and Narrative*, 3:149.
19. Collingwood, *Idea of History*, 187.
20. T. S. Eliot, *Four Quartets* ("Burnt Norton II"), in *Collected Poems, 1909–1962* (London and Boston: Faber and Faber), 192.
21. See also the work of Howard Erskine-Hill, esp. *The Social Milieu of Alexander Pope: Lives, Example, and the Poetic Response* (New Haven and London: Yale University Press, 1975). Erskine-Hill fixes on the *Essay*'s tribute to Erasmus and the reference to contemporary religious controversy (66); but Erasmus's praise of fools also had implications for Pope's satire of critical as well as religious folly and for the insidious interweaving of religious and critical dogmas.
22. The paradox is that antiexclusionism, as yet far from perfectly achieved, or even

minimally approached, is itself an "Enlightenment" value—as Ellis has argued at length in *Literature Lost*.

23. These lines record what Pope's contemporary Addison was later seen by Pope *not* to do in the famous satirical portrait of "Atticus" from "An Epistle to Dr. Arbuthnot," in *Imitations of Horace*, ed. John Butt, vol. 4 of *The Twickenham Edition of the Poems of Alexander Pope*, ed. John Butt (London: Methuen, 1939), 109–11, lines 192–214.

24. For Pope's construction of himself as the subject of the *Essay*, see Dustin H. Griffin, *Alexander Pope: The Poet in the Poems* (Princeton: Princeton University Press, 1978), 83–87.

Afterword

1. Parrinder, *Authors and Authority*, 339. Cf. Easthope, *Literary into Cultural Studies*, 65: "[A]t one end literary study becomes increasingly indistinguishable from cultural studies while at the other what originated as cultural studies makes incursions into the traditionally literary terrain of textuality."
2. Roland Barthes, "The Two Criticisms" (1963), reprinted in *Critical Essays*, 251.
3. The Deesse first appeared at the London Motorshow in 1955.
4. Roland Barthes, *Mythologies*, trans. Annette Lavers (1972; reprint, London: Vintage, 1993), 88.
5. Roland Barthes, "The New Citroen," in ibid., 88.
6. Freadman and Miller, *Re-Thinking Theory*, 92.
7. This situation may change as supermarkets increasingly enter the bookselling trade. Does the policy on returns for a defective jar of olives cover complaints about the defective plot of a "pulp" novel?
8. See, for example, the withering comments by Duke Maskell, "In Praise of the Contemporary Critic," *CQ* 5, no. 4 (summer/autumn 1971), 327–34: "Mr Hoggart isn't . . . bidding us merely to re-create the variegated surfaces of contemporary life as the poet or novelist does but to devise an 'adequate vocabulary for describing their cultural meanings.' He isn't bidding us to engage our imaginations directly with things, to go out into the world and catch the look of things, the colour, the relief, the expression, the surface-substance of the contemporary human spectacle, to look up mini-skirts or into that vivid slit in the maxi-coat [in 1971], but to ponder their 'inner meanings,' which as he says, 'are not easily read or dismissed. At Birmingham we have learned this most of all by working in long weekly seminars over two or three months on a single short story from a women's magazine. . . .'" For a further, more probing and developed satirical analysis, see Stefan Collini, "Grievance Studies: How Not to Do Cultural Criticism," in *English Pasts: Essays in History and Culture* (Oxford: Oxford University Press, 1999), 252–68.

Bibliography

Abrams, M. H. *Doing Things with Texts: Essays in Criticism and Cultural Theory*. New York and London: Norton, 1989.

———. *A Glossary of Literary Terms*. 6th ed. London and New York: Harcourt Brace, 1993.

Aden, John. "'*First* Follow Nature': Strategy and Stratification in *An Essay on Criticism*." *JEGP* 55 (1956): 604–17.

Addison, Joseph, *The Spectator*. Ed. Gregory Smith. 4 vols. New York: Everyman, 1970.

Arnold, Matthew. "The Function of Criticism at the Present Time." 1864. Reprinted in *The Oxford Authors Matthew Arnold,* ed. Miriam Allott and Robert H. Super, 317–42. Oxford: Oxford University Press, 1986.

———. *Essays in Criticism: Second Series*. Ed. S. R. Littlewood. 1938. Reprint, London: Macmillan, 1969.

———. "The Study of Poetry." 1880. Reprinted in *Selected Poems and Prose, Matthew Arnold,* ed. Miriam Allott, 225–49. London: Everyman, 1993.

Auerbach, Erich. Review of *History of Modern Criticism,* by René Wellek. *Romanische Forschungen* 62 (1956): 387–97.

Baldick, Chris. *Criticism and Literary Theory: 1890 to the Present*. London and New York: Longman, 1996.

———. *The Social Mission of English Criticism: 1848–1932*. Oxford: Clarendon Press, 1987.

Bann, Stephen. "Semiotics." In *From Formalism to Poststructuralism.*, ed. Raman Selden, 85–109. Vol. 8 of *The Cambridge History of Literary Criticism*, Cambridge: Cambridge University Press, 1995.

Barnes, Annette. *On Interpretation: A Critical Analysis*. Oxford: Blackwell, 1988.

Barthes, Roland. *Mythologies*. Trans. Annette Lavers. 1972. Reprint, London: Vintage, 1993. Originally published in French in 1957.

———. *Critical Essays*. Trans. Richard Howard. Evanston, Ill.: Northwestern University Press, 1972.

Battestin, Martin C. "Historical Criticism and the Question of Contemporaneity." *AJ* 12 (2001): 361–79.

Beardsley, M. C. *Aesthetics: Problems in the Philosophy of Criticism*. New York: Harcourt, Brace, and World, 1958.

———. *The Possibility of Criticism*. Detroit: Wayne State University Press, 1970.

Belsey, Catherine. *The Subject of Tragedy: Identity and Difference in Renaissance Drama.* London and New York: Methuen, 1985.

Bergonzi, Bernard. *Exploding English.* Oxford: Oxford University Press, 1990.

Bloom, Harold. *The Anxiety of Influence: A Theory of Poetry.* Oxford: Oxford University Press, 1973.

———. *The Western Canon: The Books and School of the Ages.* New York: Harcourt Brace, 1994.

Boswell, James. *The Life of Samuel Johnson, LL.D.* Ed. John Wilson Croker. London, 1831.

Bouhours, Dominique. *The Art of Criticism.* Trans. "A Gentleman of Quality." London, 1705.

Bradford, Richard, ed. *The State of Theory.* London and New York: Routledge, 1993.

Bradley, F. H. *The Principles of Logic.* Oxford: Oxford University Press, 1928.

Brooker, Peter, and Peter Widdowson, eds. *A Practical Reader in Contemporary Literary Theory.* London: Harvester Wheatsheaf; New York: Prentice-Hall, 1996.

Brooks, Cleanth. "The Formalist Critic." 1951. Reprinted in *Twentieth-Century Literary Theory: A Reader,* ed. K. M. Newton, 45–48. London: Macmillan, 1988.

Brower, Reuben A. *Alexander Pope: The Poetry of Allusion.* Oxford: Oxford University Press, 1959.

Brown, Alan. "On the Subject of Practical Criticism." *CQ* 28, no. 4 (1999): 293–327.

Brown, Laura. *Rereading Literature: Alexander Pope.* Oxford: Blackwell, 1985.

Brownell, Morris. *Alexander Pope and the Arts of Georgian England.* Oxford: Clarendon Press, 1978.

Butler, Christopher. "What Is a Literary Work?" *NLH* 5 (1973): 17–29.

Butler, Judith, John Guillory, and Kendall Thomas, eds. *What's Left of Theory? New Work on the Politics of Literary Theory.* New York: Routledge, 2000.

Campbell, Jill. "In Defence of Literature: A Response to Martin C. Battestin." *AJ* 12 (2001): 381–98.

Carey, John. *The Intellectuals and the Masses: Pride and Prejudice among the Literary Intelligentsia, 1880–1939.* London: Faber and Faber, 1992.

———. *Original Copy: Selected Reviews and Journalism, 1969–1986.* London: Faber and Faber, 1987.

Carroll, Joseph. "In a Corrupt Shadow." *TLS,* 12 June 1998, 27.

Cohen, Ralph, ed. *The Future of Literary Theory.* New York and London: Routledge, 1989.

———. *New Directions in Literary History.* London: Routledge and Kegan Paul, 1974.

Collingwood, R. G. *An Autobiography.* Oxford: Oxford University Press, 1939.

———. *An Essay on Metaphysics.* 1940. Reprint, ed. Rex Martin, Oxford: Clarendon Press, 1998.

———. *An Essay on Philosophical Method.* 1933. Reprint, Bristol: Thoemmes Press, 1995.

———. *The Idea of History.* Ed. Jan van der Dussen. Oxford: Oxford University Press, 1994.

———. *The New Leviathan.* 1942. Reprint, ed. David Boucher, Oxford: Oxford University Press, 1992.

———. *The Principles of Art.* Oxford: Clarendon Press, 1938.

Collini, Stefan. "Grievance Studies: How Not to Do Cultural Studies." In *English Pasts: Essays in History and Culture,* 252–68. Oxford: Oxford University Press, 1999.

Cox, R. G. "Auden as Critic and Poet." *Scrutiny* 18, no. 2 (autumn 1951): 158–61.
Crews, Frederick. "In the Big House of Theory." *NYRB,* 29 May 1986, 36–42.
Culler, Jonathan. *Framing the Sign: Criticism and Its Institutions.* Oxford: Blackwell, 1988.
———. *On Deconstruction: Theory and Criticism after Structuralism.* 1983. Reprint, London: Routledge, 1994.
Cunningham, Valentine. *Reading after Theory.* Oxford: Blackwell, 2002.
Davies, Stephen. *Definitions of Art.* Ithaca and London: Cornell University Press, 1991.
Day, Gary. "Leavis and Post-Structuralism." In *F. R. Leavis: Essays and Documents,* ed. Ian MacKillop and Richard Storer, 174–89. Sheffield, U.K.: Sheffield Academic Press, 1995.
de Man, Paul. "Literary History and Literary Modernity." In *Blindness and Insight: Essays in the Rhetoric of Contemporary Criticism,* 142–65. 2d ed. London: Routledge, 1983.
———. "The Resistance to Theory." In *Modern Criticism and Theory: A Reader,* ed. David Lodge, 354–71. London and New York: Longman, 1988.
Derrida, Jacques. *Of Grammatology.* Trans. Gayatri Chakravorty Spivak. Baltimore: Johns Hopkins University Press, 1974.
Dollimore, Jonathan, and Alan Sinfield, eds. *Political Shakespeare: New Essays in Cultural Materialism.* Manchester: Manchester University Press, 1985.
Dryden, John. *"Of Dramatic Poesy" and Other Critical Essays.* Ed. George Watson. 2 vols. London: Everyman, 1971
Eagleton, Mary, ed. *Feminist Literary Criticism.* London and New York: Longman, 1991.
Eagleton, Terry. *Criticism and Ideology: A Study in Marxist Literary Theory.* London: New Left Books, 1976.
———. *The Function of Criticism: From the Spectator to Post-Structuralism.* London: Verso, 1984.
———. *Literary Theory: An Introduction.* Oxford: Blackwell, 1983.
———. *Marxism and Literary Criticism.* London: Methuen, 1976.
———. *The Significance of Theory.* Oxford: Blackwell, 1990.
———. "Value in Art: An Exchange." *New Left Review* 142 (November–December 1983): 76–90.
Easthope, Antony. *British Post-Structuralism since 1968.* London: Routledge, 1988.
———. *Literary into Cultural Studies.* London: Routledge, 1991.
Eco, Umberto, with Richard Rorty, Jonathan Culler, and Christine Brooke-Rose. *Interpretation and Overinterpretation.* Ed. Stefan Collini. Cambridge: Cambridge University Press, 1992.
Eliot, T. S. *Collected Poems, 1909–1962.* London and Boston: Faber and Faber, 1974.
———. "The Frontiers of Criticism." 1956. Reprinted in *On Poetry and Poets.* London: Faber and Faber, 1957.
———. "The Function of Criticism." 1923. Reprinted in *Selected Essays.* London: Faber and Faber, 1932.
———. *The Sacred Wood: Essays on Poetry and Criticism.* London: Routledge, 1989.
———. *Selected Essays.* London: Faber and Faber, 1932.
———. *"To Criticize the Critic" and Other Writings.* London: Faber and Faber, 1965.
———. *The Use of Poetry and the Use of Criticism.* London: Faber and Faber, 1933.
Ellis, John M. *Against Deconstruction.* Princeton: Princeton University Press, 1989.

———. *Literature Lost: Social Agendas and the Corruption of the Humanities*. New Haven: Yale University Press, 1997.

———. "The Logic of the Question 'What Is Criticism?'" In *What Is Criticism?*, ed. Paul Hernadi, 15–29. Bloomington: Indiana University Press, 1981.

———. *The Theory of Literary Criticism: A Logical Analysis*. Berkeley: University of California Press, 1974.

Empson, William. *The Structure of Complex Words*. 1951. Reprint, Harmondsworth, England: Penguin Books, 1995.

Erskine-Hill, Howard. *The Social Milieu of Alexander Pope: Lives, Example, and the Poetic Response*. New Haven and London: Yale University Press, 1975.

Fairer, David. *The Poetry of Alexander Pope*. Harmondsworth, England: Penguin, 1989.

Felperin, Howard. *Beyond Deconstruction: The Uses and Abuses of Literary Theory*. Oxford: Clarendon Press, 1985.

Fish, Stanley. *Is There a Text in This Class? The Authority of Interpretive Communities*. Cambridge: Harvard University Press, 1980.

Foucault, Michel. *The Archaeology of Knowledge*. Trans. A. M. Sheridan Smith. 1972. Reprint, London: Routledge, 1995.

———. "What Is an Author?" In *The Foucault Reader*, ed. Paul Rabinow, 101–20. Harmondsworth, England: Penguin, 1980.

Freadman, Richard, and Seumas Miller. *Re-Thinking Theory: A Critique of Contemporary Literary Theory and an Alternative Account*. Cambridge: Cambridge University Press, 1992.

Frye, Northrop. *Anatomy of Criticism: Four Essays*. Princeton: Princeton University Press, 1957.

Fuller, David, and Patricia Waugh, eds. *The Arts and Sciences of Criticism*. Oxford: Oxford University Press, 1999.

Furbank, P. N. "Blowing in a Discordant Gourd." Review of *Critical Essays*, by Ford Madox Ford. *TLS*, 10 May 2002, 36.

Gadamer, Hans-Georg. *Truth and Method*. Trans. Joel Weinsheimer and Donald G. Marshall. 2d rev. ed. London: Sheed and Ward, 1989.

Goldgar, Bertrand A., ed. *Literary Criticism of Alexander Pope*. Lincoln and London: University of Nebraska Press, 1965.

Gooneratne, Yasmine. *Alexander Pope*. Cambridge: Cambridge University Press, 1976.

Gordon, Ian. *A Preface to Pope*. 2d ed. London and New York: Longman, 1993.

Graff, Gerald. *Literature against Itself: Literary Ideas in Modern Society*. Chicago: Elephant Paperbacks, 1995.

———. *Professing Literature: An Institutional History*. Chicago: University of Chicago Press, 1987.

Graham, Gordon. *The Shape of the Past*. Oxford: Oxford University Press, 1997.

Graves, Robert. *Goodbye to All That*. 1929. Reprint, Harmondsworth, England: Penguin Books, 1981.

Greenblatt, Stephen. *Renaissance Self-Fashioning: From More to Shakespeare*. Chicago and London: University of Chicago Press, 1980.

Greene, Donald. "An Anatomy of Pope-bashing." In *The Enduring Legacy: Alexander Pope: Tercentenary Essays*, ed. G. S. Rousseau and Pat Rogers, 241–81. Cambridge: Cambridge University Press, 1988.

———. "'Logical Structure' in Eighteenth-Century Poetry." *Philological Quarterly* 31 (1952): 315–36.

Griffin, Dustin H. *Alexander Pope: The Poet in the Poems*. Princeton: Princeton University Press, 1978.

Gross, John. *The Rise and Fall of the Man of Letters: English Literary Life since 1800*. 1969. Reprint, Harmondsworth, England: Penguin Books, 1991.

Harris, Wendell V., ed. *Beyond Poststructuralism*. University Park: Pennsylvania State University Press, 1996.

———. *Dictionary of Concepts in Literary Criticism and Theory*. New York and London: Greenwood Press, 1992.

———. *Literary Meaning: Reclaiming the Study of Literature*. London: Macmillan, 1996.

Hartman, Geoffrey. *Saving the Text: Literature/Derrida/Philosophy*. Baltimore and London: Johns Hopkins University Press, 1981.

———. "The State of the Art of Criticism." In *The Future of Literary Theory*, ed. Ralph Cohen, 86–101. London and New York: Routledge, 1989.

Harwood, John. *Eliot to Derrida: The Poverty of Interpretation*. London: Macmillan, 1995.

Heath, James A., and Michael Payne. *Text, Interpretation, Theory*. Lewisburg, Pa.: Bucknell University Press, 1985.

Heidegger, Martin. *Being and Time*. Trans. John Macquarrie and Edward Robinson. Oxford: Blackwell, 1962.

Hernadi, Paul, ed. *What Is Criticism?* Bloomington: Indiana University Press, 1981.

———. *What Is Literature?* Bloomington: Indiana University Press, 1978.

Hirsch, E. D., Jr. *The Aims of Interpretation*. Chicago: University of Chicago Press, 1976.

———. *Validity in Interpretation*. New Haven and London: Yale University Press, 1967.

Holloway, John. "Language, Realism, Subjectivity, Objectivity." In *Reconstructing Literature*, ed. Laurence Lerner. Oxford: Blackwell, 1983.

Hooker, Edward Niles. "Pope on Wit: *The Essay on Criticism*." In *Essential Articles for the Study of Alexander Pope*, ed. Maynard Mack, 175–97. London: Frank Cass, 1964.

Hopkins, Gerard Manley. *The Journals and Papers of Gerard Manley Hopkins*. Ed. Humphry House. London: Oxford University Press, 1959.

James, Clive. *The Metropolitan Critic: Non-Fiction, 1968–1973*. London: Macmillan, 1994.

———. "These Staggering Questions." 1980. Reprinted in *From the Land of Shadows*, 195–208. London: Pan Books, 1983.

James, Henry. "*Daniel Deronda:* A Conversation." *Atlantic Monthly*, December 1896.

Jauss, Hans-Robert. "Literary History as a Challenge to Literary Theory." *NLH* 2 (1970–71): 7–37.

Jefferson, Ann, and David Robey, eds. *Modern Literary Theory: A Comparative Introduction*. London: Batsford, 1982.

Johnson, Samuel. *Dictionary of the English Language*. London, 1755.

———. *Johnson on Shakespeare*. Vols. 7 and 8 of *The Yale Edition of the Works of Samuel Johnson*, ed. John H. Middendorf. New Haven and London: Yale University Press, 1968.

———. *Lives of the English Poets*. Ed. George Birkbeck Hill. 3 vols. Oxford: Clarendon Press, 1905.

———. "Preface to the Dictionary." 4th ed. 1773. Reprinted in *Johnson: Prose and Poetry*, ed. Mona Wilson. London: Hart-Davis, 1968.

———. *The Yale Edition of the Works of Samuel Johnson*. General ed. John H. Middendorf. New Haven and London: Yale University Press, 1958–.
Jonson, Ben. *Timber or Discoveries: Made upon Men and Matter*. London: Dent, 1951.
Kant, Immanuel. *Critique of Pure Reason*. Trans. Norman Kemp Smith. 1929. Reprint, London: Macmillan, 1993.
Keller, Hans. *Criticism*. London: Faber and Faber, 1987.
Kennedy, George A. Preface to *Classical Criticism*. In vol. 1 of *The Cambridge History of Literary Criticism*., ix–xv. Cambridge: Cambridge University Press, 1989.
Kermode, Frank. "Art among the Ruins." *NYRB*, 5 July 2001, 59–63.
Knellwolf, Christa. *A Contradiction Still: Representations of Women in the Poetry of Alexander Pope*. Manchester: Manchester University Press, 1998.
Knight, G. Wilson. *The Imperial Theme: Further Interpretations of Shakespeare's Tragedies including the Roman Plays.*. 3d ed. London: Methuen, 1931.
———. *The Wheel of Fire: Interpretations of Shakespearean Tragedy*. London: Methuen, 1930.
Kristeva, Julia. *Desire in Language: A Semiotic Approach to Literature and Art*. Oxford: Blackwell, 1981.
LaCapra, Dominick. "Writing the History of Criticism Now?" In *History and Criticism*, 94–114. Ithaca and London: Cornell University Press, 1985.
Lamarque, Peter. *Fictional Points of View*. Ithaca and London: Cornell University Press, 1996.
Lamarque, Peter, and Stein Haugom Olsen. *Truth, Fiction, and Literature: A Philosophical Perspective*. Oxford: Oxford University Press, 1994.
Lawrence, D. H. *Selected Literary Criticism*. Ed. Anthony Beal. 1956. Reprint, London: Heinemann, 1967.
———. *Women in Love*. Ed. David Farmer, Lindeth Vasey, and John Worthen. Harmondsworth, England: Penguin, 2000.
Leavis, F. R. *The Critic as Anti-Philosopher: Essays and Papers by F. R. Leavis*. London: Chatto and Windus, 1982.
———. "Literary Criticism and Philosophy." In *The Common Pursuit*, 211–22. London: Chatto and Windus, 1952.
———. "Johnson as Critic." *Scrutiny* 12, no. 3 (summer 1944): 187–204.
———. *The Living Principle*. London: Chatto and Windus, 1975.
———. *New Bearings in English Poetry*. London: Chatto and Windus, 1932.
———. *Revaluation: Tradition and Development in English Poetry*. 1936. Reprint, London: Peregrine Books, 1967.
———. "The Responsible Critic, or The Function of Criticism at Any Time." *Scrutiny* 19, no. 3 (1953): 162–83. Reprinted in *A Selection from Scrutiny*, 2:280–303. 2 vols. Cambridge: Cambridge University Press, 1968.
———. *"Valuation in Criticism" and Other Essays*. Ed. G. Singh. Cambridge: Cambridge University Press, 1986.
Lewis, C. S. *An Experiment in Criticism*. Cambridge: Cambridge University Press, 1961.
Lodge, David. *Working with Structuralism: Essays and Reviews on Nineteenth- and Twentieth-Century Literature*. London: Routledge, 1981.
———, ed. *Modern Criticism and Theory: A Reader*. London and New York: Longman, 1988.

———. *Twentieth-Century Literary Criticism: A Reader*. London and New York: Longman, 1972.

Mack, Maynard. *Alexander Pope: A Life*. London: Yale University Press, 1985.

Mack, Maynard, and James A. Winn. *Pope: Recent Essays by Several Hands*. Brighton: Harvester Press, 1980.

MacKillop, Ian. *F. R. Leavis: A Life in Criticism*. London: Allen Lane, 1995.

MacKillop, Ian, and Richard Storer, eds. *F. R. Leavis: Essays and Documents*. Sheffield, U.K.: Sheffield Academic Press, 1995.

Marvell, Andrew. *The Oxford Authors Andrew Marvell*. Oxford: Oxford University Press, 1990.

Maskell, Duke. "In Praise of the Contemporary Critic." *CQ* 5, no. 4 (summer/autumn, 1971): 327–34.

Mason, H. A. "An Introduction to Literary Criticism by Way of Sidney's *Apologie for Poetrie*." *CQ* 12, nos. 2 and 3 (1983): 79–173.

———. "The Miraculous Birth, or The Founding of Modern European Literary Criticism." *CQ* 11, no. 2 (1982): 281–97.

Mason, Tom, and Philip Smallwood. "Introducing the Long Eighteenth Century: Literary History and the New Pedagogy." *CQ* 29, no. 3 (2000): 191–213.

Mink, Louis O. "History and Fiction as Modes of Comprehension." In *New Directions in Literary History*, ed. Ralph Cohen, 107–24. London: Routledge and Kegan Paul, 1974.

Mitchell, W. J. T., ed. *Against Theory: Literary Studies and the New Pragmatism*. Chicago: University of Chicago Press, 1985.

Montaigne, Michel de. *Essays of Michael Seigneur de Montaigne*. Trans. Charles Cotton. 2d ed. London: William Benton, 1963.

Mulhern, Francis. *The Moment of Scrutiny*. London: New Left Books, 1979.

Newton, John. "Literary Criticism, Universities, Murder." *CQ* 5, no. 4 (summer/autumn 1971): 335–54.

———. "*Scrutiny*'s Failure with Shakespeare." *CQ* 1, no. 2 (spring 1966): 144–77.

Newton, K. M., ed. *Theory into Practice: A Reader in Modern Literary Criticism*. London: Macmillan, 1992.

———. *Twentieth-Century Literary Theory: A Reader*. London: Macmillan, 1988.

Norton Anthology of English Poetry. Ed. Alexander W. Allison et al. 3d ed. New York and London: W. W. Norton, 1983.

Ogden, C. K., and I. A. Richards. *The Meaning of Meaning*. New York: Harcourt Brace, 1956.

Olsen, Stein Haugom. "The Canon and Artistic Failure." *BJA* 41, no. 3 (July 2001): 261–78.

———. *The End of Literary Theory*. Cambridge: Cambridge University Press, 1987.

———. *The Structure of Literary Understanding*. Cambridge: Cambridge University Press, 1978.

Parker, G. F. *Johnson's Shakespeare*. Oxford: Clarendon Press, 1989.

Parrinder, Patrick. *Authors and Authority: English and American Criticism, 1750–1990*. London: Macmillan, 1991.

———. "Having Your Assumptions Questioned: A Guide to the 'Theory Guides.'" In *The State of Theory*, ed. Richard Bradford, 127–44. London: Routledge, 1993.

Peer, Willie van. "Canon Formation: Ideology or Aesthetic Quality?" *BJA* 36, no. 2 (April 1996): 97–108.

Pope, Alexander. *The Dunciad*. Ed. James Sutherland. Vol. 5 of *The Twickenham Edition of the Poems of Alexander Pope*, ed. John Butt. London: Methuen, 1965.

―――. *Imitations of Horace*. Ed. John Butt. Vol. 4 of *The Twickenham Edition of the Poems of Alexander Pope*, ed. John Butt. London: Methuen, 1939.

―――. *Pastoral Poetry and "An Essay on Criticism."* Ed. E. Audra and Aubrey Williams. Vol. 1 of *The Twickenham Edition of the Poems of Alexander Pope*, ed. John Butt. London: Methuen, 1961.

―――. "Peri Bathous." In *Selected Poetry and Prose*, ed. W. K. Wimsatt Jr. New York: Holt Rinehart, 1951.

―――. Preface to *The Iliad of Homer*. 1715. In *Translations of Homer*, ed. Maynard Mack, 3–25. Vols. 7–10 of *The Twickenham Edition of the Poems of Alexander Pope*, ed. John Butt. London: Methuen, 1967.

Poulet, Georges. "The Self and Other in Critical Consciousness." 1972. Reprinted in *Twentieth-Century Literary Theory*, ed. K. M. Newton, 80–84. London: Macmillan, 1988.

Pound, Ezra. *ABC of Reading*. 1934. Reprint, London: Faber and Faber, 1991.

―――. *Literary Essays of Ezra Pound*. Ed. T. S. Eliot. London: Faber and Faber, 1954.

Reeves, James. *The Reputation and Writings of Alexander Pope*. New York: Barnes and Noble, 1976.

Rice, Philip, and Patricia Waugh, eds. *Modern Literary Theory: A Reader*. London and New York: Edward Arnold, 1992.

Richards, I. A. *Practical Criticism: A Study of Literary Judgement*. 1929. Reprint, London: Routledge, 1991.

―――. *Principles of Literary Criticism*. London: Routledge and Kegan Paul, 1924.

Ricks, Christopher. "Literary Principles as against Theory." In *Essays in Appreciation*, 311–32. Oxford: Oxford University Press, 1996.

Ricoeur, Paul. *Time and Narrative*. Trans. Kathleen Blamey and David Pellauer. 3 vols. Chicago and London: University of Chicago Press, 1984–88.

Robson, W. W. *Critical Essays*. London: Routledge and Kegan Paul, 1966.

―――. *"The Definition of Literature" and Other Essays*. Cambridge: Cambridge University Press, 1982.

Rorty, Richard. *Contingency, Irony, and Solidarity*. Cambridge: Cambridge University Press, 1989.

Rosslyn, Felicity. *Alexander Pope: A Literary Life*. London: Macmillan, 1990.

Rousseau, G. S., and Pat Rogers, eds. *The Enduring Legacy: Tercentenary Essays*. Cambridge: Cambridge University Press, 1988.

Rylance, Rick, and Judy Simons, eds. *Literature in Context*. Houndmills, U.K.: Palgrave, 2001.

Ryle, Gilbert. *The Concept of Mind*. 1949. Reprint, Harmondsworth, England: Penguin Books, 1990.

Rymer, Thomas. *The Critical Works of Thomas Rymer*. Ed. Curt A. Zimansky. New Haven: Yale University Press, 1956.

Said, Edward. *The World, the Text, and the Critic*. London: Faber and Faber, 1984.

Saintsbury, George. *A History of Criticism and Literary Taste in Europe*. 2d ed. 3 vols. Edinburgh and London: William Blackwood and Sons, 1902–6.

Salusinszky, Imre. *Criticism in Society*. New York and London: Methuen New Accents, 1987.

Scruton, Roger. *The Aesthetics of Music*. Oxford: Oxford University Press, 1997.

Searle, John. "Literary Theory and Its Discontents." In *Beyond Poststructuralism,* ed. Wendell V. Harris, 101–35. University Park: Pennsylvania State University Press, 1996.

Selden, Raman. *A Reader's Guide to Contemporary Literary Theory*. Brighton, England: Harvester Press, 1985.

———, ed. *From Formalism to Poststructuralism*. Vol. 8 of *The Cambridge History of Literary Criticism*. Cambridge: Cambridge University Press, 1995.

Shusterman, Richard. "Essence, History, and Narrative: T. S. Eliot on the Definition of Poetry and Criticism." *Monist* 71, no. 2 (April 1988): 183–96.

Smallwood, Philip. *Modern Critics in Practice: Critical Portraits of British Literary Critics*. New York: St. Martin's Press, 1990.

———. "'More Creative than Creation': On the Idea of Criticism and the Student Critic." *Arts and Humanities in Higher Education* 1, no. 1 (June 2002): 59–71.

———. "'The True Creative Mind': R. G. Collingwood's Critical Humanism." *BJA* 41, no. 3 (July 2001): 293–311.

Smith, Barbara Herrnstein. *Contingencies of Value: Alternative Perspectives for Critical Theory*. Cambridge: Harvard University Press, 1988.

Spacks, Patricia Meyer. *An Argument of Images: The Poetry of Alexander Pope*. Cambridge: Harvard University Press, 1971.

———. "Imagery and Method in *An Essay on Criticism*." In *Pope: Recent Essays by Several Hands,* ed. Maynard Mack and James A. Winn, 97–106. Brighton, U.K.: Harvester Press, 1980.

Sparshott, F. E. *The Concept of Criticism*. Oxford: Clarendon Press, 1967.

———. "The Problem of the Problem of Criticism." In *What Is Criticism?,* ed. Paul Hernadi, 3–14. Bloomington: Indiana University Press, 1981.

Steiner, George. "F. R. Leavis." In *Twentieth-Century Literary Criticism: A Reader,* ed. David Lodge, 622–35. London and New York: Longman, 1972.

Strickland, Geoffrey. *Structuralism or Criticism? Thoughts on How We Read*. Cambridge: Cambridge University Press, 1981.

Tallis, Raymond. *Not Saussure: A Critique of Post-Saussurean Literary Theory*. 2d ed. London: Macmillan, 1995.

———. "The Survival of Theory." In *Theorrhoea and After,* 29–72. New York: St. Martin's Press, 1999.

Taylor, Helen. "Leaving Parties and Legacies: Reflections across the Binary Divide on a Decade of Englishes." In *The State of Theory,* ed. Richard Bradford. London and New York: Routledge, 1993.

Tillotson, Geoffrey. *Pope and Human Nature*. Oxford: Clarendon Press, 1958.

Todorov, Tzvetan. *Genres in Discourse*. Trans. Catherine Porter. Cambridge: Cambridge University Press, 1990.

Tolstoy, Lev Nikolaevich. *What Is Art?* 1898. Reprinted in *Tolstoy on Art,* ed. Aylmer Maude, 121–357. New York: Haskell House, 1973.

Tormey, Alan. "Critical Judgments." *Theoria* 39 (1973): 35–49.

Treglown, Jeremy, and Bridget Bennett, eds. *Grub Street and the Ivory Tower: Literary Journalism and Literary Scholarship from Fielding to the Internet*. Oxford: Clarendon Press, 1998.

Veeser, H. Aram, ed. *The New Historicism*. New York and London: Routledge, 1989.

Watson, George. *The Literary Critics: A Study of English Descriptive Criticism*. London: Chatto and Windus, 1964.

Watts, Cedric. "Bottom's Children: The Fallacies of Structuralist, Post-structuralist, and Deconstructionist Literary Theory." In *Reconstructing Literature,* ed. Laurence Lerner, 20–35. Oxford: Blackwell, 1983.

Weitz, Morris. *"Hamlet" and the Philosophy of Literary Criticism*. London: Faber and Faber, 1965.

Wellek, René. *Concepts of Criticism*. New Haven: Yale University Press, 1963.

———. *A History of Modern Criticism: 1750–1950*. 8 vols. London: Jonathan Cape; New Haven: Yale University Press, 1955–92.

Wellek, René, and Austin Warren. *Theory of Literature*. 1949. Reprint, Harmondsworth, England: Penguin Books, 1993.

Wells, Robin Headlam, Glenn Burgess, and Rowland Wymer, eds. *Neo-Historicism*. Studies in Renaissance Literature, History, and Politics 5. Cambridge: D. S. Brewer, 2000.

White, Hayden. *Tropics of Discourse: Essays in Cultural Criticism*. Baltimore: Johns Hopkins University Press, 1978.

Widdowson, Peter. "'Literary Value' and the Reconstruction of Criticism." *Literature and History* 6, no. 1 (1980): 138–50.

Wilcocks, Robert. "Letters to the Editor." *TLS,* 31 July 1998, 15.

Wilde, Oscar. "The Critic as Artist." 1891. Reprinted in *The Complete Works of Oscar Wilde*, 1108–55. Glasgow: Harper Collins, 1994.

Williams, Raymond. *Keywords: A Vocabulary of Culture and Society*. Rev. ed. London: Fontana, 1988.

Williamson, Timothy. *Vagueness*. London and New York: Routledge, 1994.

Wilson, Penelope. "Engendering the Reader: 'Wit and Poetry and Pope' Once More." In *The Enduring Legacy: Alexander Pope: Tercentenary Essays,* ed. G. S. Rousseau and Pat Rogers, 63–75. Cambridge: Cambridge University Press, 1988.

Wimsatt, William K., Jr., and Cleanth Brooks. *Literary Criticism: A Short History*. New York: Alfred A. Knopf, 1957.

Winters, Yvor. *The Function of Criticism: Problems and Exercises*. 1957. Reprint, London: Routledge and Kegan Paul, 1962.

Wittgenstein, Ludwig. *The Blue and Brown Books*. 1958. Reprint, Oxford: Blackwell, 1993.

———. "Lectures on Aesthetics." In *Lectures and Conversations on Aesthetics, Psychology, and Religious Belief*, ed. Cyril Barrett, 1–40. Oxford: Blackwell, 1966.

———. *On Certainty*. Trans. Denis Paul and G. E. M. Anscombe. Oxford: Blackwell, 1969.

———. *Philosophical Remarks*. Ed. Rush Rhees. Trans. Raymond Hargreaves and Roger White. Oxford: Blackwell, 1990. Originally published in German in 1964.

Womersley, David, ed. *Augustan Critical Writing*. Harmondsworth, England: Penguin, 1997.

Wordsworth, William. *The Prose Works of William Wordsworth*. Ed. W. J. B. Owen and J. W. Smyser. 3 vols. Oxford: Clarendon Press, 1974.

Index

Abrams, M. H., 106, 186n. 25; *Doing Things with Texts: Essays in Criticism and Critical Theory*, 197n. 18
Addison, Joseph, 41, 163, 201n. 7
Aden, John, 202n. 16
Adorno, Theodor, 177
Aesthetics: Problems in the Philosophy of Criticism (Beardsley), 18
Aesthetics of Music, The (Scruton), 202 n. 15
Against Deconstruction (Ellis), 18, 185 n. 14, 188n. 26, 193n. 14
Against Interpretation (Sontag), 115
Alcott, Louisa May: *Little Women*, 36
Alexander Pope (Gooneratne), 200n. 1
Alexander Pope: A Life (Mack), 202n. 14
Alexander Pope: A Literary Life (Rosslyn), 200n. 1
Alexander Pope: The Poet in the Poems (Griffin), 205n. 24
Alexander Pope: The Poetry of Allusion (Brower), 201n. 7
Alexander Pope and the Arts of Georgian England (Brownell), 202n. 8
Althusser, Louis, 177, 180–81
Anatomy of Criticism, The (Frye), 70
Apologie for Poetrie, An (Sidney), 106, 144
Archaeology of Knowledge, The (Foucault), 199n. 16
Argument of Images, The: The Poetry of Alexander Pope (Spacks), 203n. 17
Aristotle, 31, 131, 136, 169; *Poetics (Treatise on Poetry)*, 131, 136, 163; as "standard case" of criticism, 163; on unities of time and place, 141. *See also* Stagyrite

Arnold, Matthew, 50, 137, 163, 166, 187nn. 14 and 19; his claim that poetry is "the criticism of life," 59; on criticism's function, 38–40, 42, 68, 106, 174; ethical grounds of his criticism, 145; as evaluative critic, 91, 99; "The Function of Criticism at the Present Time," 68; as source of cultural theory, 22, 176, 178; on Milton, 124; on Wordsworth, 122
Ars Poetica (Horace), 58
Art of Criticism, The (Bouhours), 201n. 7
Arts and Sciences of Criticism, The (Fuller and Waugh), 190n. 41
Audra, E., 200n. 1
Auerbach, Erich, 198n. 6
Augustan age, 24
Augustan Critical Writing (Womersley), 201n. 4
Authors and Authority: English and American Criticism, 1750–1950 (Parrinder), 199nn. 12 and 20
Autobiography, An (Collingwood), 184 n. 11
Ayer, A. J., 127

Baldick, Chris, 51, 132–34, 136–37
Balzac, Honoré de, 179
"Band Plays On, The" (Tallis), 103
Bann, Stephen, 138
Barnes, Annette, 119
Barnes, Julian, 30
Barthes, Roland, 50, 53, 72; on criticism as discourse, 42; on criticism as science, 92; method in cultural studies, 178–80. Works: *Mythologies*, 179; "The New

Citroen," 180; *The Pleasure of the Text*, 138, 179; "The Two Criticisms," 178
Battestin, Martin C., 183 n. 3
Beardsley, M. C., 18, 50, 124
Being and Time (Heidegger), 15
Belsey, Catherine, 185 nn. 21 and 24
Ben Hur, 36
Benjamin, Walter, 177
Bennett, Bridget, 192 n. 12
Bergonzi, Bernard, 24
Beyle, Henri (pseud. Stendhal), 83
Beyond Deconstruction: The Uses and Abuses of Literary Theory (Felperin), 185 n. 24
Beyond Poststructuralism (Harris), 183 n. 1, 186 n. 29, 194 n. 3
Biographia Literaria (Coleridge), 54
Blake, William, 118
Bloom, Harold, 23, 50, 72, 172, 176, 187 n. 12
Blue Book, The (Wittgenstein), 73
Book of Laughter and Forgetting, The (Kundera), 165
Bouhours, Dominique, 201 n. 7
Bradley, F. H., 156
British idealism, 20
British Post-Structuralism since 1968 (Easthope), 85
Brooker, Peter, 109–10, 113, 194 n. 7
Brooks, Cleanth, 33, 50, 137, 139
Brower, Reuben, 201 n. 7
Brown, Alan, 191 n. 7
Brown, Laura, 201 n. 4
Brownell, Morris, 202 n. 8
Browning, Robert, 125
Burgess, Glenn, 185 n. 17
Burns, Robert, 123
Butler, Judith, 186 n. 1
Byron, George Gordon, Lord, 123, 164

Cambridge History of Literary Criticism, The, 107, 138–39
Campbell, Jill, 183 n. 3
"Canon and Artistic Failure, The" (Olsen), 187 n. 12, 203 n. 23
Canons (von Hallberg), 187 n. 12
Carey, John, 50, 83, 87, 92, 94, 100; *The Intellectuals and the Masses*, 87; *Original Copy*, 83
Carroll, Joseph, 183 n. 3

Chaucer, Geoffrey, 59, 102, 168
Chesterton, G. K., 125
Cocktail Party, The (T. S. Eliot), 118
Coetzee, John, 135
Cohen, Leonard, 116–17
Coleridge, Samuel Taylor, 54, 163–64, 187 n. 19; *Biographia Literaria*, 54
Collingwood, R. G., 161, 184 n. 12, 186 n. 4, 198 n. 53, 200 n. 28; on consciousness, 169; on definition and history, 20–21; on "empirical" and "transcendental" concepts, 150; on history as a "world," 140–41; theory of the "scale of forms," 46. Works: *An Autobiography*, 184 n. 11; *An Essay on Metaphysics*, 186 n. 4, 200 n. 33, 201 n. 5; *An Essay on Philosophical Method*, 45–48, 155; *The Idea of History*, 60–62, 198 n. 53; *The Principles of Art*, 64–65, 67, 74
Collini, Stefan, 115, 205 n. 8.
Common Pursuit, The (Leavis), 68
Concept of Criticism, The (Sparshott), 18, 192 n. 1
Concept of Mind, The (Ryle), 143
Concepts of Criticism (Wellek), 183 n. 4
Contingencies of Value: Alternative Perspectives for Critical Theory (Smith), 193 n. 10
Contingency, Irony, and Solidarity (Rorty), 143
Contradiction Still, A: Representations of Women in the Poetry of Alexander Pope (Knellwolf), 201 n. 4
Cowley, Abraham, 124, 148; on Crashaw, 165; *Miscellanies*, 124; "Ode on Wit," 148
Cowper, William, 123
Cox, R. G., 50, 52
Crabbe, George, 125
Crashaw, Richard, 165
Crews, Frederick, 24
"Critic as Artist, The" (Wilde), 43, 72, 190 n. 43
criticism: academic methods of, 84; aesthetic model of, 15; confusion in the concept of, 64–65, 105; crisis in, 162; defining conditions for, 29–30; essence of, 42–45, 66, 68–69; emotion in, 119–20; empirical and transcendental concepts of, 150; existence of, 61;

criticism *(continued)*
    feminist, 71; finalist definition of, 30, 61, 62, 63, 73; function of, 25, 38–41, 90; historical representation of, 17, 65, 133–34; idea of, 16, 21–23, 29–30, 60, 67, 74, 88, 104, 156–58, 160–62, 204 n. 5; language of, 23, 66, 171–72; and literary history, 101; modernity of, 15; point of view on, 147–50; poststructuralist forms of, 63, 70–71, 87, 106, 123, 138–39, 169; as science and/or art, 57, 84; as social construct, 58, 61; value judgments in, 54, 86. *See also* theory; literature
Criticism (Keller), 81
Criticism and Ideology (Eagleton), 90, 202 n. 12
Critique of Pure Reason, The (Kant), 150
Crow (Hughes), 116
Culler, Jonathan, 107, 110, 186 n. 1, 199 n. 24
cultural studies, 18, 59, 65, 86, 139, 176–82
Cunningham, Valentine, 19, 176, 192 n. 12

Daniel Deronda (G. Eliot), 102
"*Daniel Deronda:* A Conversation" (James), 190 n. 43
"Date Line" (Pound), 68, 70
Davies, Stephen, 187 n. 5, 202 n. 9, 204 n. 8
Day, Gary, 185 n. 21
Decline and Fall of the Roman Empire, The (Gibbon), 34, 37
deconstruction, 16, 110, 138, 161, 200 n. 32; deconstructive attitudes, 25, 155
definition: absolutist theories of, 48; as against proposition, 61; dictionary, 53–54, 60, 105, 162; honorific, 35, 38, 53; ostensive, 34; poetic mode of, 156; of philosophical concepts, 155; prohibition against circularity in, 60; and social conventions, 34; types of, 161; working, 64, 162
Definition of Literature and Other Essays, The (Robson), 19, 34–37, 192 n. 7
"Definition of Love, The" (Marvell), 108
Definitions of Art (Davies), 187 n. 5, 202 n. 9, 204 n. 8
de Man, Paul, 15, 105, 107, 167, 169
Dennis, John, 154
De Quincey, Thomas, 202 n. 16
De Rerum Natura (Lucretius), 102

Derrida, Jacques, 115, 139, 142, 184 n. 12, 200 n. 39
Desire in Language (Kristeva), 85
Dickens, Charles, 36, 136
Dickinson, Emily, 164
Dictionary of the English Language (Johnson), 49
Dillon, Wentworth, Earl of Roscommon, 201 n. 7
Doing Things with Texts: Essays in Criticism and Critical Theory (Abrams), 197 n. 18
Dollimore, Jonathan, 127, 185 n. 24
Donne, John, 59, 118
Dostoievsky, Feodor Mikhailovich, 92
Dowson, Ernest, 37
Dryden, John, 59, 69, 96, 103, 125–26, 154, 164, 166; on Oldham, 165; on Shakespeare, 122, 124
Dunciad, The, 85, 119, 169
Dylan, Bob, 69

Eagleton, Terry, 29, 31, 53, 90–91, 164; definition of "literature," 36–38, 48, 190 n. 42, 202 n. 12; definition of "theory," 108, 110; on the eighteenth century, 122; on fact and value, 95; on the function of criticism, 41–42, 68, 174; as historian of criticism, 137–38; influence of tradition on, 178, 185 n. 21; on rubbish in the canon, 98. Works: *Criticism and Ideology*, 90, 202 n. 12; *The Function of Criticism: From the Spectator to Poststructuralism*, 41, 68; *Literary Theory: An Introduction*, 36–38, 41, 85, 104, 127, 138, 190 n. 42, 191 n. 20
Easthope, Antony, 191 n. 16, 193 n. 15, 205 n. 1
Eco, Umberto, 115
eighteenth-century studies, periodization of, 20
Eliot, George, 102, 164; *Daniel Deronda*, 102; *Middlemarch*, 140
Eliot, T. S., 58, 139, 166, 200 n. 36; on cases of literary greatness, 126; on consciousness, 169–70; on criticism as not a science, 190 n. 39; definition of criticism, 50, 53, 71–72, 74; on the function of criticism, 40–42, 68–69, 174; on interpretation, 118; on Keats,

124; as "magisterial" critic, 193n. 10; on Milton, 124; as source of cultural perspective in criticism, 176; as "standard case" of criticism, 163. Works: *Four Quartets*, 41, 66, 169–70, "The Frontiers of Criticism," 41, 77, 118, 190n. 39; "The Function of Criticism," 40–41, 68; *The Sacred Wood*, 200n. 36

Eliot to Derrida: The Poverty of Interpretation (Harwood), 19

Ellis, John M., 19, 31, 144, 148, 150; definition of literature, 32–37; definition of theory, 25. Works: *Against Deconstruction*, 18, 185n. 14, 188n. 26, 193n. 14; *Literature Lost: Social Agendas and the Corruption of the Humanities*, 18, 171, 183n. 3, 187n. 11, 204n. 22; "The Logic of the Question: 'What Is Criticism?,'" 43–44, 64, 72, 189n. 37; *The Theory of Literary Criticism*, 32–37, 57, 123

Empson, William, 202n. 11

End of Literary Theory, The (Olsen), 18, 194n. 30

Enduring Legacy, The: Alexander Pope: Tercentenary Essays (Rousseau and Rogers), 201n. 4, 202n. 16

"Engendering the Reader: 'Wit and Poetry and Pope' Once More" (Wilson), 201n. 4

English Pasts: Essays in History and Culture (Collini), 205n. 8

Erasmus, Desiderius: *The Praise of Folly*, 145

Erskine-Hill, Howard, 204n. 21

Essay on Criticism, 15–18, 20, 22, 48, 58, 63, 77, 88, 90, 106, 114, 116, 127, 131, 142, 144–55, 159–60, 167–75

"Essay on Dramatic Poesy, An" (Dryden), 96

Essay on Man, An, 153, 156, 202n. 12

Essay on Metaphysics, An (Collingwood), 186n. 4, 200n. 33, 201n. 5

Essay on Philosophical Method, An (Collingwood), 45–48, 155

Essay on Poetry (Sheffield), 201n. 7

Essay on Translated Verse, An (Roscommon), 201n. 7

Essay upon Unnatural Flights in Poetry, An (Granville), 201n. 7

Essential Articles for the Study of Alexander Pope (Mack), 202n. 11

"Evaluative Criticism and Criticism without Evaluation" (Robson), 93, 192n. 7

Faerie Queene, The (Spenser), 36, 118

Fairer, David, 200n. 1

Felperin, Howard, 113, 185n. 24

feminism, 70; feminist critical approaches (to literature), 16, 71; feminist criticism, 99

Fictional Points of View (Lamarque), 19, 187n. 8

Fiction and the Reading Public (Q. D. Leavis), 141

"'*First* Follow Nature': Strategy and Stratification in *An Essay on Criticism*" (Aden), 202n. 16

Fischer, Michael, 197n. 18

Fish, Stanley, 186n. 25

Fiske, John, 179–80, 192n. 9

Flaubert's Parrot (Barnes), 30

Foe (Coetzee), 135

Forester, C. S., 142

Foucault, Michel, 65, 199n. 16; *The Archaeology of Knowledge*, 199n. 16; "What Is an Author?" 190n. 4

Four Quartets (T. S. Eliot), 41, 66, 169–70

Framing the Sign: Criticism and its Institutions (Culler), 199n. 24

Freadman, Richard, 19, 106, 111–12, 181, 203n. 19

F. R. Leavis: A Life in Criticism (MacKillop), 187n. 19

F. R. Leavis: Essays and Documents (MacKillop and Storer), 185n. 21

From the Land of Shadows (James), 83

"Frontiers of Criticism, The" (T. S. Eliot), 41, 77, 118, 190n. 39

Frye, Northrop, 42–43, 50, 70–72, 92, 99

Fuller, David, 190n. 41

Fuller, Peter, 98

"Function of Criticism, The" (T. S. Eliot), 40–41, 68

Function of Criticism, The: From the Spectator to Poststructuralism (Eagleton), 41, 68

"Function of Criticism at the Present Time, The" (Arnold), 68

Gadamer, Hans-Georg, 19, 159–60, 184 n. 12
Gallagher, Catherine, 20
Gallie, W. B., 21
Genres in Discourse (Todorov), 187 n. 5
Gibbon, Edward, 34, 37
Goethe, Johann Wolfgang von, 126
Goldgar, Bertrand A., 200 n. 1
Goldsmith, Oliver, 122
Gooneratne, Yasmine, 200 n. 1
Gordon, Ian, 200 n. 1
Graff, Gerald, 117, 185 n. 23, 194 n. 5
Graham, Gordon, 137
Granville, George, Lord Landsdowne, 201 n. 7
Graves, Robert, 91
Gray, Thomas, 59, 122
Great Expectations (Dickens), 136
Greenblatt, Stephen, 20, 185 n. 24
Greene, Donald, 202 n. 16
"Grievance Studies: How Not to Do Cultural Criticism" (Collini), 205 n. 8
Griffin, Dustin H., 205 n. 24
Gross, John, 24
Grub Street and the Ivory Tower: Literary Journalism and Literary Scholarship from Fielding to the Internet (Treglown and Bennett), 192 n. 12
Guillory, John, 186 n. 1

Hallberg, Robert von, 187 n. 12
Hamlet (Shakespeare), 30, 53, 118, 124, 136, 165
Hardy, Thomas: *Jude the Obscure*, 163
Harris, Wendell V., 19, 197 n. 11; *Beyond Poststructuralism*, 183 n. 1, 186 n. 29, 194 n. 3; definition of criticism, 53, 162; on dispensability of theory, 186 n. 29; *Literary Meaning: Reclaiming the Study of Literature*, 19, 194 n. 12, 197 n. 11; on redefinition of theory, 194 n. 12
Hartman, Geoffrey, 102, 109, 115
Harwood, John, 19, 113
Heath, James M., 115
Hegel, Georg Wilhelm Friedrich, 115, 159
Heidegger, Martin, 15, 24
Hernadi, Paul, 18, 187 n. 5, 189 n. 37
Hirsch, E. D., Jr., 50, 91, 115
History of Modern Criticism, 1750–1950 (Wellek), 133

Hoggart, Richard, 178–79, 205 n. 8
Holloway, John, 103
Homer, 30, 123, 135, 156, 165, 169
Hooker, Edward Niles, 202 n. 11
Hopkins, Gerard Manley, 113, 114, 135, 164
Horace (Quintus Horatius Flaccus), 58, 168–69, 202 n. 14
Horatian Ode, An (Marvell), 29
Hughes, Ted, 103, 116, 164; *Poetry in the Making*, 164; *Shakespeare and the Goddess of Complete Being*, 164
"Hunting the Highbrow" (Woolf), 88

Ibsen, Henrik, 29
Idea of History, The (Collingwood), 21, 60–62, 198 n. 53
Idler (Johnson), 102
Iliad, The: Pope's translation of, 123, 169
"Imagery and Method in *An Essay on Criticism*" (Spacks), 203 n. 17
Imperial Theme, The: Further Interpretations of Shakespeare's Tragedies including the Roman Plays (Knight), 196 n. 6
"In Praise of the Contemporary Critic" (Maskell), 205 n. 8
Intellectuals and the Masses, The (Carey), 87
Interpretation: An Essay on the Philosophy of Literary Criticism (Juhl), 196 n. 6
Interpretation and Overinterpretation (Collini), 115
"In the Big House of Theory" (Crews), 19, 185 n. 13
"Introducing the Long Eighteenth Century: Literary History and the New Pedagogy" (Mason and Smallwood), 201 n. 4
Is There a Text in This Class?: The Authority of Interpretive Communities (Fish), 186 n. 25

Jacobson, Howard, 165
Jakobson, Roman, 35
James, Clive, 50, 72, 132
James, Henry, 58, 113, 137, 164, 190 n. 43
Jauss, Hans-Robert, 19
Jefferson, Ann, 109, 191 n. 20
Johnson, Samuel, 54, 58, 102, 141, 178; on conjectural criticism, 117–18; on Cowley, 124; as creator-critic, 164; on

definition of criticism, 49, 160; definition of theory, 105; definitions, 29, 49; on Dryden and Pope, 125–26; on epitaphs, 169; as evaluative critic, 91, 99–100; on *Hamlet*, 124; on *King Lear*, 119, 122, 124; Leavis on, 21, 187 n. 19; on the natural and new, 146; neglect of his criteria, 23; praise of Pope's *Essay on Criticism*, 156; on Shakespeare, 123, 138, 158, 168; as successor of Pope, 20; his theorizing, 106. Works: *Idler*, 102; *Lives of the Poets*, 124, 156; Preface to a *Dictionary of the English Language*, 49; Preface to Shakespeare, 54, 106, 138, 158, 168; *Rambler*, 29
Johnson's Shakespeare (Parker), 185 n. 19
Jonson, Ben, 105, 118, 164, 183 n. 4; "On the Death of His First Sonne," 118; on Shakespeare, 165; *Timber or Discoveries: Made Upon Men and Matter*, 183 n. 4
Journals (Hopkins), 114
Joyce, James, 36, 122
Jude the Obscure (Hardy), 163
judgment: different textual proportions of, 96; form of, 123; of literary greatness, 124; rating and weighing in, 123; rightness of, 94; types of, 121
Juhl, P. D., 115, 196 n. 6

Kant, Immanuel, 60, 122, 150, 153–54
Kastan, David Scott, 20–21
Keats, John, 123, 164–65
Keller, Hans, 97
Kermode, Frank, 20–21
Keywords (Williams), 109, 204 n. 5
King Lear (Shakespeare), 119, 124
King Solomon's Mines (Haggard), 36
Knellwolf, Christa, 170, 201 n. 4
Knight, G. Wilson, 196 n. 6, 201 n. 2
Knight's Tale, The (Chaucer), 102
Kundera, Milan, 165

La Bruyère, Jean de, 126
Lacan, Jacques, 164
LaCapra, Dominick, 184 n. 12
Lamarque, Peter, 19, 52, 187 n. 8; *Fictional Points of View*, 19, 187 n. 8; *Truth, Fiction, and Literature* (with Stein Haugom Olsen), 19, 187 n. 8

La Rochefoucauld, François de Marsillac, Duc de, 126
Laureate of Peace, The: On the Genius of Alexander Pope (Knight), 201 n. 2
Lawrence, D. H., 165, 190 n. 40; definition of criticism, 55–57; his outspoken evaluations, 92, 96, 100, 122
Leavis, F. R., 41, 58, 139, 178; *The Common Pursuit*, 68; as evaluative critic, 99; definition of criticism, 143, 162; on the function of criticism, 68; on Johnson, 21–22; 140; on the judicial, 120–21, 127; his objection to philosophical definition, 66, 166; on Q. D. Leavis, 141; "The Responsible Critic, or the Function of Criticism at Any Time," 143; self-historicizing, 131, 198 n. 1; on Shelley, 96, 122; as source of cultural theory, 176; on valuation, 90–91, 93; "Valuation in Criticism," 93; on Wordsworth, 124
Leavis, Q. D., 141
Lee, Hermione, 192 n. 12
Lerner, Laurence, 184 n. 9
Letters of John Keats, The, 164
Lewis, C. S., 126, 132
Literary Criticism: A Short History (Wimsatt and Brooks), 137, 139
Literary Criticism of Alexander Pope, The (Goldgar), 200 n. 1
"Literary History and Literary Modernity" (de Man), 15
"Literary in Theory, The" (Culler), 186 n. 1
Literary into Cultural Studies (Easthope), 191 n. 16, 193 n. 15, 205 n. 1
Literary Meaning: Reclaiming the Study of Literature (Harris), 19, 194 n. 12, 197 n. 11
"Literary Theory and Its Discontents" (Searle), 204 n. 9
Literary Theory: An Introduction (Eagleton), 36–38, 41, 85, 104, 127, 138, 190 n. 42, 191 n. 20
literature: canon of, 35, 37; as commodity, 81; conceptual indispensability of, 94; its definition, 31–38, 187 n. 5; its existence, 93, 161; as fiction, 34; language of, 32–33; "middlebrow," 36; in relation to criticism, 17, 29–31, 62, 66, 78, 163; its replacement by "text," 23. *See also* criticism; theory

Literature Lost: Social Agendas and the Corruption of the Humanities (Ellis), 18, 171, 183 n. 3, 187 n. 11, 204 n. 22
Little Women (Alcott), 36
Lives of the Grammarians, The (Suetonius), 135
Lives of the Poets (Johnson), 124
Locke, John, 127
Lodge, David, 54, 108, 163, 190 n. 40
"Logical Structure in Eighteenth-Century Poetry" (Greene), 202 n. 16
"Logic of the Question, The: 'What Is Criticism?'" (Ellis), 43, 72, 189 n. 37
Longinus, Cassius, 150, 169
Lucretius (Titus Lucretius Carus), 102
Lyrical Ballads (Wordsworth), 59, 113

Mack, Maynard, 202 nn. 11 and 14
MacKillop, Ian, 185 n. 21; *F. R. Leavis: A Life in Criticism*, 187 n. 19
Madonna, 179–80
Martin, Rex, 186 n. 4
Marvell, Andrew, 29, 36, 111; "The Definition of Love," 108, 148; *An Horatian Ode*, 29; "To His Coy Mistress," 116
Marxist criticism, 16, 110; contrast with evaluative criticism, 99; "Marxist" as subdivision of criticism, 71; and "radical scepticism," 161; its technical terminology, 64
Maskell, Duke, 205 n. 8
Mason, H. A., 51; on critical urbanity, 173; on defining criticism, 74, 144–47
Mason, Tom, 201 n. 4
Middlemarch (G. Eliot), 140
Midnight's Children (Rushdie), 165
Miller, Hillis, 58, 187 n. 5
Miller, Karl, 192 n. 12
Miller, Seumas, 19, 106, 111–12, 181, 203 n. 19
Milton, John, 122, 124, 126, 163; *Paradise Lost*, 36, 181
Mink, Louis O., 141
Miscellanies (Cowley), 124
Mitchell, W. J. T., 107
Modern Criticism (Saintsbury), 198 n. 5
Modern Critics in Practice: Critical Portraits of British Literary Critics (Smallwood), 185 n. 21
Modern Language Association of America (MLA), 105
Modern Literary Theory: A Comparative Introduction (Jefferson and Robey), 191 n. 20
Modern Literary Theory: A Reader (Rice and Waught), 194 n. 7
Montaigne, Michel, Seigneur de, 127, 135
Mulhern, Francis, 50
Mythologies (Barthes), 179

Nature (and Judgment), 153
Neo-Historicism: Studies in Renaissance Literature, History, and Politics (Wells, Burgess, and Wymer), 185 n. 17
"New Citroen, The" (Barthes), 180
"New Criticism," 18, 22, 65, 116
New Historicism (Veeser), 183 n. 2
"New Historicism," 16, 21, 127
New Humanism, 25
New Left Review, 98
New Musical Express (NME), 82
New Statesman, 145
Newton, John M., 114
Newton, K. M., 109, 194 n. 7, 196 n. 42
Nietzsche, Friedrich Wilhelm, 87
Norton Anthology of Theory and Criticism, The, 194 n. 2, 201 n. 7
Not Saussure: A Critique of Post-Saussurean Literary Theory (Tallis), 185 n. 22

"Ode on Wit" (Cowley), 148
Odyssey, Pope's translation of, 169
Of Grammatology (Derrida), 85
Oldham, John, 165
Olsen, Stein Haugom, 18–19, 52, 123, 171, 187 nn. 8 and 12; on criticism as a social practice, 203 n. 23; on criticism's relation to philosophy, 42. Works: "The Canon and Artistic Failure," 187 n. 12, 203 n. 23; *The End of Literary Theory*, 18, 194 n. 30; *The Structure of Literary Understanding*, 18; *Truth, Fiction, and Literature* (with Peter Lamarque), 19, 187 n. 8
Omeros (Walcott), 30
On Interpretation (Barnes), 119
"On Liberty of Interpreting" (Robson), 116

"On the Death of His First Sonne" (Jonson), 118
"On the Idea of Criticism and the Student Critic" (Smallwood), 191 n. 7
"On the Subject of Practical Criticism" (Alan Brown), 191 n. 7
Original Copy (Carey), 83
Othello (Shakespeare), 95–96

Paglia, Camille, 176
Paradise Lost (Milton), 36, 181
Parker, G. F., 185 n. 19
Parrinder, Patrick, 110–11, 199 nn. 12 and 20
Payne, Michael, 115
Peeping Tom (Jacobson), 165
Peer, Willie van, 187 n. 12
"Peri Bathous" (Pope), 102
Perloff, Majorie, 192 n. 12
Philosophical Remarks (Wittgenstein), 155
Philosophy and Historical Understanding (Gallie), 21
Plato, 134
Pleasure of the Text, The (Barthes), 179
Poetics (Aristotle), 131, 136. See also *Treatise on Poetry*
Poetry in the Making (Hughes), 164
Poetry of Alexander Pope, The (Fairer), 200 n. 1
Polanyi, Michael, 66
Political Shakespeare: New Essays in Cultural Materialism (Dollimore and Sinfield), 185 n. 24, 198 n. 53
Pope, Alexander, 122; as author of criticism in poetry, 58; on books and humankind, 178; and the canon, 98; compared with Dryden, 125–26; criteria of, 23; and current definitions of criticism, 24, 183 n. 4; on the ends of writing, 104; on Homer, 123, 135; on the idea of criticism, 163; and judgment, 127; Leavis on, 58; on stooping to understand, 106. Works: *Dunciad*, 85, 119, 169; *Essay on Criticism*, 15–18, 20, 22, 48, 58, 63, 77, 88, 90, 106, 114, 116, 127, 131, 142, 144–55, 159–60, 167–75; *Essay on Man*, 153, 156, 202 n. 12; "Peri Bathous," 102; Preface to the *Iliad*, 123; *Rape of the Lock*, 165; *Temple of Fame*, 168; translation of Homer, 156, 169

Pope and Human Nature (Tillotson), 202 n. 16
"Pope on Wit: The *Essay on Criticism*" (Hooker), 202 n. 11
Postmodernism, 16, 22, 65; postmodernist novels, 30
Posttheoretical, 17, 21, 48; post-theory, 19
Poulet, Georges, 50
Pound, Ezra, 68, 70–71, 122, 125, 159–60
Practical Reader in Contemporary Literary Theory, A (Widdowson and Brooker), 194 n. 7
Practicing New Historicism (Gallagher and Greenblatt), 20
Praise of Folly, The (Erasmus), 145
precarious margins, fallacy of, 56
Preface to Pope, A (Gordon), 200 n. 1
Preface to Shakespeare (Johnson), 54, 106, 138, 158, 168
Principles of Art, The (Collingwood), 64–65, 67, 74
Professing Literature: An Institutional History (Graff), 194 n. 5

Quintilian (Marcus Fabius Quintilianus), 168

race-class-gender, 16, 171
Racine, Jean, 179
Rambler (Johnson), 29
Rape of the Lock, The, 165
Reader's Guide to Contemporary Literary Theory, A (Selden), 191 n. 20
Reading after Theory (Cunningham), 19, 176
Reading the Popular (Fiske), 179
Reconstructing Literature (Lerner), 184 n. 9
Reeves, James, 200 n. 1
Renaissance Self-Fashioning: From More to Shakespeare (Greenblatt), 185 n. 24
Reputation and Writings of Alexander Pope, The (Reeves), 200 n. 1
Rereading Literature: Alexander Pope (L. Brown), 201 n. 4
"Responsible Critic, or the Function of Criticism at Any Time, The" (Leavis), 143
Re-Thinking Theory (Freadman and Miller), 19, 106, 203 n. 19
Rice, Philip, 110, 194 n. 7, 195 n. 31

Richards, I. A., 187n. 14; definition of criticism, 42, 50, 65, 73, 90; definition of poetry, 53; on judgment, 92; on the proper use of a word, 52
Ricks, Christopher, 109
Ricoeur, Paul, 19, 169
Rise and Fall of the Man of Letters, The (Gross), 78
Robey, David, 109
Robson, W. W., 19, 31, 63, 93, 192 n. 7; on alienation of criticism from authors and readers, 24; on criticism's title to exist, 61; definition of literature, 34–37; on distinction of fiction and history, 142; on Lewis and Chesterton, 125–26. Works: *The Definition of Literature and Other Essays*, 19, 34–37; "Evaluative Criticism and Criticism without Evaluation," 93; "On Liberty of Interpreting," 116
Rochester, John Wilmot, Earl of, 148; on Waller, 165
Rorty, Richard, 142–43, 166, 170
Roscommon, Wentworth Dillon, Earl of, 201 n. 7
Rosencrantz and Guildenstern Are Dead (Stoppard), 30
Rosslyn, Felicity, 200n. 1
Rushdie, Salman: *Midnight's Children*, 165
Ryle, Gilbert, 143, 164
Rymer, Thomas, 95

Sacred Wood, The (T. S. Eliot), 200n. 36
Said, Edward W., 50, 52, 72, 109, 111
Saint-Beuve, Charles-Augustin, 83
Saintsbury, George, 133–34, 136–37, 198n. 5
Salusinszky, Imre, 38
Scott, Sir Walter, 123
"*Scrutiny*'s Failure with Shakespeare" (J. M. Newton), 114
Scruton, Roger, 202n. 15
Searle, John, 55, 183n. 1, 204n. 9
Selden, Raman, 107, 110
Sexual Personae (Paglia), 176
Shakespeare, William, 29, 36–37, 122–24; Ted Hughes on, 164. Works: *Hamlet*, 30, 53, 118, 124, 136, 165; *King Lear*, 119, 14; *Othello*, 95–96; *Sonnets*, 95, 113, 185 n. 24; *Troilus and Cressida*, 59

Shakespeare after Theory (Kastan), 20
Shakespeare and the Goddess of Complete Being (Hughes), 164
Shape of the Past, The (Graham), 137
Shaw, George Bernard, 29
Sheffield, John, Earl of Mulgrave, 201 n. 7
Shelley, Percy Bysshe, 69, 96, 103, 122–23, 166
Shusterman, Richard, 161
"Sick Rose, The" (Blake), 118
Sidney, Sir Philip, 103, 106, 144
Simons, Judy, 142
Sinfield, Alan, 127, 185n. 24
Smallwood, Philip, 185n., 201n. 4
Smith, Barbara Herrnstein, 95, 99, 187 n. 12
social construction, 57
Social Milieu of Alexander Pope, The: Lives, Example, and Poetic Response (Erskine-Hill), 204n. 21
Songs and Sonnets (Donne), 59
Sonnets (Shakespeare), 95, 113, 185 n. 24
Sontag, Susan, 115
Spacks, Patricia Meyer, 203n. 17
Sparshott, F. E., 18, 115, 131
Spectator (Addison and Steele), 201n. 7
Spectator, 145
Spenser, Edmund, 36, 118, 122
Stagyrite, 168. *See also* Aristotle
Stein, Gertrude, 122
Steiner, George, 50
Stendhal. *See* Beyle, Henri
Stephenson, Fr. A. J., 198n. 1
Sterne, Laurence, 59, 100
Stoppard, Tom, 30, 165
Storer, Richard, 185n. 21
Strickland, Geoffrey, 90, 193 n. 17
Strindberg, August, 92, 100
Structuralism, 84, 110
Structuralism or Criticism? Thoughts on How We Read (Strickland), 90, 193 n. 17
Structure of Literary Understanding, The (Olsen), 18
Subject of Tragedy, The: Identity and Difference in Renaissance Drama (Belsey), 185n. 24
Suetonius (Gaius Suetonius Tranquillus), 135

"Suzanne Takes You Down" (Cohen), 116–17
Swift, Jonathan, 58

tacit inference, logic of, 66
Tallis, Raymond, 103, 114, 184n. 9, 185n. 22
Taylor, Helen, 110
Temple of Fame, The, 168
Theorrhoea and After (Tallis), 184n. 9
theory, 17–20, 194n. 13, 196n. 42; as against criticism, 74, 102–16, 161, 171; as against idea, 156–58; as against judgment, 120; as against literary journalism, 90; and antihumanism, 179; as constituent of criticism, 128; and critical renewal, 25; guides to, 18, 70, 104–5; and practice, 199n. 10; and theorizing, 106; skepticism about, 84; sociopolitically uncommitted, 19; terminological chaos of, 23. *See also* posttheoretical
Theory into Practice: A Reader in Modern Literary Criticism (K. M. Newton), 194n. 7, 196n. 42
Theory of Literary Criticism, The (Ellis), 32–37, 57, 123
Theory of Literature, The (Wellek and Warren), 31–32
Thomas, Kendall, 186n. 1
Tibetan Book of the Dead, The, 98
Tillotson, Geoffrey, 202n. 16
Timber or Discoveries: Made upon Men and Matter (Jonson), 183n. 4
"To Criticize the Critic" (T. S. Eliot), 69
Todorov, Tzvetan, 187n. 5
"To His Coy Mistress" (Marvell), 116
Tolstoy, Lev Nikolaevich, 34, 103, 164, 187n. 5
Tormey, Alan, 127
Tragic Muse, The (James), 113
Treatise on Poetry (Aristotle), 163. See also *Poetics*
Treglown, Jeremy, 192n. 12
Trilling, Lionel, 164, 176
Tristram Shandy (Sterne), 59, 100
Troilus and Cressida (Shakespeare), 59
Tropics of Discourse (White), 131
Truth and Method (Gadamer), 159, 160
Truth, Fiction, and Literature (Lamarque and Olsen), 19, 187n. 8

Twentieth-Century Literary Theory (K. M. Newton), 109
"Two Criticisms, The" (Barthes), 178

Ulysses (Joyce), 36
"Upon Nothing" (Rochester), 148

Vagueness (Williamson), 186n. 3
valuation, implicit and explicit, 94–96
"Valuation in Criticism" (Leavis), 93
Veeser, H. Aram, 183n. 2

Walcott, Derek, 30
Walsh, William, 154
War and Peace (Tolstoy), 34
Warren, Austin, 31–32, 34–36
Watson, George, 133, 137
Watts, Cedric, 184n. 9
Waugh, Patricia, 110, 190n. 41, 194n. 7, 195n. 31
Weitz, Morris, 53
Wellek, René: definition of criticism, 50, 183n. 4; definition of literature, 31–32, 34–36; on the history of criticism, 133–34, 136–37. Works: *Concepts of Criticism*, 183n. 4; *History of Modern Criticism, 1750–1950*, 133; *The Theory of Literature* (with Austin Warren), 31–32
Wells, H. G., 92
Wells, Robin Headlam, 185n. 17
Western Canon, The: The Books and School of the Ages (Bloom), 176, 187n. 12
What Car?, 82
"What Is an Author?" (Foucault), 190n. 4
What Is Art? (Tolstoy), 187n. 5
What Is Criticism? (Hernadi), 18, 189n. 37
What Is Literature? (Hernadi), 187n. 5
What's Left of Theory? New Work on the Politics of Literary Theory (Butler, Guillory, and Thomas), 186n. 1
Wheel of Fire, The: Interpretations of Shakespearean Tragedy, 196n. 6
White, Hayden, 131
Widdowson, Peter, 93, 109–10, 113, 187n. 5, 194n. 7
Wilcocks, Robert, 183n. 3
Wilde, Oscar, 43, 50, 58, 72, 190n. 43; "The Critic as Artist," 43, 72, 190n. 43

Williams, Raymond, 126–27, 204 n. 5; compared with Leavis, 120–21; on the cultural aspect of criticism, 176, 178; definition of theory, 109; on getting rid of the critical habit, 139

Williamson, Timothy, 186 n. 3

Wilson, Penelope, 201 n. 4

Wimsatt, W. K., Jr., 133, 137, 139

Winters, Yvor, 41, 193 n. 10

"Wit Governing Wit: *An Essay on Criticism*" (Spacks), 203 n. 17

"Wit in the *Essay on Criticism*" (Empson), 202 n. 11

Wittgenstein, Ludwig, 52, 73, 94, 117, 155; *Philosophical Remarks*, 155

Women in Love (Lawrence), 165

Womersley, David, 170, 201 n. 4

Wordsworth, William, 134, 164; on epitaphs, 169; on the decline of poetry, 121–22; and Johnson, 141; Leavis on, 124; *Lyrical Ballads*, 59, 113; Matthew Arnold on, 122–23; his poems on capital punishment, 98; his poetry as instrument of politics, 69; Preface to *Lyrical Ballads*, 164; his theory (and practice) of poetical diction, 113

Working with Structuralism: Essays and Reviews on Nineteenth- and Twentieth-Century Literature (Lodge), 84, 190 n. 40

Wymer, Rowland, 185 n. 17